GOOD MORNING, Mr SARRA

GOOD MORNING, Mr SARRA

My life working for a stronger, smarter future for our children

CHRIS SARRA

First published 2012 by University of Queensland Press
PO Box 6042, St Lucia, Queensland 4067 Australia

www.uqp.com.au

Cataloguing-in-Publication entry is available from the
National Library of Australia
http://catalogue.nla.gov.au/

978 0 7022 3888 8 (pbk)
978 0 7022 4907 5 (ePDF)
978 0 7022 4908 2 (ePub)
978 0 7022 4909 9 (kindle)

Typeset in 12/17 pt Bembo by Post Pre-press Group, Brisbane
Printed in Australia by McPherson's Printing Group

University of Queensland Press uses papers that are natural, renewable and recyclable products made from wood grown in sustainable forests. The logging and manufacturing processes conform to the environmental regulations of the country of origin.

Contents

A hundred years from now it will not matter what my bank account was, the sort of house I lived in, or the kind of car I drove . . . but the world may be different because I was important in the life of a child.

Forest E. Witcraft (1894–1967)
Scholar, teacher and Boy Scout administrator

Prologue

'The tide of low expectations of Indigenous children in Australian schools has changed!'

'Did I just hear myself say that?' Could it really be that we have made possible what many never dared to imagine? Despite my firmest intentions and efforts not to be, I am nervous. I am in the Sofitel, one of the flashiest hotels in Brisbane, in front of a crowd of about five hundred people. The deputy prime minister is in the audience and she is looking at me. I am supposed to be supremely confident at this moment but the truth is I'm not and I am annoyed with myself. I had got up early this morning to run on the tread-mill just to get that confident feeling yet here I am, flustered.

The crowd is here for our Inaugural Stronger Smarter Summit on Indigenous education. It is indeed a very swish affair. Four weeks earlier we had bets on the number of people that would turn up. Most of my colleagues thought we would not get over two hundred and fifty participants. I said there would be around four hundred and sixty. There were four hundred and sixty-two registrations. As I look out I see many of the faces that have been part of the journey to this tipping point, beyond which we hoped for a brighter future for Indigenous children.

On the stage I am reading from the Summit Communiqué I had drafted just a few days earlier.

The 2009 Stronger Smarter Summit symbolises a tipping point beyond which we now demand high expectations for all Indigenous students. We demand leadership with high-expectations schools, and high-expectations teacher/student relationships. The tide of low expectations of Indigenous students in our schools has changed. Rather than hope for a brighter future for Indigenous students, we now expect it. There is no place in any education jurisdiction for educators with stifled perceptions of who Indigenous students are, or what they can achieve. We need educators to work in partnership with community, using whole-school strategies to deliver brighter futures for all Indigenous students.

We recognise that while the tide has changed, positive results across the country are yet to flow in some places. Indigenous students will develop and embrace a positive sense of their own cultural identity as Aboriginal or Torres Strait Islander people. We now expect dramatically improved results will be delivered and Indigenous students will enjoy educational outcomes that are comparable to any other Australian child. We recognise that delivering on the promise of a stronger smarter future for all Australian children will require exceptionally hard work – innovative approaches to teaching, quality curriculum and quality relationships with Indigenous students, their parents and communities.

This is a human right that we as educators must deliver on, with the full support of state and federal governments.

After I've read it deputy prime minister Julia Gillard makes her way to the stage to give a stunning speech. While she may have some critics I really like what she has done for education in Australia, particularly Indigenous education. She announces a sixteen million-dollar investment into the work of our Stronger Smarter Institute and a huge cheer goes up in the crowd. Even though I knew this announcement was coming I am still somewhat blown away by it. I can't help wondering what my mum would think about this, and also what my dad would think of it if he were here today. I figure he probably wouldn't say much; rather, he would have his real proud look of a puffed-up chest, smug smile and shining Italian eyes.

Moments later I return to the lectern and say, 'I would like to thank you Ms Deputy Prime Minister for the sixteen thousand dollars you are giving us.' There is an expected murmur in the audience as people down in the front section are whispering politely to me, 'Sixteen million. Sixteen million!'

I looked out to the crowd, then at Ms Gillard and say with feigned surprise, 'What? Sixteen million!'

I pretend to be short of breath and about to faint on the stage. The people who know me best quickly figure I am playing the clown again. The entourage of television and radio journalists looks bewildered. Even in the most serious moments I can't help myself. I should perhaps be a little bit more focussed at a time like this.

My entire career has been dedicated to changing the tide of low expectations of Indigenous children in schools. So if the tide has indeed changed, what do I do now? It was a strange, yet pretty special, feeling. In some ways it was euphoric and in others surreal. In many ways I think my life experiences had crafted and shaped me for this moment and this announcement. Some may find it strange, but in many ways I am quite certain that even before I was born there were events and circumstances conspiring to bring me to this moment.

1

Humble beginnings

I was born on 21 September 1967, the last in our family of ten children. My father's name was Pantaleone Sarra. He was born in 1924 and came from a little Italian village called Miglianico, which is in the Chieti province of the Abruzzo region, east of Rome and bordering the Adriatic Sea. The village church is called St Pantaleone, so I guess he was probably named in honour of that saint. Like a lot of Europeans who made that dramatic journey abroad after the Depression in search of work, a new beginning and a brighter future, his beautiful lyrical name was bastardised by those who could not pronounce it. He was called Peter.

Dad never spoke too much about his family in Italy. My Italian grandfather was killed by German soldiers trouncing through Abruzzo during the Second World War. At the time my father's brother, *Zio* (Uncle) Raffaele, was just ten years old. He ran over to help, only to be shot in the leg with a bullet that ensured he walked with a limp for the rest of his life.

In Italy Dad worked extremely hard, married Emma in his

early twenties and together they had three children, Venere, Maria and Guilio. The times must have been tough as he made, what I am sure, the difficult decision to leave Europe in the early 1950s. Our Italian grandmother, from all accounts a strong matriarch, must have been broken-hearted when her son moved to Australia, never to be seen by her again. Dad left his wife and three children behind with a view to reconnecting with them when he got his money and circumstances sorted. As it turned out, they never came here and he would get back only for a short time in 1984.

On my mother's side my grandmother and great-grandparents were descendants of the Gooreng Gooreng – there are a few variations to this spelling – people in the north of Bundaberg. My grandfather and his people were of the Bunda people from in and around Bundaberg. Some people say Bunda, some say Tarebilang Bunda. History is circumspect in its discussion about my people, especially the massacre of our people on the Burnett River's Paddy's Island but both Aboriginal and non-Aboriginal historians agree that many were slaughtered there in 1849.

In the June of that year some local Aborigines in the Gin Gin area killed two young shepherds who worked for Gregory Blaxland and William Forster, the white settlers who had taken land there. Retribution of this nature was common throughout Australia; Aboriginal people were, understandably, hostile about the arrival of the white people and their herds. A group of settlers consequently avenged the shepherds' deaths by shooting a large number of Aborigines at their camp near Bingera. Some months later, Blaxland was killed. Forster organised another punitive party and they were responsible for the Paddy's Island massacre.

It seems the land to which my people belonged was too rich and fertile, and too proximal to the southeast, to escape the rapacious clutches of the colonisers. In spite of this, for me there is an enduring richness and strength about knowing that you grew up in a place where your people walked for thousands of years. To some extent I am certain that this made us solid.

Mum's mother was Kate Williams. Kate's mother was Ellen Cameron and her father James Williams. As well as Kate, Ellen and James had Annie, Ivy, Fannie, and James Junior. James Williams was a well-regarded, hard-working Aboriginal man around his area. He was held in such high regard he was offered a selection of land at Berajondo, near Baffle Creek just north of Bundaberg. This was quite unheard of at this time.

Mum's other grandfather was John Broom, a well-regarded horseman in the northern parts of Bundaberg. Grandfather Broom's partner was Emma. Together they had Alexander, Steven, Sarah, Tom, Bill, Cecelia and Kate. All are long gone now but I still remember Uncle Steve as a wonderful and gentle man who married Aunty Elsie, from Innisfail. He loved to paint and even today I keep at home an old shield upon which he painted Aboriginal men in traditional dance. I also remember very well Aunty Kate and Aunty Cecelia, who we knew better as Aunty Seal, who both lived long lives as devout Christian women held in high regard and with a sense of elegance, particularly in their best church dresses and with their long flowing silver hair.

Great-grandfather Johnny Broom outlived his wife by many years and would go on to live with Mum's father, Alexander, and sometimes with Great Uncle Steven at Avondale. Grandfather Broom worked as a labourer on Loeskow's Fairymead Station north of Bundaberg. Like my other great-grandfather, James Williams, he too was held in high regard for his extraordinarily solid work ethic. So much so, Mum recalls he was promised a parcel of land on the northern parts of the Burnett River as payment and acknowledgement of his efforts by Mr Loeskow. Shamefully, when they went to the courthouse to finalise the paperwork they were told it was not possible, as Aboriginal people were not entitled to own land. This was a source of great pain for such a proud Aboriginal man wanting to secure the well-being of his family, and Mum says it ultimately rendered him unwell, only to die of a broken heart.

Like me, Mum was youngest in her family. She was born Norma Broom in November 1929. She had two older brothers, Alex and Harold. Both were renowned Aboriginal boxers in their day. They were well-built and robust men commanding respect in local boxing circles, particularly in the Jim Sharman tents. Mum's older sisters were Molly and Mae. Aunty Molly would make it known that, as Mum was the youngest, she was by far the most spoilt, unlike me.

Aunty Molly would laugh as she recalled their 'get square' adventures, when they would take Mum for a walk in the bush and let her have it, only to discover, and rediscover, that Mum had a tendency to dob them in when they got back to the house. The usual result was a paddling for being nasty to poor little Norma, ensuring they would have to make up for it next time, and further ensuring perpetuation of the 'get Norma, get paddled' cycle.

In many ways I am exceedingly grateful that none of my immediate descendants were ever rounded up and imprisoned in missions like Cherbourg or Woorabinda, under the haze of the dreadful assimilation policy of that time. Notwithstanding, it was something that, like a grim reaper ushering in the death of one's sense of freedom, made its presence known. On occasions Mum would tell us that the old people lived with a constant sense of fear and mistrust of white people they didn't know well.

'Don't go near them white people,' she recalls them saying.

'Don't talk lingo!'

'Don't look them in the face!'

'Don't be cheeky to them!'

'They'll steal you. They'll kill you!'

I suspect the incredibly hard work ethic of our family played some part in ensuring they were allowed to live with some degree of freedom. It was clear, though, that this could never be something taken for granted. There were times when Grandfather Broom would have to write to the authorities of the day to plead with them to understand they were hardworking people with no desire to be separated or taken away to some mission.

Mum's childhood was spent living between Loeskow's paddock with her dad's people, and further north at Berajondo with her mum's kin. During her working years Mum spent some time in north Queensland, but most of her life was in and around Bundaberg, mostly working in domestic house roles for white people. She enjoyed going to the dance halls with her cousins and together they would check out the local talent. The influx of European men spiced the events up a bit, and there was one who was just too smooth and too charismatic to resist: one Pantaleone Sarra of Miglianico, Abruzzo, Italia.

By this stage Mum already had my eldest sister Amanda. She was born in 1952. It is difficult to know whether it was the 'Miglianico mojo' or the flash Fiat he had at the time, but something clicked. Romance blossomed, yet no doubt there were trials and tribulations. The result of the magic, though, was the children that would flow from this union. And flow they did. Cameron was born soon after, followed by Athena, more commonly referred to as Tina, Zac, Grant, Tracie, Dean, Lieba, Simon and finally me. We all carried our mum's surname until 1972, when it was decided we would change it to match our father's.

The Sarra family lived at 21 Whittred Street, on the east side of the town, just across the road from the Millaquin sugar mill and in the same street as the Bundaberg Rum distillery. I often say to others that my real claim to fame is that when you read the label of a Bundy bottle, no matter where you are in the world, it says, 'Whittred Street, Bundaberg'. So I get to puff up my chest with pride and say, 'That's my street!'

As a kid there was a lot to like about growing up in Bundaberg in the 1970s. Just down from us was the Burnett River, and a big paddock by our house kept us occupied with endless games of cricket in the summer, and Rugby League in the winter. We called it the 'SCG', 'Sarra's Cricket Ground', and it was the venue for many games, sometimes a few fights, but mostly lots of fun. One of the great things about being in a large family is we always had the numbers to make two teams for whatever game was on the program. We also managed to drag in plenty of the stray kids from around the neighbourhood as well, and for us this was just normal. Mum taught us to be nice to other kids and to stick up for those who could not stick up for themselves. Anyone who might have been a misfit had a place at the SCG.

Number 21 was a crowded house yet it didn't seem to bother us. We were three to a room: the big boys, Cameron, Zac and Grant in one; the girls Tina, Lieba and Tracie in another; and Simon, Dean and me in the third. We had to share beds; sometimes we had bunk beds and sometimes we slept top-to-toe. Mum and Dad had their own room. I can't remember living with Amanda, as she left home when I was still a toddler.

Growing up, there were a number of morning rituals in our home. First there was the sound of my father's footsteps from his bedroom to the kitchen. Then, almost on cue, I would hear that smoker's cough getting his body going for the hard work that would certainly follow. Close behind would be the sound of the radio with some dry voice from 4BU in Bundaberg, or the sound of the ABC trumpets kicking off the news at the top of the hour. My father would then make his way into our room.

'Chris!'

'Hmm,' I would respond sluggishly.

''Ere, reada my star!' he would say in his broken English. It was the usual astrological dribble but my father would always be attentive.

'Today you will face many challenges but do not trust the people around you. Look for the positives and good things will come your way,' or some other generic lines. If I was feeling a bit livelier I would throw in a few lines on the end.

'Be nice to your youngest son. Treat him kind and buy something good for him from the shop.'

His eyes would crinkle up momentarily, but then he would say, 'Ah don't talk a bull-a-shit!'

I would get out the cereal while my father sat and dipped his toast into the really strong coffee that he'd made. I could never work out why he would do this but I treasure those early morning memories of my father.

The kitchen was always a pretty lively place. Often the meat in our evening meals consisted of a hare our father had shot, or pigeons or chooks we had to kill and pluck, or a cow, pig or goat that had been knocked on the head. I always used to feel sorry for them as they met their fate. There were even times when our pet lamb, goat or hare was known to mysteriously disappear so cruelly, yet reappear so tenderly. So sad, yet so delicious!

Things were always oversized in our kitchen as I remember. Big thirty-kilogram bags of sugar, big sacks of potatoes, big bags of flour, and even a big bread bin. Appetites were always big, too. In their early teens the girls did the cooking and sometimes it was whatever they had brought home from their Home Ec. classes at high school. It was usually the type of meals that were useful in big families – a huge pot of stew and rice, often with dog bones from the butcher because they were cheap, or a huge pot of spaghetti. None of us would complain as we all loved spaghetti, and with a firm mother like ours it was not a good idea to complain about what was dished up.

Dinnertime was always much anticipated. We would wait eagerly for the call. We might be down playing on the SCG as the sun was setting or watching the black-and-white TV with half an ear on the kitchen. Even today I still jump and think about making a dash when I hear someone say, 'Dinner's ready!' We would race into the kitchen with just a split second to scan for the biggest plate, and then make our grab for it. We had to live with our decision as the rest of plates were soon taken. I must have had a good reaction time to 'the call' as somehow I ended up with the nickname 'Fats' and 'Tubby', despite my body resembling that of a finely tuned machine – at least that is what my good self-esteem enabled me to see in the mirror.

We had a huge table that would seat five on each side, sitting on a long bench, and Mum and Dad at each end. There were often times when we had to bring a table up from downstairs to put at the end of the main table in order to make room for extended family or other hangers-on. I loved sitting around that table. Not just because of the good food we ate, but because it was a time when we were all together and having a good yarn, each of us having a valid voice at the table. Mum encouraged us to have a say and ask whatever questions we liked. There was no such thing as a silly question. One night Mum was telling us all about how babies were made and it must have sent our cousin Kenny Roberts' mind racing. After she explained how the baby is inside an egg in the mother's belly Kenny piped up and asked what happens to the shell after the baby is born. I then had images of a newborn baby with its mother, and this huge eggshell lying broken on the ground.

Sometimes our older brothers would talk about dramas they were having with people at school calling them racist names. Mum would say to us things like, 'You're more of a man if you can walk away from a fight!' When we talked about racist taunts on the sports field she would say, 'They must be feeling inferior to you because that must be the only way they can put you down.'

'We are blackfullas, and that's just how it is! Don't let anyone ever try to put you down or make you feel ashamed of that!'

'Treat others how you want to be treated!'

These were pretty profound messages being drummed into us. We learned a lot about life at that table. It was an excellent place to put things into perspective. I believe it was this that enabled us to grow into strong identities, not enslaved by racism and the attitudes that came with it. There was a sense of a real humanity nurtured in all of us and I think that made us powerful in our own ways to cope with the challenges of life. So much so that we could withstand and tolerate the guy next door calling us 'fucking little black bastards', yet still be generous enough to pick him up and help him stumble home after he had fallen off his bike, which had miraculously carried him so far while blind drunk from the East End Hotel in the afternoon, or to mow his grass after he had his leg chopped off.

We would never dare ignore the humanity of others, particularly those within our own family. Even though our mum shielded us from some of the chaos, we were honest enough to recognise that some of our extended family really struggled with life and, like others succumbing to such challenges, resorted to alcohol, perhaps as a means to escape or, at the very least, to add some sense of purpose to get through the day.

'That's your family, and don't you ever look down on them. You don't ever turn your back on family,' Mum would say of our uncles or cousins, who could be spotted under the Burnett River bridge, 'getting on the charge' with their mates.

Mum also encouraged us to think about the future, even after Zac at an early age announced his grand plan. When he grew up he wanted to buy a big truck so he could pick up all the cockroaches in our house, load them up, and then take them to the dump. Today, as a Magistrate in Brisbane, Zac still thinks that is a good idea.

In our younger years Mum was more your stop-at-home mum. Later she would take up work as a social worker and played a key role, along with others, in setting up organisations such as the Aboriginal Housing Cooperative in Bundaberg. She was involved in many activities to do with land rights and women's rights. My father wasn't sure at first how to deal with these ventures, but he was told by Mum to just do so. I remember once a discussion at the table in which Aunty Mabel, who had grown up on the Cherbourg mission, chided Mum.

'Norma,' she said, 'what are you going on about all this rubbish for? You've just got to forget all this stuff.'

Mum would hold her ground and I remember feeling really proud of her for doing so. What she was doing was important to her and I knew it was. She would stand up for herself and for other blackfullas in Bundaberg. Even when they were stabbing her in the back she would defend them because she was not the kind to live with injustice and indignity. She would even stick up for people too silly to do it for themselves. One day she was trying to help a guy organise guitar lessons from someone in town and she asked him, 'What this guy's name now and I will get his number from the phone book and ring him up to organise these lessons for you?'

'Oh, gee, I forget his name there, Norma. His number will be there in the phone book but!'

Sometimes she could have a laugh while working, but most of the time she had a serious fight on her hands. On another day she and a few other campaigners went to the Gin Gin Council to protest about them wanting to erect a sign on the side of the road. It was a painting of two naked and traditional Aboriginal women with the words, 'Welcome to Gin Gin'.

'What's the big deal?' the people at the council asked. In all of her feistiness she pointed to the women in the picture and said, 'That's a gin, and that's a gin!' It was the genesis of a huge uproar, with some half-wits having no idea how offensive this representation was. As Mum and her colleagues unleashed their fury I remember feeling so proud about how she had taken up the fight, particularly when she could have done what so many others did and just ignored the issue.

I know there were times when it took it out of her. All I could do was watch when she came home and slumped down in the chair, talking about the frustrations of the day. Some days she would be arguing the case for someone to some small-minded bureaucrat, and on other days she was organising meetings for big-time people coming to town to meet with members of our Aboriginal community. It was pretty amazing to be a part of this as a young kid, particularly as I was always keen to get a sense of what was really going on. I recall Mum taking us to get our eyes checked in what must have been one of Fred Hollows' efforts, and also sitting in on discussions with someone who I am pretty sure must have been the eminent historian Henry Reynolds. I remember Mum at one point in the conversation saying, 'That might be what your history books say, but I believe we were here from the start!' Everyone in the audience cheered for her and I was suitably impressed. After the meeting the guy came looking specifically for her and wanted to sit down and have a yarn.

Sometimes her activism led to a bit of travel. Like a lot of Aboriginal people in that era there was a degree of mobility due to the Catholic Council holding a range of conferences with an Aboriginal rights' agenda. Looking back it was pretty amazing. At a young age I got to hear what people had to say about land rights, fights against racism and setting up housing cooperatives, legal aid and health centres just for blackfullas. I remember listening to some pretty prominent people, like Mum Shirl from Sydney and the statesman-like Pat Dodson from the Kimberley, who took part in the discussions.

My father seldom had time to get to these events as he was so busy working, but at one he managed to meet Pat Dodson.

'That man is like a saint!' he said to Mum later. I'm sure Mum was pleased as punch that he thought of so highly of him.

Dad worked for the Bundaberg City Council and was well regarded by his mates on his team. He often said he would have been the foreman but for the fact that he could not read or write English. His gang was responsible for the kerbing and channelling around the town and even today, as I drive around Bundaberg, I am reminded of his work in various places.

In earlier years Dad cut cane – the old-fashioned, hard way, with the cane knife. It was dirty sweaty work but he never ever feared hard labour. He was well connected to his Italian mates who had also made the long journey from the father country and would meet with them every Sunday evening at their 'Across the Waves' Soccer Club. He also undertook some share farming with his good mate John Botta. Together they would work the land, producing small crops including zucchinis, pumpkins, tomatoes, cucumbers, eggfruit and a whole range of other things. You name it, they had a go if they could get a good price at the Melbourne markets. Their other partner was a mysterious and elusive Mr D. Rocco. We never saw much of him but he always seemed to be a very handy and good colleague for our father.

In the summer holidays we would help out by picking watermelons and tobacco. I picked watermelons for Mr Facciano and tobacco for Mr Gorza, both mates of my dad. Sometimes they sent us to tell one of the others a message in Italian. We had no idea what they were but knew they were 'interesting' by the smiles on their faces. I suspect now they were a bit bawdy and the joke was on us. The work was pretty hard going at times but the toughest part was getting up in the morning. Our father would chase us to bed early and wake us some hours later. It was a struggle waking for work when it was dark outside. On some mornings we would get up, drearily spoon some Cornflakes or Rice Bubbles into our mouths and strike up some energy to open our lethargic eyes to check the clock only to find, to our exasperation, that we were awake an hour earlier than we needed to be. This left us with a dilemma: jump back into bed or stay awake. Tough decisions! Once we got into the swing of the day, though, things were fine.

I loved those days of picking tobacco. Not just because we got paid to do it, but also because it was the Sarra boys working alongside their father. To me there was something entirely priceless about that. Like my older brothers I started working in the fields while I was pretty young. We would go out with the bigger boys at about seven or eight years old and potter around a bit, picking some crop here and there, and sometimes sitting on the tractor trailer helping to load. For this we might get about a dollar an hour. Then by the time we were thirteen we would be well into it the swing of it, picking our own row and collecting money for it – about six or eight dollars an hour. I loved waiting around to collect our cheques when the work was done. We'd load the barns and be pretty tired after labouring in the sun all day, for ten hours straight, but there was something deeply satisfying about watching the boss sign your cheque and hand it over.

I grew to appreciate and love this work as to me it was an honourable trajectory into manhood. Picking alongside grown men and earning the same money as them brought with it the realisation that in many ways people saw me as a man. Of course, to live up to my father's expectation we all had to work and act like men. This didn't mean it was always serious out there in the field; in fact, my father was the chief joker in many ways, entertaining the gang with his funny stories and antics. There was something special about the good-humoured working-class banter that went on. Nothing pompous or precocious, but of course we would sort out all of the world's problems out there under the sun.

At the end of each row, which was often a hundred to a

hundred and fifty metres long, we would sit down and have a yarn while the smokers puffed their cigarettes, as if there wasn't enough tobacco around the place. It was always a treat when new people joined the gang, as we would talk about the snakes we saw while we picked.

'What? Snakes! Out here?' they would ask, with trepidation.

'Yeah, big ones too. King browns!' we'd say, which was not always a fabrication.

Then we would start on the next row and one of us would sneak up behind the new guy, knowing that brown snakes were fresh in his mind, and rub a stick or a piece of grass against his leg. Their reaction would entertain us no end as they jumped almost six-foot high and threw their hard-picked leaves every-where. Our victims were always pretty jovial with us once their nerves calmed down and we had handed them the toilet paper we always kept on the tractor for such occasions.

2

School days

I have vague recollections of my first day at Bundaberg East State School in 1973. The school was a huge building with high ceilings. My teacher was Miss Petersen. She was the nicest lady in the world. My brother Cameron thought she was pretty cool, too, and was always saying he was going to come up to the school for a meeting with Miss Petersen. I couldn't understand why as Mum did all the meetings with the teachers. Not that I think our teachers were too keen to meet with Mum as she wasn't shy about coming to school to set things straight from time to time. Most often she met with Dean's teachers. Right throughout his schooling he had a way of 'brokering' conversations between Mum and his teachers.

On school days in our house it sometimes felt like Central Station in the mornings. By the time I was in Year 1 there were eight of us having to get into the rhythm of the rush of bodies to wash, uniforms to iron, breakfasts to get down. Luckily, for the boys, we could walk across the road with towel and soap in hand to have a shower in the Millaquin Mill showers. There were about eight stalls of steaming hot showers, one for each of us, and no girls screaming at the door saying, 'Hurry up.' It was great, too, because I got to hang out with my big brothers. Sometimes on our way back home we would jump on the back of the cane trolleys and sail along while doing our best to hang on. Mum would give us a good whack and growl us if she caught us doing this. I could never understand why.

During the morning we also had to attend to our two cows, Josephine and Mavis. Josephine was the gorgeous brown Jersey, and Mavis was the feisty black and white Friesian. They were the unpaid curators of the SCG. They always did a great job fertilising and keeping the grass mowed. In the mornings before school we would take them across the road to tie them up where there was plenty of grass. Occasionally one or both of them would make a run for it, to various parts of East Bundaberg, and we had to chase them down and drag them back. Sometimes I would try to out-psyche them by looking them in the eyes to see if they were in the mood to bolt or not. I used to think I could tell if they had that glint in their eyes, doing their best to conceal an elaborate bovine getaway plan.

Once Josephine and Mavis were settled and secured we rushed back to the house to wash our feet and head out for school. In my early primary years it was Tracie, Dean, Lieba, Simon and me who trounced off together to Bundaberg East. Over time our party dwindled down to just Simon and me. Some days we would trek through the sugar mill or Burnett Sawmill. These days, with workplace health and safety rules, we would never be allowed to roam as we did, particularly through the mill. We'd gleefully race in and out of sheds, and up and down ladders to reach into the huge toffee vats as they steamed away. In other parts of the mill we would run into the huge storage sheds where they stockpiled the sugar before carting it off. They were like indoor sand dunes. We'd run up to the top and roll all the way to the bottom with sugar in our hair, our clothes and, conveniently, our mouths. I imagine this sugar ended up on other people's tables and I wondered what they would have thought about these little black kids rolling around in it and having such fun.

All the workers at the mills knew the Sarra kids. Some would even share their lunch leftovers with us when we were on our way home from school. On other days we would take the long way and stick to the roads. Whichever route we chose we seemed to have the food part of it pegged. We knew the exact location of every guava, mango, Brazilian cherry, banana, bush lemon tree, and every prickly cucumber or cherry tomato bush that was growing freely. Actually, the banana trees weren't really growing wild, but if they hung over the fence we considered them to be 'free'.

Food was a big thing in our lives. When we got home in the afternoons we'd get stuck into a loaf of bread, usually to make Vegemite or peanut paste sandwiches. Sometimes we'd even have a crack at cooking a piece of meat if we found some lying around in the fridge. After this we go to the SCG for a game of football or cricket, and we'd even play if there were only enough of us for one person on each team. Gender wasn't an issue in these games, and Lieba is testimony to this. She would run the football up with elbows cocked to cause maximum damage.

Somewhere between our game and dinnertime we'd have to retrieve Josephine and Mavis and someone would milk them. The bigger boys usually did this, but, even though I was pretty young,

I would sometimes give the milking a go. Grant hailed himself as the number one, 'fill the most buckets', milking champion of the family. He claims he had some type of special relationship with Josephine, and that he would get more milk if he played her the right music on the radio.

When I was in Year 7 I started to deliver the afternoon *Telegraph* around East Bundaberg for Mr Chapman, who owned the newsagent up the road. I must have been a sight with my big bag of papers hanging off my shoulder and my little leather money pouch around my waist. I would walk up and down Princess Street, stopping at Petersen's Hardware store, Mr Hazard's store, the furniture shop and the pubs, the Prince of Wales and the East End. I used to wonder about what the men got out of just sitting around drinking beer in the afternoon. I felt a bit of embarrassment as I sang out to everyone in the bar, 'TEL–LEEE!' at the top of my lungs. In my head I was thinking, 'Big shame job, this one!' Sometimes, just to make it more interesting, I would go right up close to someone who was half asleep in their chair, fill my lungs with air and then scream out that famous call just to watch them jump half out of their drunken skin.

It didn't pay as well as the tobacco. Sometimes the tips were okay and sometimes they were lousy. The best tip I got was from some guy in a pub who dumped all of his change on me. I noticed one coin that looked a bit strange and so I showed it to Mum when I got home. Mum took it to a coin dealer who checked it out. Turns out it was some kind of gold sovereign, which made my Mum excited. At the time I didn't really know what the fuss was all about, but I still have that coin somewhere.

As I neared high school it was decidedly uncool to continue a career as a paperboy, and I traded my hessian bag for a Stanley knife and began packing groceries and pushing trolleys for Jack 'swish swish', The Slasher. It was a great job lined up for me by my good mate Tim Lenz. We worked Thursday nights and Saturday mornings. With red-blooded hormones bouncing all around our adolescent bodies, we cruised up and down the shopping aisles and in and out of the car park, taking moments when we could, while we worked hard of course, to check out the checkout girls and any other spunky chicks that came into the number one no-frills retailer. It was never flash work, but it paid well enough to enable us to buy our own clothes, so we could tell our mum not to worry about second-hand school uniforms anymore. All of the work I did at an early age taught me the disciplines of having to front up and do the job I was paid to do. It wasn't always work, though. We had plenty of time to enjoy just being kids.

I liked to get to school early so we had a good go at kicking the ball around, or playing football, soccer, cricket, or red rover. Simon and I were in the same class and grade all through primary school. I was the funny one in the class. Simon was often serious, although he did have a funny side to him and I enjoyed it when he was in the mood to be light-hearted. Overall I found school to be fun enough, I did it because I had to. While I could do all the work and I enjoyed the company of all the other kids, there were some parts that weren't so fun.

In our middle primary years I remember sitting in class learning about 'The Aborigines'. Me, Simon and Debbie Williams were the only blackfullas in the classroom. Debbie was good fun and we got on well with her, despite her later dobbing us in for stealing soft drink from the tuckshop in Year 7. So here we were learning about The Aborigines – interesting!

'The Aborigines live in housing shelters called gunyahs!' All the kids turned to stare at us with a strange look on their faces. It was difficult to know how to respond, especially as we were only about eight or nine years old.

'For food they eat wild berries from the bush, yams they dig from beneath the ground, and also . . . *snakes* and *goannas*!'

'Eeerrgh yuck!' the other kids squealed as they screwed up their faces at us, as if saying, 'What kind of people are you?'

I felt so angry. It was a kind of rage more fierce than I felt when they would tease us and call us skinhead after Mum had done her amateur job of cutting our hair. I wanted to punch them in the mouth to wipe the smirks well and truly off their faces. Of course, I couldn't do that in the classroom, but it was a different story in the playground. When kids asked us if we had snake or goanna for breakfast or on our sandwiches, we would just let them have it.

The part of school that I loved best was sport. I'd look forward to athletics day, even though I was never a fast runner or good jumper. I remember well the school athletics carnival of 1977, when I was in Year 5. I was the final runner in the mixed relay and the fate of our house team, Millaquin, rested in my hands – actually, more in my legs and their ability to finish first. The atmosphere was tense. As I took the baton there was only one thing between me and the glory that was our destiny: Julie Reynolds. I passed her at about the sixty-metre mark and was able to cross the line first, carrying not only the baton, but the hopes, dreams and euphoria of victory for my house team. The atmosphere was electric and the crowd went wild with rapturous cheering, all seventy of them. It was an historic day for me at school that day.

John Paul Young was big at that time, and the next day I woke up singing to everyone who would listen: 'Take a look at me I'm yesterday's hero! Yesterday's hero!' They were the only words I knew of that song but it kind of just worked for me.

I played sport in the mornings before school, during little lunch and big lunch, and couldn't wait for Friday afternoons when we were bussed to Salter Oval to play Rugby League or cricket. Our cricket coach was Mr Baulch and he would take us to the games and then be the umpire. In class Mr Baulch was really strict, but even with the strictest teachers I seemed to test the boundaries. The kids we played against often had nice cricketing whites while we just wore whatever range of colours we happened to choose that morning. On one particular Friday afternoon, in our usual ragtag way, Simon and I opened the batting and I had on my rainbow-coloured singlet, grey shorts, one batting pad on my left leg and, as usual, no shoes. The strap of the batting pad was rubbing against back of my ankle causing me some pain with the blister that was developing. At the end of one over Mr Baulch put his hand on my shoulder.

'Chris, what's wrong with your leg?'

'I got this blister, sir!'

'Let me have a look,' he said.

He bent down beside me to check it out and then took his handkerchief from his chest pocket to put between the pad strap and the blister, in order to relieve the pain. I remember feeling very weird at the time because it was a kind of caring and closeness I had never really experienced with any other teacher. I was thinking, 'This guy must really care for me.' Because of that gesture alone I decided I would never ever again play up on Mr Baulch. I was going to try hard in class because I knew that was what he wanted from me and I did not want to disappoint him.

That gesture offered an enduring lesson that would feature

prominently in my career as an educator. The role of the teacher is to be respected, but it becomes difficult to respect if we get so caught up in the role of 'the teacher' that we relinquish our sense of being a decent human being. Some teachers get this; some don't. Mr Baulch certainly got it.

During the school year holidays we would either potter around home or go to Brisbane and hang out with Aunty Molly and Uncle Andy. Aunty Molly was always fun to be with. Uncle Andy was from the Torres Strait Islands. He was good for a laugh and had potentially the driest jokes of anyone on the planet. For the summer holidays we would usually pick tobacco in the mornings and then go to the beach in the afternoons.

My eldest brother Cameron was like a god to me, and to many of the local girls, too. I just wanted to be like him. He would throw us into his flash blue Valiant Pacer, which we helped him wash and wax and polish just about every weekend, and head for Kelly's Beach, Bargara. Lieba, Simon and I would swim for hours between the creek and the ocean while Tracie and Tina worked on their tan and talked about whatever they talked about. Zac, Grant and Cameron would have the occasional swim in the surf, and then come out with chests puffed up and looking as muscular as they could for the girls. Dean would swing between torment-ing us little ones and hanging out with the big boys. When the sun started to go down we would gather up our towels and wash the sand and salt off our bodies, because we would not dare put either in Cameron's car. Heading home we would sometimes stop at the doughnut or the fish and chips shop for a feed. They were pretty special days, feeling tired and yet absolutely content from a few hours of sun, surf and sand with a belly full of fried food.

On other school holidays we went to Berajondo and hung out

with Aunty Mabel. This part of the world was a pretty special place for all sorts of reasons. At various times some of the older generations in our extended family on my grandmother's side lived there. It is also where my great-grandparents on my grandmother's side are buried. Mum and Aunty Molly talked about spending a lot of time there when they were little. It is where Mum took her first steps. As kids we would just run with our cousins and have all sorts of adventures in the surrounding bush. The possibilities were limited only by our imaginations. There was a cave where we could catch 'lobbies', as we called them, with a long string and a small piece of meat. Someone had the grand idea that if ever a world war three broke out, then we could hide in our cave at Berajondo. I'm not sure I shared that sense of optimism about it being good enough to protect us from the inevitability of a colossal and destructive nuclear bomb, but none of that mattered, because as kids anything was possible in our imaginations.

We could roam free anywhere on the hundred and twenty acres at Berajondo and just go back to the house when we were hungry. Sometimes we got our feed out and about, from bush lemons or guavas. One day, Mum and our Uncle Michael Williams took us out to show us how to get witchetty grubs, or *booyums* as we were taught to say in our lingo. Uncle Michael was pretty impressive and I remember being mesmerised as he honed in on the tree with the wood shavings, a sign of their presence, and then worked his magic to pull out this huge fat and creamy grub. I remember thinking just how deadly we were being able to read those natural signs and work such magic.

The Berajondo night sky was always so big. After a huge feed of corned beef and vegies or stew and rice, topped off with some of Aunty Mabel's bread and butter pudding, we would sit on the front verandah of the old house by the kerosene lanterns, yarning about all sorts of things and playing cards, Scrabble or whatever game was going. Off in the distance we could hear and see the lights of *The Sunlander* as it cruised by without even noticing this little bunch of blackfullas watching from beneath the blanket of darkness.

Sometimes we would take off from the property and go camping along Baffle Creek, another special place that we called the 'billabong'. Throughout the day we kids would swim, fish or play football or cricket with our cousins, while the older people sat around yarning, occasionally joining us in our adventures to cool off in the creek or demonstrate their aged but sporting prowess. There would always be a fire going nearby to boil the billy and, more often than not, a blanket on the ground with a card game in full swing. Sometimes there was some serious coin being tossed around, but mostly it was just for fun. On every occasion there was plenty of laughter.

Fishing at the billabong was good, too. You could catch a jewfish, a nice fat eel, or a catfish. I remember one time getting up before everyone else to check the lines. To my delight I pulled in a huge catfish. Uncle Michael came down as I was pulling the fish in. I showed it to him with a big grin on my face. He grinned back at me saying, 'Good on you son. Your blood's worth bottling!' I beamed with pride at his compliment but I could not help being perplexed by it. I wandered around all day thinking in my own naive way, 'What this fulla want to put my blood in a bottle for?' For ages I had this image of some old bottle sitting on the shelf with my blood in it. Was this any way to treat the number one fish catcher in the family?

Aunty Mabel loved having us around, although there was an occasion when she wasn't so happy with us. As usual we were staying there with lots of cousins, Eddie and David Tyson, Michael and Stephen Kiss and Clinton and Brandon Thompson. We did the usual things but on this particular holiday we were into making slingshots. We would head off into the bush with our tomahawk to find a tree with a branch with a nice strong fork in it. Then we'd cut up an old tyre tube for the sling part. The only piece left to find was something with which to make a small pouch for the rocks, our weapon of choice, to sit in.

In our efforts to outdo everyone else, Eddie and I found an old leather bag in the shed out the back. We were so pleased with ourselves and I can still see Eddie's smiling face as he cut the old leather bag with a sharp knife.

'Oooh . . . look at that writing there. Pure leather!'

'Deadly 'ay?'

I was puffing my chest up really proud, too. There was no way the others would match the quality of our kit.

Oddly enough, my chest wasn't so puffed up when I heard Aunty Mabel screaming out at us with anger and sadness at the same time. The bag was Aunty Fay's first-ever school bag and it had been kept for sentimental reasons for more than fifty years. We scattered to avoid her wrath, until we got hungry. We were even hungrier by the next morning as we had to go to bed without dinner that night.

Mum knew how to draw the line on our behaviour; she was the disciplinarian at home, giving us a whack when she thought we needed it. There were plenty of times when we had to line up as Mum tapped us with the egg flip or jug cord. Behaviour management wasn't a fashionable term back then, but one of her favourite 'aids' was the bottle of Epsom salts. If we were fighting she'd say, 'You kids have got shit on the liver.' Then she'd line us up, get the old brown cups that are still in the house today, and we'd have to drink the salts, easily the worst taste I have ever encountered in my life. Of course, it worked. We stopped fighting because we didn't want another dose. The salts also usually cleaned us out proper, even if I was never sure if the cleanout actually stopped us from wanting to fight each other, or if we were just too afraid of exerting too much physical energy for fear of getting some aggressive energy going in the back of our pants.

Once when I was in grade eight Mum took me, Lieba and Simon up to Berajondo for a drive to see Aunty Mabel for the day. It was a trip like the many others we had made, just Mum and the three little ones. Lieba was in the front of our old Ford Falcon XB, and Simon and I were fighting in the back.

'If you boys keep fighting I'll stop this bloody car and you can get out and walk!'

Still we kept fighting.

'Gorn then! Keep it up and you'll be walking home directly!'

By this stage we were out of town – fourteen kilometres away in fact. We figured there was no way Mum would make us walk home. That would be cruel. But then she pulled the car to the side of the road.

'Gorn youse two wasters. Get out! I told you! You wanna keep fighting you can bloody well walk home! Now get!'

In disbelief we got out of the car and watched it disappear up the road towards Berajondo. After a period of waiting it became clear she was not turning around and coming back to pick us up so there was only one thing left to do. Walk home!

It was a long walk home, but a good time to think. We didn't walk together, and in my private thoughts I contemplated how behaviours bring consequences, and, when those consequences are signalled by our mother, it is best to take them seriously. Years later Mum confessed she was worried sick about us for the remainder of the day.

For the record I was home first, by at least twenty minutes, and somehow this convinced my brother-in-law, Gooze, that I was some kind of cross-country champion. Boy did he misread the form guide! It was not so much my athletic prowess that got me home first, more wanting to get there quickly for a feed. I did have some sporting prowess, though, as I did okay at cricket, hockey and Rugby League all right.

In Year 8 at Kepnock State High School in 1980, Simon and I would be reunited with Dean, who was in Year 12, and Lieba in Year 10. Lieba was quite introverted and quiet at school. Dean, on the other hand, was like the Godfather. He was captain of the open Rugby League team with a giant stature and a giant personality. I was nervous starting high school but I knew there was no need to be as Dean perpetuated the reputation established by Cameron, Zac and Grant, and hopefully passed on to me, as boys not to be messed with. What I loved about Dean was how all of the stray kids from the fringes, who often got picked on, knew to come to him for protection.

Our primary school had barely a hundred and thirty students, and our high school had almost a thousand. Despite the dramatically increased number of students around us I adjusted pretty easily. The hardest thing for me was getting used to wearing shoes every day. I could do the work, although it never seemed to excite me that much, and there were not that many teachers going out of their way to get my intellectual juices flowing. It didn't take me long to settle into the role of class clown. It worked for me, the kids around me and, I guess, the teachers. As long as I knew when to pull my head in I pretty much got away with most things, except the day I was playing the role of the mad scientist in grade eight science. I was tipping water from one test tube to the other, with all of the other kids looking on and giggling as I performed for them with my best, deranged and irregular face. Their giggling and jeering egged me on. Without thinking, I lifted the test tube to my mouth, drinking down the water and pretended to be even more crazy. It was kind of funny, at least until I looked up and saw Mr Collingwood staring straight at me from his big science bench at the front.

'Get out here, Sarra!'

It's amazing how things can be not so funny in a moment. I got a lecture about the types of chemicals that go into test tubes and this curbed my exuberance for drinking from them. By the time I had written out 'I will not drink from test tubes again' several hundred times, my interest was well and truly purged.

Rugby League was the game I loved passionately. The Sarra boys were renowned locally as great players. Cameron was a gun centre and played for Natives, one of the local teams. Zac and Grant were also gun players and played for Queensland schoolboys Rugby League in the late 1970s. Dean was very Arthur Beetson-like on the rugby field and people learned, often the hard way, not to mess with him. He was multi-talented, as he was also good at baseball, cricket and boxing. Simon was a pretty handy football player, too. The girls all excelled in softball and hockey. As for me, well I just cruised through on their coat tails.

By 1984 our high school had only won the Open Rugby League grand final two times: in 1979 when Grant and Zac had played in the team and in 1984 when Simon and I played. We played against Bundaberg State High School at their ground and beat them in an epic match. Bundy High's coach, Kerry Short, and their official, Terry Doherty, agreed I should have the honour of keeping the game ball. At least that's how I recall it. At the time it seemed like winning that game was the most important achievement of our entire lives. Alan Rennick was our coach and we would do anything for him. We had a 'star-studded' team, none of whom went on to play professionally of course, but we were legends in our own lunchtime. My good mate David Spediacci was our main strike weapon. He was big like a man, and hairy like a gorilla. Even today we still tease him about that grand final match when, after just three minutes, he was taken off to hospital in the back of an ambulance, knocked out cold, with no recollection of that momentous day.

Like many teenage kids I was watching the rugby games on television. Brisbane Rugby League was big and we would watch it on Sunday evenings, especially since Zac had become something of a superstar and was playing first grade for Brisbane Easts. We would see him on the TV and then go to school the next day feeling proud as the teachers and kids would ask, 'Did you see your big brother on the TV last night?' While the bigger boys played team Rugby League predominantly, Simon and I were only allowed to play school football. It was a rule set by my mother as our family ended up 'boycotting' the Bundaberg Rugby League. A situation arose with the guy that lived behind our house. He was also the scorekeeper at Salter's Oval, where all games were played. We copped abuse from him in many ways, which made no sense to me as his daughter was in our class at school and we were pretty good friends. Occasionally we would find rocks being thrown into our yard, and the dad would hurl some quite vitriolic abuse at us.

'Black cunts!'

'Black niggers!'

'Black boongs!'

'Black gin!' he would say about my mum.

I remember one day when he swerved his car towards me while I was standing near the side of the road. As a young kid I had no idea what this was all about. Finally, Cameron, Zac and Grant had had enough. They confronted him at the football, trying to coax him out of the scorer's box. But the bravado that enabled him to abuse us escaped him and he stayed put. My older brothers backed off and walked away but Dean worked as the bait, kicking the wheel of his car.

'This is a shitty car!' he said, in his best brazen-yet-bulky fourteen-year-old self. The apparent departure of the bigger boys must have somehow restored the old man's warped sense of right-eousness, as he got out of the box and down the ladder. On the ground he was met by my big brothers and it must have been an ugly scene. There was a huge uproar and the boys were hauled in before a hearing.

Mum went along to stand up for them and Zac did his very best to justify his unsavoury actions.

'How would you like it if your mother was being called a black gin, or a black slut? How would you like it?'

I doubt they would have any insight into the anger and hurt being articulated. The fact that we had ignored the abuse over many years counted for nothing. Despite our best efforts, we were blackfullas, and the people on the other side of the table would never have understood what was going on. This was Queensland

after all. Further north blackfullas, on Joh Bjelke-Petersen government's orders, were being herded out of their communities in
the middle of the night to make way for mining companies to
dig up their land; police were killing blackfullas and getting away
with it; blackfullas were being denied access to housing, entry to
pubs and clubs for no civil reason. This was Queensland and there
were no racial vilification laws back then. What chance did we
have of getting anyone to understand?

Zac was given a hefty suspension. Mum fought back in the
only way she could, declaring that none of her boys would play
Rugby League for them ever again. It was a decision that would
hurt us younger ones, especially since our mates at school would
hound us to come and play on the weekends, and occasionally
some coach would pull up at home to beg Mum to let us play
in their team. Mum was fierce and staunch in her resolve. And I
profoundly respected her for this.

Simon and I ended up playing team hockey for most of our
teenage years. Every Saturday morning we would head over the
bridge to Hinkler Park, lace up our boots and get it on. Tina,
Tracie and Lieba played, too. We had to find our own way to training two nights a week after school. Mum would say, 'If they want
you to play then they can come and pick you up!' Tom or Dan
McCullough were kind enough to come and get us. They were
really decent guys. Tom was older and in a very Wayne Bennett-
like way he would not only coach us, he also played a part in
guiding us through the tumultuous transitions from adolescence
to young men. By the time we were fifteen, we were regulars in
the A grade men's team. There were times when I would get feisty
and get sent off for being a bit too aggressive, or for abusing the ref.
Just one go at actually being a ref cured me of that.

While we fought each other constantly at home, we always stood by each other if any of us even looked like being in a fight away from home. Our blood truly was much thicker than water. There were undoubtedly times when our family struggled, but somehow, whether it was through hard work, the support of our extended family, and a sense of loyalty to a belief about what is right and decent, we always managed to get by. We didn't live in luxury, but we certainly never felt impoverished in any way, materially or spiritually. In many ways I think we were energised by our togetherness. Perhaps we didn't realise it at the time but I think that sense of 'togetherness' and strong and hardworking parents enabled us to survive and succeed the challenges of school.

There was another joker in our class, Wayne Dallan, who was also Aboriginal. We were often in competition with each other to be the funniest, but we were really good mates as well. We had lots in common, and this was most notable when people from the Commonwealth education department came to visit. Wayne, Simon and me would be called out of class: 'Them three have to come to A Block for an Aboriginal meeting.' I am not sure what the others felt, but for me there was a little bit of shame in it. Not about being Aboriginal, but being singled out and taken out of class. I am not sure how it could have been arranged differently, though, as I would have been dirty about meeting during lunch-time or before or after school. That was my time to be on the oval playing sports.

In those meetings the people would ask us how we were going and if we needed any support. I remember saying something about help in maths would be handy, and never thought too much more about it until a few days later a lady arrived at my door to be my maths tutor. For a few weeks she would come to my house twice a week and sit with me, going through my maths homework. She was really nice but in the end I gave up because I was just too shy and felt extraordinarily uncomfortable in this one-on-one situation. I remember the other kids in my maths class saying how lucky I was to have a tutor, and looking back I guess I was, but this arrangement was never going to work for me.

A guy also tutored us for woodwork. I would go to his house on a Monday afternoon, and Simon would go on a Wednesday. Mum would drop us off and he would drop us home. For some reason this worked a bit better for me and I actually enjoyed it because we learnt some good skills and made some pretty flash stuff, like kitchen cupboards, coffee tables and other useful things. I remember feeling pretty deadly because I had crafted a set of wooden wine goblets and a tray on his wood lathe.

These were opportunities for us, but I could not understand why they were not offered to other students. I never understood either why we got money to go to school. Of course, I understand very well now why such opportunities were extremely important, but at the time I couldn't, let alone explain it to others. I would actively avoid any questions about it. If I had known then what I know now I would have explained to people that these small amounts of money and the access to tutoring took the edge off some of the challenges we faced as Aboriginal kids in a school system that my mum and her family were never allowed to participate in. It was a way of enabling us to succeed in a system that had failed us so dramatically. If misunderstood, as it often is, it is easy to assume it's an unequal opportunity. I can, in part, understand why some people develop a sense of outrage about it, but this outrage is fuelled by ignorance about the full context of this matter.

On the surface it actually did appear unequal. So for a moment I can empathise with those who harbour a sense of disapproval about the apparent inequity. Only for a moment, though. My empathy soon dissipates when I ask where this sense of indignation was when Aboriginal kids were so readily left on the scrapheap, and not given any access to schooling, just because they were black. If those people did not complain about inequity then, they cannot complain about efforts to remedy it now. I never complained about getting money, mind you. It did help out a lot and we would certainly have struggled to get through school without it.

Every second Wednesday in junior high school we would receive a cheque with our name on it for the princely sum of three dollars. We'd usually take it to the shop at the front of the school, because we had to pay off our tab from when we had 'booked up'. Once our bill was paid we still had a bit left to buy a can of Coke and a Chiko Roll, and a little bit more to get us to the end of the week. Then we would just go and book up again. The shopkeeper never worried about us saying 'Just put it on my tab, my cheque is coming next week!' He always knew we were good for it, and we always were. I yearned for the day I would be in grade eleven, because our cheques doubled then to the even more princely sum of six dollars. Not only could we book up a Chiko Roll and a Coke, we could go for hamburger and a Drumstick if we wanted.

The teachers I had at high school were mostly pretty good, but there were some who seemed to get off on their sense of power over the kids. I didn't realise it at the time but school was pretty much about being straight down the middle. If you could get through the day without interrupting what was going on, without letting anyone know you didn't have a clue what was going on, or without letting anyone know that you were bored out of your head, then most teachers just left you alone. Looking back it seemed many of them were going through the motions as much as I was. There were some teachers who stood out, though.

In Year 9, Mr Rimmer, my history teacher, clearly loved his subject. So much so we could not help but get into the subject. He would not only tell us stories about the wars in Europe, but also show us pictures he had taken of the graves of the people we were talking about. He would play bits of music relevant to the topic and he had us enthralled by his lessons. Some kids and teachers thought this English man with slightly dark skin was a bit mad, but none of that matters if you can have a class of teenage boys eager to get to their next history lesson. While his eccentric and passionate approach to his history lessons was something to remember, it was not the main thing that stuck in my mind about him.

'Here, Sarra! You've got some ability, you know. It'd be a shame to see you waste it,' he would tell me in the playground or when he kept me back for a moment after class. He would also ring up my mum or go and see her to talk about how smart I was. At the time I could not understand why this guy was going out of his way like this.

In Year 10 he hunted me down in the playground to tell me about Speech Day. Speech Day at Kepnock High was to me one of the most boring days of the school calendar. A mammoth task to endure, sitting for about three hours and listening to the principal give a speech, then the P&C president give his speech, and then all the academic and sports award winners trounce across the stage.

'Listen, tomorrow's Speech Day,' he said with his English

accent, 'you won't want to miss it. It's a pretty important day. I rang your mother, and told her to make sure she comes along.'

'What's this fulla doing ringing up my Mum to come to this?' I wondered.

The next afternoon I sat in the assembly, as insanely bored as I had been in years 8 and 9, watching the procession of goody two-shoes students sauntering across the huge stage in front of students and parents, with each parent popping up to momentarily be part of it as the name of their child boomed out over the PA system. I sat, and I sat, and I sat. The senior mistress then announced over the microphone, 'The winner of the AL Stewart Award for Citizenship is Chris Sarra!'

'Holy shit!' I thought. 'So that's what Mr Rimmer was carrying on about.'

It seemed to take forever to walk up to collect this nice flash trophy sponsored by a prominent local car dealer. By the time I collected my prize they were already calling out the winner of the next award.

Mum was pleased for me, even though she chipped me about wearing my dirty old sandshoes on the stage. It reminded me of the time when we had a family photo taken and she told me off for wearing my comfy sandshoes. They were good for me, especially as I hadn't seriously worn any shoes for the first thirteen years of my life.

Mr Rimmer went to Mum afterwards to chat and I could see Mum was proud. Strangely enough, Mr Rimmer seemed proud, too. For a moment I wondered if it was because he was a little bit black like us. I respected him a great deal and he taught me to love history. He helped me to love Rugby League more passionately, too, although I am not sure this was part of the learning objectives. He took time out to explain to us that Rugby League originated in the north of England because 'the toffs of the upper class refused to play Rugby Union against those workers in the coal mines', so the miners, in consultation with God, made up their own game, Rugby League. Something about this resonated quite strongly with the 'working class warrior' inside of me. Forever my sense of passion for Rugby League would be conversely matched by my sense of dispassion for Rugby Union and I resolved that I would never sell out. If Mr Rimmer had continued to be our history teacher I would have retained a love for this subject, rather than selling out on it as I did; just as quickly as one teacher unearths a deep sense of passion for a particular subject, the next teacher can bury it so callously.

While my passion for history died, a new one was nurtured by Mr Woodman, the teacher we had for earth science. Strangely enough he was another foreigner; an American with a persisting accent. It was exciting to watch and learn from him. He was so enthusiastic about getting us to understand how continents shifted via plate tectonics, how volcanos formed, how tsunamis and earthquakes occurred. Sadly, the joy of learning was eroded, yet again, by the teachers that followed, who just made us read the textbook and answer the questions at the end of the chapter. On one occasion I recall the lesson was so boring I fell asleep in class, only to be awoken by the other kids laughing at me.

I loved physical education the most. The practical part got us out of the classroom and running about, but I was also into the theory. I was always fascinated by the human body and loved to understand how it worked physiologically, and anatomically. Part of this passion I guess was fuelled by my regular visits to the gym with my mates, Tim Lenz and Pat Cumner. At least three afternoons a week after school we would be gulping down the protein drinks and up to the Trimshape Gym at East Bundaberg to pump iron. We'd try our best to look impressive to the girls in their gym gear, and at the same time trying to steal a glance at our muscles in the mirror when we thought nobody was watching.

I was pretty good at English, too, although I was never a top student. I used to think that just getting a pass was good enough and so I never bothered to study hard, or try too much. Apart from Mr Rimmer, I never had a teacher who really went out of their way to push me to do better. For English I would occasionally get Bs and so I never really felt the need to push to get As. I used to think there was no point as my teachers had me pegged at that level. I felt that even if I had had an Oxford Scholar complete an assignment for me to hand in, then I would still get a B at best. It didn't really matter that much to me, as I never felt that tuned in to what school was all about. As far as I was concerned we just had to go, get our senior certificate, and then go and look for a job. The thought of going on to tertiary education never seriously entered my mind. They never seemed like a place Aboriginal people would go.

During my schooling it's fair to say I was not particularly conscious of the extent to which my sense of Aboriginal identity really came into play. I knew very well who I was and where I came from and I made it known to others. There was, of course, the odd occasion where someone would call me black coon or black nigger, but in many ways it was incidental and never usually bothered me that much. I had my mother to thank for my good self-esteem, and against this background being called black was something positive. It was not something I was hung up on or took too seriously. There were times, though, when I would let the jovial mingle with the complex.

Our Year 11 English teacher really was an English teacher. Dave Swindell was a pommie, who was also pretty good. He retained his English accent and skin colour that was almost albino-like, but had a red face from the Aussie sun. Sometimes I would tease him about how he pronounced his words, and on one particular day he asked us about what we wanted to be when we left school.

'I want to be white!' I said jokingly.

I immediately knew this made him uncomfortable, as he wasn't sure how to respond. All the other kids laughed, as they always did when I cracked a gag.

'You want to be . . . white?' he stammered, with half a smile and a look of apprehension.

'Yeah!' I replied. 'Then I wouldn't have to put up with the shit I gotta put up with . . . and I could run with you mob and do whatever I want in this place – on my land!'

The others laughed, but I am certain they had no idea about what they were laughing at. I was doing my best to invoke the voice and message of those Aboriginal leaders I had listened to from the sidelines of the Catholic conferences. In some ways it was all a bit of fun but in others it was my way of saying, 'I'm not like you, but I expect to get a fair go too!' I guess it was my way of also exposing them to a message many would never have come up against before. These kind of complex conversations are not always so light-hearted, though.

In Year 12, a teacher was encouraging a conversation about Aborigines. I was feeling okay about it until some of the students started to direct comments and questions at me.

'How come, when the government gives a perfectly good house to an Aboriginal family, they just pull the timber off and use it for firewood?'

'How come Aborigines drink so much?'

'How come you get your school trips paid for by the government?'

'How come they get free cars?'

I was put on the spot and didn't know what to say. I remember mumbling some inadequate words like, 'Yeah, well, it doesn't make sense to me either. My family doesn't burn our house. I guess people have to find a way to move forward and learn to live a modern life.' I wish that I had known then what I know now. I simply didn't have the intellectual capacity to articulate an appropriate response back then; I was fifteen years old!

The teacher had no clue about how to harness a safe and productive conversation to achieve more thoughtful and constructive insights. To me it felt like she was on their side. I was left to flounder alone, albeit with the moral support of my good mate Sheree James, who could do little more than understand I was feeling brutally hurt at this time. After the lesson she said, 'I'm so proud of you.'

'What for?' I asked.

'Well you just took all those questions from everyone and gave it your best. And it wasn't fair,' she said. 'I wouldn't like to be put in that situation.'

It was very decent of her. But in spite of her support my head whirled with that 'lesson' for a long time. Emotionally and intellectually I was a raging torrent of raw emotion – adolescent frustration swirling with juvenile confusion among rapids of intense anger.

I remember thinking I should have said, 'If you want to know you have to fucking ask *why*, and you keep asking.' If there is some old blackfulla drunk in the street, ask *why*? Why is he drunk in the street? Maybe he's drunk because he has had a shitty life. Well, *why* has he had a shitty life? Because he's lived around a whole bunch of halfwits who've treated him like shit. But *why* have they treated him like shit? Because he's black, because his ways are different, because he's lost his pride as a man, because people have got it in their heads that he is inferior. Somehow he now thinks he is inferior and so he acts like he is. I also wanted to say, 'Why do I have to explain myself and my people to you?' When do you ever have to explain to me why some white people are so fucked up? Your people get pissed. Your people bash their women. Your people get stuck into drugs. It's not pretty, and no race is perfect!

Fortunately I was strong enough, and smart enough, to just contain this sense of adolescent rage and confusion. I'd learned to use humour, and how not to alienate others. All of our family had been strengthened by the lessons from our mother: be proud, hold your ground. I knew that there would be no turning back if I went down the anger track. It would only lead to more marginalisation, more confirmation of negative attitudes. I'm sure this sense of frustration is still felt by black kids in schools today. It is more frustrating to 'check' our response. The perception that Aboriginal kids are angry and violent exists in contrast to the reality. A black child can ignore someone putting them down ninety-nine times, but if on the hundredth they yield and punch another kid in the mouth for it, all of a sudden that perception is confirmed as reality.

'See, I told you they were angry and violent.'

I've watched others break under the pressure of the stereotype.

It is a constant that many Aborigines have to contend with. We have to watch every move we make, while others of a certain type can stumble along unchecked in their own ignorant bliss or stupidity with no sense of accountability to anyone. Fortunately for me such torrid days were little more than sporadic. I genuinely hurt for kids who have to encounter and contend with such dynamics regularly and without the strength and support of strong parents.

Towards the end of 1984, I kept hearing other kids talk about some thing called QTAC. It was a mystery to me. I never went to any of the information sessions about university; it just went over my head as being of no relevance to me. When everyone started talking about it, though, I figured it must be important so I went to see the career guidance officer, something I'd never done before. Like most of the people at school the guidance officer seemed a pretty good bloke.

'What's this QTAC thing?' I asked him.

'QTAC stands for Queensland Tertiary Admissions Centre,' he said, with a sense of authority that I accepted.

'So what does it do, this QTAC thing? I've heard the other kids talking about it.'

'Well, it's a form that you have to fill out to say what your preferences are for university courses.'

'Do I have to do anything for it?' I asked vaguely.

'Well let's have a look,' he said, and headed off into another office to retrieve some obscure-looking orange piece of cardboard that turned out to be my student record card.

'Hey', he said with a smile and some surprise. 'It looks like you have the right number of Board subjects! By the looks of this it seems like you are pretty smart, too, you know.'

He must have sensed I was trying hard to seem interested and so he sat beside me and showed me my marks from Year 7.

'Have a look at this. This is your TOLA score. You got ten out of fifteen. That means you must be pretty bright!'

'Okay,' I said, wondering what it was. He told me it was the Test of Learning Ability and I had a vague recollection of doing it but not why. He convinced me to fill out a QTAC form.

'What courses would you like to list?'

'I dunno!'

'What do you reckon is the best job in the world?'

'I dunno! Maybe a Phys. Ed. teacher,' I said, looking out the window at the PE teacher and her class just outside. It kind of made sense. I loved the theory and practical elements of the subject. Why not?

With that he wrote down some numbers on my QTAC form for the PE teaching course at the Brisbane College of Advanced Education.

'You probably won't get into that course,' he said, 'but we will put it down just in case. Let's just put courses down so you have a chance of getting in somewhere.' The other courses were at Gatton Agricultural College.

Even though I pretended to get it, I never really did. By that stage what was most important to me was getting out of that room and away from another know-all adult. Like any shy black kid I was intent on telling him whatever I thought he needed to hear from me to wrap things up.

The last day of school rolled around with little fanfare. I don't know what I expected, and I wasn't into pulling any last-minute pranks. I just remember grabbing my stuff and making that my final walk across the parade ground, stopping to punch some smart-arse

Year 9 kid in the mouth. He was big-noting himself in front of his mates by calling me names and probably figured that while he was in the manual arts classroom with a teacher, he could say something smart and get away with it. I reached in through the window and jobbed him, unbeknown to the teacher, and headed for the bike racks. I had never been a troublemaker or swung my fists in all of my years of high school until that eleventh hour. I got on my old blue pushie and rode off into the sunset.

Those twelve years of school made very little sense to me. I did okay. I had a good time. Yet still that enduring question continued to haunt me: 'What the hell was that all about?'

The next few years would see me wrestle seriously with this question, and in many ways the answers I discovered were not that nice.

3

A revelation

In January 1985 our family travelled to Leeton in New South Wales, packed like black sardines in a hired minibus. A car full of Sarras on a twenty-seven-hour trip proved interesting – strong-headed Mum and strong-headed Zac made sure of that. My enduring memory is of them having the most animated of arguments all the way. Over the years Dad had occasionally gone down south in search of seasonal fruit-picking work. We were heading there now, though, to attend Dean's wedding. He had met a local girl when he went to Leeton for work a few years earlier. Being a Sarra, he quickly got into the local Rugby League scene, too.

The trip occupied my mind and I hadn't thought much about what I'd be doing the following year. My TE score was seven hundred and fifty, which was average, but good enough for me. A few weeks after finishing high school I had received a letter in response to my application from the Brisbane College of Advanced Education. I had been invited to an interview to see if I was suitable for a program aimed at getting more Aboriginal teachers into

Queensland's secondary schools. To say I was surprised would be an understatement. None of this would have happened if I hadn't, almost on a whim, taken up that fifth Board subject for Senior. In many ways it was a fluke.

At Kelvin Grove I met a whole bunch of other Aboriginal kids. Ken Southgate, the head of Physical Education, and Hope Neill, a prominent Indigenous educator at that time, interviewed me. We also met a few of the college's staff, namely Clarrie Diefenbach, Stewart Pow, Paul Thomas and Gary MacLennan. They had conceived the idea of running this program and spent the morning explaining why they wanted more Aboriginal and Torres Strait Islander teachers in secondary school. Later in the day we had been asked to write an essay about why we wanted to be a part of the program. I vowed that I would not let those who established the course down and would prove it was not a Mickey Mouse scheme.

I came back to Bundy from Leeton feeling pretty pumped. Then I waited. And waited. I didn't hear a thing. I rang my brother Grant, who had a Commonwealth Public Service job in Brisbane, to see if he could find out what was going on. He rang Clarrie Diefenbach, who was very surprised I hadn't been con-tacted. He said that they definitely wanted me on the course and he chased it up immediately. I had the feeling of a near miss. If Grant and Clarrie had not intervened, I might have been left in limbo.

That holiday season I worked in the tobacco fields as usual. Having been up since four o'clock in the morning, I came home one afternoon, tired and covered in dust, sweat and nicotine stains, and saw the big chunky envelope addressed to me. Inside was my Secondary Physical Education teacher-training offer. Now it felt real. Mum and Dad were both chuffed. There had never been a teacher in my family. I could hardly believe it, but I had no doubt that if I started this, I would finish it. Many years later, I was on a plane with Professor Paul Thomas and he told me about the fights he and Clarrie and the others had had to get their fellow academics to agree to the establishment of the program. He knew about my career and what that opportunity had meant for me. As I thanked him and we shook hands I knew this was a very special moment.

At the end of January 1985 I jumped on a McCafferty's bus and headed to the city. Brisbane didn't scare me as it might have done if we hadn't spent lots of time there during school holidays. As kids we loved riding the suburban trains to Fortitude Valley with Aunty Molly, who was a regular at Big Valley Bingo. As she put in a few solid hours at Bingo, Lieba, Simon and I made our own way around the shopping centres, up and down escalators, in and out of shops and all along Brunswick Street. If we weren't in the Valley, we went up to Cloudland for a game. This magnificent ballroom had been built in 1940 and was a much-loved Brisbane icon. It suffered the same fate as many other beautiful old buildings around that time – Joh Bjelke-Petersen had it knocked down in the middle of the night to make way for 'development' in 1982.

By the time I moved to Brisbane, Aunty Molly and my sister Lieba were living at 16 Mars Street in Wilston. It was a grand old Queenslander that had been broken up into three flats by a fun and friendly Italian landlord named Frank Mollo. He was always good for a yarn and reminded me in some ways of my father and the guys he used to knock around with in Bundaberg. I would often tease Aunty Molly saying that if she ever married him then her name would be Molly Mollo.

'Oh, Chris. You're cracked!' she would say, giggling away.

Aunty Molly and Uncle Andy were in flat one and Lieba lived in number two. I bunked down in Lieba's flat for the first two weeks until I found a place of my own. Lieba put an advertisement in the paper for me in the hope that I could find somewhere to board, which seemed to make more sense than getting my own flat. I ended up boarding with Ian and Nerida Arney, a very nice couple with two quite young girls. I lived in a room under their Newmarket house and I had told them I was happy to work around the yard and help with household chores in order to maintain the board at a reasonable price. They were very good to me. To get to college from their place I had to catch the 19B bus that ran along Banks Road. On the way home I'd get the 19A and get off at McDonald's on Newmarket Road to walk that treacherous uphill stretch along Banks Road to Bearsden Avenue.

When I arrived at college for Orientation Week I didn't have a clue about where I was supposed to go or what to do. Luckily enough I bumped into Alan Wason, an Aboriginal guy from Mareeba who was at the same interviews I attended some months earlier.

'Hey, you made it in too, 'ay?'

'Yeah! You know where we supposed to be going?' I asked him.

'Nuh!' was Alan's reply.

Alan was a chunky kind of straight-haired, green-eyed black-fulla with about the same complexion as me. We didn't really talk much at the interviews but our shared confusion at O Week ensured we connected immediately. Eventually we stumbled upon the right room, along the way noticing and commenting on the girls like kids in a candy shop. Alan had seen nothing like this in Mareeba, and I had seen nothing like it in Bundaberg. I knew then I was going to like being at college.

We found the right room but it didn't take long for confusion to revisit as they bamboozled us with talk about subject codes, timetables and room numbers. I noticed other students seemed quite at ease with what was going on. If they did encounter anything they weren't sure about they would just put their hands up and ask questions as confident as you like. There were all sorts of questions swirling around in my head but I was too shamed to put my hand up. Alan felt the same. There were no other blackfullas and in some ways it felt like I was there under false pretences. It was almost as if I was unworthy, and this was heightened during the break when I got to mingle with the other students.

The usual line of question and conversation went, 'How you going? What's your name? Where you from? What school did you go to?' All of which I could handle well enough, despite my almost crippling feeling of shyness. The next part of the conversation was where I did whatever it took to disengage as best as I could.

'What TE score did you get?'

I knew it would come up. All the other students had to have TE scores above nine hundred and ten to get in. So I was feeling something like an imposter, yet I understood why I was here. There was clearly a need for more Aboriginal teachers. I had not come across any during my school years, so I was going to have to live with my sense of guilt, get over it, and do my best to explain why I was afforded such an opportunity. It was never easy, mind you. While most of our new classmates were pretty good, there was the odd one who went out of their way to make a point about how their mate missed out on getting in despite having the right score.

Our first major learning experience was the O Week camp for our PE group. We went somewhere on Moreton Island. The thing that struck me as a sign of our age was that we were allowed to take alcohol with us. It wasn't a big thing for me, but there were a few other students who were working themselves into a frenzy about what type and quantities of drinks they were taking. The camp was the usual kind of getting-to-know-you bonding experience, with the ropes and team-building activities, a bit of swimming here and there, and then a final night concert. The third-year student mentors did a bawdy rendition of 'Old McDonald had a farm'. It was very funny and I'm sure it was done at every camp by the older dudes to impress the 'freshies'. I was getting into the evening, and after a few beers my shyness was wearing off. I was getting to know the people around me and when it came to making people laugh, it was my time to shine. Then one of the others guys got up to tell some of his jokes.

'How many coons can you fit in a falcon?'

'What do you call an Abo with a job?'

Out they rolled. A range of racist diatribe that wasn't even particularly funny. That they rolled from his lips so easily was palpable. Also palpable was that nobody seemed that jarred by such commentary, not even the lecturers. It did me, though!

I don't know if it was a sense of outrage or if I was feeling a bit more courageous with a few beers in me, but I piped up when their laughter subsided and said, 'Yeah, my mum's Aboriginal, you know. And I'm Aboriginal, too!'

There was a bit of a jeer in the crowd and he seemed to cower a bit. There is always a feeling of not knowing where to go in the wake of such circumstances. I was just there to fit in and be part of the crowd. I didn't want to be the angry blackfulla who everyone tiptoed around. I just wanted to hold my place with dignity. But I wasn't going to put up with this type of behaviour either. I have never really liked the uneasiness that emerges when you call them on it. I would rather it didn't happen because it makes everyone uncomfortable. But I didn't want to enable comfort by being passive when others set out to trash my people.

For me, humour has always been the best train on which to depart such a toxic and unsavoury station, and so with a few more beers under my belt I got up and did my own stand-up show. Making people laugh has been one of my talents and I seemed to be doing okay that night. With the racist trash and its discomfort behind us, I had the whole camp laughing with blackfullas' humour. Proper deadly style! Mind you, we were all pretty charged by this stage and I think this made my work a bit easier. The more they laughed the more I pushed the limits by getting cruder and cruder. Eventually I must have pushed too far as I recall Tom Cuddihy, one of our lecturers, frogmarching me off the stage to the cheers of my new college buddies.

Some years later Tom and I recalled this night, and he was somewhat reverential in his reflection. He said he admired me for standing up and signalling that I was not going to put up with that kind of talk.

'You stood up for yourself and your mother and your people, and then you got up and told your own jokes and they were really funny, you know!'

In February the first semester of college started. Because Alan and I were part of this 'special entry' program, we had four subjects, while the 'normal' student had six, knowing that it meant we would take at least four years to complete our teaching diploma, while the others would be done in three. With this reduced workload I was convinced I could take on the challenges of tertiary education, in spite of my TE score. As it turned out, it didn't take much to get into the rhythm of college and I actually enjoyed myself.

I had some great lecturers, like Graham Nimmo, who would teach us the intricacies of communication within a classroom and take us through the micro-skills of teaching and lesson planning. I found it really fascinating and hadn't experienced this kind of learning before. I enjoyed all of my subjects, particularly those in psychology, sociology and philosophy. Clarrie also provided extracurricular lessons when he picked me and Alan up in his car and drove us around some suburbs in Brisbane, such as the West End and out to Inala and Goodna.

'Have a look at the houses, boys. What kind of money do you think the parents in those houses would be making? Do you reckon they would have finished high school? Do you reckon anyone who lives in this suburb would have a university degree?'

These were questions we had never entertained before. Then Clarrie said, 'Think about the teachers in this school and how they see the kids from this suburb. Do you think they have enough money to go on school excursions? Do you reckon they think they are lining them up to go to university when they finish school? Do you reckon they even think these kids will finish high school?'

We told him what we thought as we cruised along. At Inala and Goodna the houses looked a bit like the ones we grew up in. The kids playing on the footpaths reminded me of me back in East Bundaberg after school. I doubted those kids would have been thinking about going to college.

'Let's go and have a look at Kenmore and we will check some

houses near my house at The Gap!' he said, asking us the same questions as we drove around. Our answers, of course, were very different as the houses were bigger and more spacious, and the cars were flashier. There was definitely more money in these places. The kids were more than likely thinking about going to college and their parents would probably have gone, too.

Clarrie was stretching our thinking. It was an extraordinary learning experience. Some years earlier he had written a PhD thesis on teacher expectations, but, because it was loaded with honest empirical evidence about the racism that existed in the attitudes and expectations of teachers, it was rejected by one of the examiners. It seems it was a message that the profession was not yet ready to hear. This was clearly a great disappointment to Clarrie. For years he had been trying to convince anyone who would listen that there were Indigenous people who could teach successfully in Queensland secondary schools. For years nobody in the department of education seemed interested, but Clarrie persisted. He was intensely passionate about the need for Indigenous teachers as role models. He could also see that unless there were special measures established to recruit and support them it would be a very long time before it occurred.

In setting up the program back in the early 1980s, Clarrie Diefenbach, Stuart Pow and Paul Thomas went out on a limb. These men with good academic careers didn't have to go out of their way for people like me. Their lives could have continued along happily but they saw an injustice and were not prepared to sit by and do nothing. I guess they knew that when you say or do nothing about injustice you actually say, 'I can live with that!'

We stopped at Clarrie's place for afternoon tea, to shoot some snooker on his huge table and meet his lovely wife, Elva. She was pleased to meet us as Clarrie must have talked a lot about us at home.

'So you're from Mareeba, Alan,' she said. 'I have relatives there. Do you know any of the Blacks in Mareeba?'

Alan looked up at her and said quite smugly, 'Yep, I know all of them!'

Clarrie and I burst out laughing.

'Not blacks, Alan! Blacks! Do you know anyone up there with the surname Black?' I'm not sure what Alan was thinking but Elva would never have asked a question like that.

The academic and social support around Alan and me was really great. It was made even more so when Clarrie sat us down in his office and said, 'Wait here, boys, I want you to meet this new guy we appointed to keep an eye on you.' Around the corner struts my uncle Michael Williams. It was a fantastic moment. I respect him immensely; he is a man of tremendous wisdom. He had walked with us in the bush at Berajondo and taught me many things when I was a kid, even if he did want to put my blood in a bottle! I had stepped into a whole new world and I was really happy that he would be with me as my mentor.

Later on the college appointed Jeannie Barney as a counsellor. Jeannie was from Cherbourg and she was such a beautiful woman. She was so kind and gentle in her way with people. She had beautiful black skin and gorgeous jet-black hair. Several times a week I would pop into her office to just sit around and yarn about anything and everything.

Clarrie and Michael assigned a tutor, Gary MacLennan, to me to help with assignments and other assessment tasks. He was the short, dark-haired, bearded guy I remembered from the interviews many months prior, a feisty Irishman with whom I would remain friends forever. Gary had a deep sense of passion and belief about sticking up for the underdogs. Like many students who sat in awe during his lectures, I loved what he had to say and how he said it. He is a real teacher, and one of the best. I would meet regularly with him to discuss my progress and he challenged me constantly to think deeply about what I was learning. Intellectually Gary grabbed me by the scruff of the neck in one hand, and with the other he shined a light on my entire world, forcing me to see it differently. Gary showed me the 'hidden curriculum' of schooling and the 'hidden agendas' of society.

On one occasion Gary urged me to do an assignment about my mother's education and contemplate what opportunities she had had access to. The idea was to see how this may have enhanced or stifled my own efforts in school. It was a great idea but I wasn't sure I was ready for what it would reveal. Mum told me that she loved to read and had dreamed of being an archaeologist. It was never going to happen, though, as she was only ever allowed to go to school until Year 3. When I asked why, she said, 'I guess they just thought of us as uncivilised natives, and that we weren't capable of learning.'

This floored me to some extent, and it got me talking with my older brothers and sisters about their experiences at school. Tracie said, 'Remember that old hag we had in Year 2? She would make us sit at the back and say she was going to bring a bath tub in to wash these Aboriginal kids because they stink!'

As I tried to imagine what this would do to the spirit of a six- or seven-year-old, how it would make them feel about school and the people there, things started making sense to me. I began to see aspects of my own past as I hadn't before. I saw more clearly the circumstances: I had been sold short by people with low expectations, I had sold myself short with limited expectations of who I was and what I could achieve, and I didn't know I'd done this.

I recalled the principal coming into the room when I was in the last year of primary school. He had a look of surprise, which played out in his voice when he announced, 'Chris Sarra got the highest score in the TOLA tests!' Looking back through the lens offered by Gary I could see that he was saying, 'I didn't expect that from you!'

I recalled the Year 11 maths teacher signalling the same when he handed back a test and jokingly said to the class, 'Sarra got seventy-five per cent! Must have been an easy test!' We all laughed, myself included. He was a good man and I really liked him. I'm sure he wasn't being malicious but in his jest he sent a message that he didn't even know he'd sent: 'I didn't really expect you to get seventy-five per cent!' At the same time, I was receiving a negative message about myself that I didn't even know I was taking in.

The connection with Gary occurred at just the right time. I sometimes wonder what my life would have been like if we hadn't met and he hadn't brought me to such revelations. Would I have just got my degree and gone through the motions of teaching? Gary taught me about social justice and how to see a bigger picture. He got me wondering about how many other black kids were being sold short when they actually had something to offer. How many were selling themselves short because there was no one to encourage them to believe differently? How many non-Indigenous kids – from poor or unhappy homes, the smelly ones, the ones with no shoes or flash lunches – were also being sold short by a teacher with a prescribed view about who they were and what they could achieve in life?

With the deep and passionate support of Gary, along with Michael, Jeannie and Clarrie, Alan and I got to the end of the first term. I went home for a few weeks holiday at Easter and being back in Bundaberg was good. My dad was really proud to tell his mates I was going to be a schoolteacher. It was really something. I think Mum enjoyed the idea as well, although she was more inclined to remind me not to get too far ahead of myself and not to forget where I came from. One afternoon Mum and I sat together, just the two of us, watching the usual shows, checking to see if Gordon was going to get back with Pat the Rat on *Sons and Daughters*. The news came on. The Joh Bjelke-Petersen government was still in power and he had just sacked almost a thousand South East Queensland Electricity Board (SEQEB) workers. My father would get up out of his chair and spit on the screen whenever Bjelke-Peterson came on and Gary had shared with me his passionate disdain for the premier. In between news items Mum and I yarned.

'So what's it like then, this college thing?'

'It's not too bad. It's a bit like school in some ways, but you gotta make sure you get your work done,' I told her. I then told her how it was pretty good because I got to work with a mentor like Gary. On the TV the frenzied SEQEB rallies in Brisbane rolled before us and we saw scores of Queensland police doing their thing. As I watched, three Queensland cops grappled and shoved this feisty little guy into the back of a paddy wagon.

'Hey, Mum, that's him!' I shouted, and jumped up to quickly point him out. 'That's the guy there now. That's Gary. That's my mentor!'

I was feeling really proud of him. As for my mum, she just looked at the TV across the top of her glasses and then back at me. I am not really sure what she was thinking.

I was launched into a whole new world of analysis and critique. It was as if my mother had kindled a fire in my belly for the rights and social justice and wellbeing of Aboriginal and poor people, and then Gary came along and threw petrol on it. His influence triggered a range of emotions. I was extremely angry, yet passionate and determined. I was so determined that I met with Clarrie, Gary and Michael before the end of the first year and announced that I wanted to catch up on what I had missed during the first year. I wanted to take on an extra workload so I could walk out at the same time as everyone else on the course. I wanted to walk out as a 'normal' student, considered just as good, if not better than them.

Clarrie was not so keen on the idea. He wanted me to take my time to make sure I got it right. Gary was not so keen either. He had seen me get Distinctions and High Distinctions and thought it was important that I retain such a scholarly standard all the way through, even if it did mean taking extra time to finish. Michael got what it was about. Blackfulla to blackfulla, he knew how important it was for me to prove myself to be as good as anyone. My newfound and unheralded sense of determination prevailed and I started my second year workload a hundred and ten per cent more than other students, and in my third year I did a hundred and twenty per cent. This also meant I had to walk away from playing Rugby League in any serious and committed way.

During the holidays at the end of first year I was back working in the tobacco fields and picking watermelons and pumpkins. I had a clear sense of purpose that summer. The old yellow 19A and 19B buses were not too bad, the view was great, but I had to get my own wheels and roll when I wanted to. I worked and worked to rack up eleven hundred dollars, enough to buy my first car with the princely sum of nine hundred dollars.

My father stitched up a deal for me with one of his Italian mates, Attilio D'addario, and I bought his old 1972 Datsun 1600. Some would say it was a meat-pie brown colour, but I liked to think of it as 'sexual chocolate'. It may not have been the flashiest car, but it was mine.

The second year at college was renowned for being particularly hard. The novelty of tertiary education had worn off and in PE we faced Ken Southgate, the head of the faculty, and his subject, anatomy. Ken was quite a short, yet pretty fierce and feisty sounding guy. His big booming voice made up for whatever he lacked in size. He would start this subject by counting up the numbers in the classroom and reflect on the success-rate percentage of previous years.

'Nine of you are going to fail this!' he screeched.

We all sat bolt upright. He had developed a reputation as a hard taskmaster and he went on to tell us how many students had come and gone, and how they had handled the major assessment task for that unit, the oral exam. We heard stories of how students vomited before going into the room, and how some sweated and then vomited during the exam. It was pretty scary, but I could not afford to be a statistic on the wrong side of his ledger.

Sometime during that year I realised this was not just about me anymore. There were many people who had gone out of their way for me and were depending on my success. I also began to think about all those black kids in schools who needed to see someone cutting through the space in order to make them believe they could embark on such a journey as well. If I could do it then so could they.

In the lead-up to the anatomy oral exam I studied like I had never before. I hooked up with my mate Nigel Grieve, who had a skeleton at his house. I'd go there and we would study until the early hours of the morning. I loved the subject because I was fascinated by the human body. At my own place I would study until late at night, and then get up in the morning when it was still dark to study some more. On the day of the exam I was nervous. Extremely nervous.

Ken Southgate welcomed me into his office and got down to business straightaway. He sat at his desk and I sat opposite. Together we gazed upon the human bones and plastic muscular models before us and I felt like a small boy. He took out a long, sharp needle and began prodding and poking at various bits.

'Tell me about this part of this bone.'

'What is the name of this little muscle running through here?'

'What movements does that muscle cause?'

I had to explain the names of the muscles, where they originated and attached, and whether they were prime movers or assistant movers in lateral or horizontal flexion or extension or whatever. It was really hard going and it was difficult to gauge how I was doing. Occasionally he would write something down on his pad and then pick up his needle again. After about an hour we stopped. The exam was over.

I looked up at him and he looked at me. He was one of the guys who interviewed me to see if I was good enough to be in his faculty before I started. At some point back then he must have thought I was worth a go. All of a sudden he smiled. I wasn't sure what to do or think.

'You've been working very hard, haven't you?'

Immediately I figured I had at least passed. I felt so overcome. I'm not sure if it was some tremendous sense of elation that I had passed or relief that it was over, but I felt like crying. I looked straight back at him and said, 'I have worked on this like I have never worked before. I don't want to let anyone down. I have to finish this!'

He told me I got a B plus. I could tell he was pleased. He had backed me, and I think he was proud he had.

In my mind, all I could think was, 'I can do this . . . I can really do this!' From then on I knew there was no stopping me.

Sadly, Alan did not get past this difficult hurdle, even after two tries. It got the better of him, as it had stumped many other students, and Alan went back to Mareeba. I was now the only Aboriginal student from the original intake. Being the last man standing added to the role-breaking pressure I was feeling. Of course, it wasn't always hard work.

Wednesday afternoons were lecture-free and so lots of students would head down to the Normanby Hotel. I wouldn't go every Wednesday as my much-needed, sixty-eight dollars a week Commonwealth-sponsored budget didn't allow it. I'd get there about once a month and had a way of making my presence known. The manager at the Normanby was Pedro, a little guy who looked like a kind of Mediterranean leprechaun with Coke-bottle glasses. He would let some of us get up and sing a few songs with whoever was on at the time. My song was 'Hurricane'. The problem for me was that it was such a long song I would always forget the lyrics. I guess a skinful of beers, bourbons, wine and orange juice, or whatever was going cheap at the time, didn't help my memory much either.

'"Pistol shots ring out in the . . ." blah, blah, blah.' Whenever I got lost I would just break back into the chorus: '"Here comes the story of Hurricane. The man the authorities came to blame."'

The crowd usually cheered me on and at some point I remember thinking, 'Gee I must be all right, 'ay!' It didn't occur to me that everyone in the Normanby was just as smashed as I was. Those once-a-month blow-outs did their thing to keep me sane in some ways and it was good just to hang out with my college buddies and loosen up. For me succeeding at college was serious business, but I was never the type to be serious all of the time.

Having Aunty Molly and Lieba close by was crucial; there is no way to measure the importance of this. Looking back, doing family things kept me well grounded at a time when I could have easily become otherwise. By the middle of second year I had moved back to Mars Street, sharing flat two with Lieba. She would kick in a few dollars to help me when things were getting really tight. I owed her so much for her support yet she was happy to help. I think all she expected from me was to finish the course and become a teacher. In the afternoons, when I got home from college, Aunty Molly would have the kettle on and pancakes cooked with jam and cream. If not pancakes it was scones or Johnny cakes. There were always cards, as well.

'Come on, we'll have a quick game,' Aunty Molly would say.

'Aunty, I gotta study!' I would sometimes say.

'Oh, come on! First to five,' she would plead.

She loved having us around. We were her children, too, and she was another mum to us.

If we weren't playing cards we would go for a cruise in my car. Aunty Molly would climb into the front passenger seat of the Datsun 1600 with Uncle Andy in the back. The turn of my ignition key was usually the cue for Dire Straits, Bruce Springsteen, Radiators or the Violent Femmes to crank up in the cassette deck. Most times, though, it was the legendary Bob Dylan engulfing us with his rasping tone and lyrics: 'Heeey, mister tambourine man play a song for me . . .'

'Oh, Chris!' Aunty Molly would say, half-giggling, half-bewildered. 'You still playing this old drunk?'

'Here, Aunty!' I would say, leaping to defend the great philosopher and poet. 'Don't talk about Bob Dylan like that! He's a legend you know!'

She would dismiss me straightaway with her usual flippant chuckle.

'Legend? Good go! Still sound like an old drunk to me!'

During the final months of college there was a lot of talk about how teaching jobs were scarce. The education department sent in their recruiters to chat with us and deliver the stark news or offer interviews. I had to consider whether or not to teach in a remote Aboriginal community or stay somewhere more provincial. In the end I didn't really mind as I was happy to take a job wherever I was sent. A guy from the department gave us some great advice about life in the country as a teacher. He said that if we fell in love with a local girl, we should come back to the city during the holidays and sit on the Queen Street Mall for an hour. If we were still thinking about that girl then there was a good chance we might be truly in love with her. It made sense, and it was advice I tucked away in my mind for the unpredictable road ahead.

My good mate Annette Walker and I had our interviews for positions on the same day and we prepared for them together. My brother Grant had loaned me some flash clothes and a sports jacket to wear. It was the first real job interview I had ever done. I wasn't sure what to expect. I got through the interview okay, I guess, but there was one question at the end that I wasn't quite expecting, and I am sure it was a question not asked of anybody else.

'So you're from Bundaberg, Chris?' he asked.

'Yes, that's right.'

'What part of Bundaberg are you from?' he probed.

'I grew up in East Bundaberg, right across the road from Millaquin Mill.'

'Over near the slums, 'ay?' he said.

I was a bit taken aback. One part of me wanted to take him on and say something like, 'Do you have a problem with that or something?' and another part wanted to say 'Go get fucked!' I was certain this would not augur well in a job interview and so in a bit of a daze I replied, 'Yeah, well . . . that's my home. That's where I come from!' It was the only response I could think of, and looking back it was the right one.

Inevitably the end of the final year rolled around. For the last exam I was up at four o'clock that morning, studying hard before going in. When the exam was finished I put down my pen and thought, 'Geez, this is it! I finished college!'

Within an hour we were down at the Normanby, and within an hour and a half I had at least one wobbly boot strapped on. It was a great night. We had been eagerly anticipating the end for some time and it was surreal to be finally living the moment of getting on the charge with the good friends I had made over the years. We were somewhat sad, too, because we knew that, just like with your old school buddies, you end up going your own separate ways afterwards – but not before I had sung the 'Hurricane' one more time. I drifted out at some stage, deciding to walk home. Somewhere in the night two lovely girls kindly picked me up in their Volkswagen and dropped me at the bottom of Mars Street to stumble the rest of the way home.

The next morning I was sleeping quite heavily when the phone rang, which did nothing for my sore head. I wondered who could be ringing at such an ungodly hour of the morning – half past ten!

'Hello,' I stammered.

A big voice at the other end of the phone came booming back down the line at me.

'Can I speak with Mr Chris Sarra?'

'Yes, this is me,' I said, trying to hold my head in some way to stop it pounding so much.

'This is Frank Underwood from the department of education,' he boomed. 'We have a job for you teaching PE and English at Cecil Plains. Will you be willing to accept this job?'

'Yes, I will take the job,' I said meekly.

'Do you know where Cecil Plains is?' he then asked.

'I've never heard of Cecil Plains, but I'll take the job,' I said.

He went on to discuss formalities and to let me know who I should contact. As he was winding up the conversation, getting ready to hang up, I asked, 'Hey, mate, you're fair dinkum now, 'ay? You're not pulling my leg or something?'

'I can assure you, Mr Sarra, this is a very serious job offer and I wish you well working in our department.'

And just like that, I was a PE teacher.

He had told me Cecil Plains was west of Toowoomba and I got out a map to look for it. 'This doesn't look too bad,' I thought. Other graduates conjured up engagements or family hardships to do whatever it took to stay east of Ipswich and south of Carseldine. I was happy to go anywhere. I wondered what the principal would be like, what the other teachers would be like, how many Aboriginal kids would be in the school. I was ready to go.

4

I'm a teacher!

If I was going to be professional then I had to get better wheels. As soon as my salary details were confirmed I went straight into the Queensland Teachers Credit Union to score a loan for a decent second-hand car. I should have been much more loyal to the old Datsun 1600. It had been exceptionally good to me – far better than the newer 1980 V6 Commodore wagon that turned out to be quite a lemon, and a sour one at that. I am amazed at how a car salesperson can ring you three to four times in one day to tell you about the latest good thing they have to sell, but when things go wrong and you are trying to ring them they are always too busy, or have just stepped out of the office or whatever.

In mid January 1988 lots of people were getting excited about the Bicentenary and Expo but not me. I used my brother's card to get through the gate at Expo but I really wasn't into it that much. I had a wagon packed with all of my life's possessions and was ready to set off for Cecil Plains, a place I had never ever heard of before but that would be my new home. Up until this point in my life everything had been safe, in that I had always been surrounded by family. Now I was heading where I knew nobody and had to make friends and connections in the town on my own. In a way this was extremely daunting, yet in another I was quite excited by the prospect.

On my way through Toowoomba I did what a lot of twenty-year-old drivers do – got pulled over for speeding. I was doing seventy-six kilometres per hour in a sixty zone. I pulled over and quickly reached into the glove box to grab a t-shirt I kept there. It had a police academy logo on it. Michael Pownell, an old schoolmate, who had just been through the academy had given it to me. I put it on, thinking it might help, and stepped out of the car. I walked towards the police car because the body language books said this was a good idea. The policeman gazed at me, and then the car.

'Looks like you're moving house,' he murmured. He raised his eyebrows on noticing my shirt. 'You a police officer?'

'No, my best mate is,' I replied, hoping desperately this would help.

'Tell you what I'll do,' he said with authority. 'I clocked you at seventy-six but I will write you down at seventy-four. That means you won't lose any points and the fine won't be as steep.'

Thank you, good buddy Michael. Thank you, t-shirt. Thank you, body language book. It was very decent of him. Like most people, I suppose, I am a bit nervous around police and I wasn't sure what would happen. Apart from Michael the only other time in my life I had directly encountered a policeman was when one pulled his car up to stop me on my bike when I was about thirteen years old. On that occasion he did the really brave act of giving me a thirty-dollar traffic infringement notice for riding my bike on the footpath of the heavily traffic-laden Princess

Street. Looking back I can't help wondering if he was only able to be courageous around little barefooted blackfullas.

I arrived at Cecil Plains, and went for a cruise around the town. Up one street, back down another then up a third, and that was it. I'd seen the town. My accommodation was a duplex, which I shared with a female teacher. I pulled into the driveway and met the bloke who lived next door. We introduced ourselves and got talking about this and that. He was a pretty scruffy looking guy who had been teaching for quite a while.

'What nationality are you?' he asked.

Not too sure where this would end up, I replied, 'I'm Aboriginal.'

He looked at me then said, 'Oh, right. Well, I'm racial prejudiced myself, you know.'

I was taken aback, thinking this wasn't exactly a badge of honour. As much as I felt like smacking his despicable ignorance and bile back down his throat there was no point. I was new in a small country town, new to the school team, and I had to work and live alongside this jerk. I didn't really want to be cast as that angry black man, notwithstanding justification. I just tucked away the experience, to be mindful of, and did my best to look for other positive things in him that I could work with. We got on well enough to the extent that he considered me a good friend and work colleague, but I never forgot his remark. Maybe this is what it means to be tolerant.

I don't really like the term tolerant, as in a 'tolerant society'. It always implies putting up with something you don't like. We tolerate things we don't necessarily like but can endure if we have to, like a sore back, loud noise next door or leaking roof. We should never see another group of people as one to be tolerated. As I got used to hearing politicians spruik on about a tolerant society, I couldn't help wondering if they would muse begrudgingly about how they had to grit their teeth and tolerate these black bastards. When political leaders speak about Australia as a tolerant society, I get the feeling they are reaching out to like-minded people with an arrogant grin that says, 'We're stuck with these black bastards so let's just tolerate them.'

I guess the strategy of looking for the good in people or situations helps to keep you sane and balanced. I can thank my mum for this. As I've said before, she instilled in us the strength to stay in control of our own emotions rather than relinquishing them so easily to others who are invariably not worth it. Racists fail to understand that when their views, beliefs and behaviours undermine the humanity of others, they actually undermine their own sense of humanity. At this point they are the ones that suffer because they stifle their capacity to show their best, or to see the best in others. Once I get to this point in my mind about such people I tend to feel sorry for them rather than angry, knowing that they have a serious problem, not me.

Fortunately, the rest of the school team, and the rest of the community, were keen to see what I had to offer, not only as a good secondary English teacher and PE teacher, but also as an Aboriginal teacher. I seriously think that many people were happy about having an Aboriginal teacher in their neck of the woods. Besides all of that, there were so many great things to love about Cecil Plains. The landscape, with its chunky gum trees and tea trees hugging a meandering Condamine River, was fantastic. The sunsets were awe-inspiring and poetic, particularly after a dry day with the dust in the air from the cotton harvesters. What I liked best, though, were the people.

Dean Hearn, one of the local young cotton farmers, dropped by just to introduce himself and welcome the new teachers to town. His primary motive, of course, was more about meeting the new female teachers but it was still a nice gesture. Rodney Baker, another young cotton farmer, pulled me up on the side of the road when I was out for a run one day to stitch me up to play Rugby League for Pittsworth, and to share the hour drive to training twice a week. Rodney was a wild man who drove his bright yellow Mitsubishi Lancer like a maniac. We would always tease him and call him 'Gobbledock', because he looked like the one making it big on the TV ads for Smiths chips. Over time I became very close mates with both Dean and Rodney, and sadly both of them would meet with tragedy. Rodney was killed in a car accident late one night somewhere between Oakey and Mt Tyson, just outside of Toowoomba. Dean became paralysed from the neck down after being thrown by a wave on his last swim at Mooloolaba. He and I still keep in touch from time to time and he still gets around quite a bit despite his injury.

The kids at Cecil Plains were great. I loved their sense of innocence and naivety that somehow did not reside with kids in schools at the city or on the coast. There were about a hundred and thirty students at the school. It had a small secondary department of just thirty. I taught English to years 8, 9 and 10 and felt really lucky in that I taught PE to every kid in the school. They were all fun in their own way. I had the primary kids eating out of my hand, especially the littlies. I would line up the kids from grade one before taking them back to their teacher and say, 'Righto, kids, listen up now. You want me to teach you some really big words before you go back to Mrs Olsen?'

'Yes!' they would all say. I would then teach them the magical big word and walk them back to class. Mrs Olsen was very sweet, petite and an incredibly experienced teacher.

'Mrs Olsen, you have to ask them if they enjoyed PE today!' I would say as twenty-eight little five-year-olds smiled and giggled. They were bursting to let out this magical and impressive big word. Mrs Olsen knew what was going on and she would nonchalantly say, 'Did you enjoy PE today, grade one?'

'IMM – MEN – SE – LY!' they hollered in remarkable harmony, somehow turning a three-syllable word into four.

The big kids were great, too, and I really enjoyed getting out and about on the oval and playing cricket and football with them. At the time I was in my physical prime – young and fit. When we played footy I would urge them to try to get a big hit on me and they loved the challenge. They would do their very best, without even realising that this was more than just fun and games. I was building some emotional capital with them so that when we were in class they would do whatever I asked of them.

There were times when I got to have quiet yarns with a few of them who struggled. At that new stage in my life I was still a fledgling teacher, but I had fresh in my mind what good, bad and ordinary teachers were like. I wanted to be one of the good teachers, one of those who would go out of his way to be there for kids in a relationship that was respectful, caring and fun. I knew it was challenging being fourteen, with your voice deepening one moment and then squeaky the next, and hormones zinging all over your body throwing the entire universe out of whack. But some kids face real hardships. I remember one young fellow who didn't have a mother. His father was a truck driver and as such was away often. He basically looked after himself and his little brother. We'd talk about food and he asked how to make spaghetti. Thanks to my home life I could look after myself in the kitchen and so I showed him a few things about cooking, which he appreciated. He was never really recognised as a bright student by others, but to me he displayed a tremendous sense of maturity and emotional intelligence.

In my work with him I wanted to expose the hidden curriculum to him. I wanted him and others to understand that in many ways school was like a game where some kids know the rules because their parents knew them, and other kids didn't. At the start of the year he hated Shakespeare as much as any fifteen-year-old country boy, but as he got to understand it within the context of the whole school game, he started to appreciate it a bit more. For their oral assessment task the entire class had to choose and recite a soliloquy from *Julius Caesar*, and I remember watching with pride as he rose above the jibes from his adolescent mates, who were giggling because he turned up in full Shakespearean costume for his recital.

His life was so gentle, and the elements
So mix'd in him that Nature might stand up
And say to all the world, 'This was a man!'

I could not help thinking that he was in many ways describing himself. He was a good young man who landed on his feet when he got an apprenticeship at a bakery in Dalby after he finished Year 10.

I loved teaching Shakespeare. I loved it even more teaching the bard to kids who expected to hate it. At first I was always pretty confident about my ability to get them to love the plays and be excited about them like I was, even if it meant resorting to the really basic by saying to grade nine boys that chicks would really dig them if they could quote Shakespeare. I loved being a teacher.

At the first term Easter break of 1988 I returned to Brisbane for our graduation ceremony. I remember feeling proud the day I graduated. All of my family turned up to see me walk across the stage to get my diploma. Mike Williams, Clarrie and Gary also showed up. As part of his important address, when the chancellor read my name out he congratulated me for being the first Aboriginal student to complete the secondary teacher program. I wasn't expecting that special mention! When I stood up everyone in the great hall clapped. It was pretty special, yet in some ways it felt strange, like I should not have been in this space, but I was. I strutted across the stage with my chest pounding and I could hear my family singing out. Unlike all of the other graduates, they let me have the stage to myself as I shook hands with the chancellor and grabbed the piece of paper. This was the culmination of three years of sweat and tears. I looked down at the paper and thought, 'This is it?'

We took so many photos and I remember thinking how great it was to have all of the family there, especially Lieba, because if it hadn't been for her support I would have struggled a lot more than I did. My mum and dad were so proud I was a teacher.

I was now enjoying and exploring some of the tricks of the trade I was learning back at Cecil Plains. Simple things, such as making eye contact with a student first when you are walking towards them so that they move out of your way rather than you having to move for them; like leaving just enough space for one student to pass between you and the door so they file orderly into the classroom rather than bumping into each other; like turning your body sideways to write on the blackboard so you can still see the class and are not turning your back on them; like open questioning and other behaviour management techniques. I felt I was pretty good at the relationships aspect of teaching, always with some room to improve. There was obviously room to develop in many of the technical aspects of teaching, like assessing where a child is at in terms of their literacy performance, setting individual learning goals, and tailoring classroom learning experiences for each child that would build upon what they knew.

It was also great to watch and learn from other, more experienced, teachers as they executed our craft. I remember being mentored by Barry Welch who was a very experienced secondary English teacher at Dalby State High School up the road. Bill Brazier, our principal, was a great bloke and I also learned a lot from him. When he talked about his time teaching at Duaringa with a lot of Aboriginal kids in the community I would hang off his every word. He loved teaching and you could tell this by the way he just loved to drop into our classrooms unannounced and take over. From Bill I learned that great teachers love kids, and they love what they do. He also taught me about being selective and strategic about what a teacher should see and hear. As he explained sometimes it is far better to pretend you didn't hear a child swear, than to damage what could be a tenuous relationship with a child who could do with a break, and was probably just letting off steam.

For me the ability to teach is a gift that should not be taken for granted. It is something special to be able to take knowledge and share it in such a way that thirty young minds can understand. While we may not get paid as much as other professions there is no remuneration that can account for that feeling you get when you realise the penny has dropped inside a child's head when they finally get it. A special moment for me was watching a young chubby kid called Graham, who did everything he could to get out of swimming because he couldn't swim, try a few moves that I had instructed him on in the pool and suddenly just take off. It was exciting to see the look in his eyes as he realised, 'I can swim!'

I found myself in that first year of teaching thinking back to Mr Baulch, my primary school teacher; in particular, about how good he made me feel as a student. He made it easy to respect and honour what he was trying to do with me. What amazed me in part, and continues to do so, is that I still remember him so clearly in a positive and respectful way, which got me to thinking about how my students would remember me. I always took my role seriously and would engage the strategy of an emotional bank account with every child. You make a deposit every time you have a positive exchange with a child, and an emotional debit when the exchange is negative. The trick is to have as much or more emotional credit, or positive interactions, with each child so that when you have to discipline them you don't end up on the red side of the ledger.

There are so many ways a teacher can have a positive exchange with a child. It can be as simple as saying, 'Great to see you here today,' or 'This might be hard but I reckon you can do this,' or even, as Mr Baulch did, helping out when they are hurting. This is part of the magic and power of teaching that I think we can sometimes underestimate. These days, when I travel to various places and talk with thousands of people, one of the things I ask is who remembers a teacher from school. Just about everyone remembers one and, more than that, they remember whether or not they made them feel good about who they were, or made them feel something less positive. It's quite a powerful position to be in.

I connected well with most students but there were some times when I didn't quite so well. I look back on those times with regrets and often think of the mistakes I made as a twenty-one-year-old rookie and how I would do some things so differently if I had the chance again. Inside the classroom the kids were always well behaved for me but as I look back I can't help wondering if it was out of genuine respect for me, or because they feared my reprimands. I was pretty firm with discipline, and in part I wonder if this was because if kids played up I construed this as wasting 'my' time in 'my' classroom. The reality, now exposed by wisdom, is it was 'our' classroom, and 'our' time. Had I been so wise at the time I might have been less firm, and more concerned about whether there was something going on for them outside the classroom, whether I was teaching in a way that they could learn, or whether or not they were truly bored out of their heads and tolerating me.

Like a lot of those country towns out west, the farm kids, who might have been financially better off, would usually go to the local primary school and then to a boarding school in Too-woomba or wherever their parents and grandparents had gone. One of the things that surprised me about the kids left at Cecil Plains in high school was just how much they were so easily conditioned to a watered-down script in the same way that I was as an Aboriginal student. Given my own experience, it was easy to see that if left unchallenged these children would sell themselves short and just go through the motions at school, coming in just below satisfactory as everyone, including themselves, expected. I was determined to get them to see differently. Just because they had been a D student didn't mean they had to be a D student forever. There were lots of students I would pull aside with their grades and challenge them to wonder about whether they truly had the potential to do better than this, or whether they were content with just being as everyone expected. Some kids responded well to such conversations, picking up their efforts and improving, while some, I'm certain, found it to be a strange and foreign type of conversation.

Living in a small country town meant that everything I did was known or at least guessed at. The kids (and no doubt their parents) always knew whether I'd gone to Dalby, Pittsworth, Toowoomba or Bundy for a weekend or for the holidays. They knew how many tries I scored and how many goals I kicked on the weekend. They knew about parties, girlfriends, everything. Sometimes it seemed that they knew what I was doing, even before I did it, like the day I came off the pushbike. I had a Year 8 PE class that I took regularly to the swimming pool one term. They were always hounding me to come in and have a swim with them. I fobbed them off, saying that I would get in with them during the last lesson of the term, which I did. It was great fun; however, when I got out and went to the changing rooms, I realised I did not have a spare pair of jocks with me. I just pulled on my shorts, planning to ride home quickly and get some underpants at little lunch.

I walked the kids back to school then borrowed a pushbike from a Year 10 student, telling him I needed to get something from home. And away I pedalled. It was springtime and the magpies were on the attack. Sure enough, I got swooped by a cantankerous one – pretty savagely – and the next moment I am arse up and tumbling off the bike and along the harsh and unforgiving gravel road. I had gravel rash and skin off all over me, and the kid's bike was the worse for wear, too – handlebars one way, wheels some other. Of course, this had to happen right in front of the rather large lady who was the Scout mistress in town.

'You all right, love?' she asked, to which I made the somewhat inane and futile reply.

'Yeah, but please don't tell anybody you saw me fall off the bike,' I whimpered. I am not sure why I bothered as she had a reputation for knowing and sharing everyone's business in town.

I straightened up the bike as best I could and raced into my place to get my jocks before heading back to the school. On the way back I stopped to see Robyn, the bush nurse. She insisted on taking me into her clinic and putting numerous dressings and bandages all over me. I told her what had happened and she rang Bill at the school. She did her best to be polite and responsible, and not to laugh at me, but I could hear Bill laughing on the other end of the phone.

'Some nurse you are,' I was thinking, 'laughing after a tragic accident!'

I left her doing her best not to laugh in my face and headed back to school. When I arrived, there were kids with their eyes popping out as they asked me if I was all right.

'What happened, sir?'

I replied, 'Nothing to worry about,' as I tried to hide the bandaging up my arms and down my legs. I had to find the kid whose bike I'd borrowed and come clean with him so he could check if his bike was okay. In no time the whole school and the whole town knew and they had a good laugh. In any event, I had to give the principal the details so he could fill in an Incident Report form, which he did with great care and ceremony. He wrote in the Action Taken column: 'Ensure that in future Mr Sarra must wear underpants when he comes to school.'

I didn't mind them having a joke at my expense. Just as it was at school, once I got to know everyone I became the clown. I would often torment Mick the groundsman in whatever ways I could and I sometimes enjoyed putting on a show in the staff-room. I often complained about how the married guys on staff would come to work with nicely packed lunches while I had to eat the standard salad rolls made down at the local shop. In an effort to make them feel guilty I bought a tin of tuna and swapped the label with a tin of cat food and sat eating it in front of them. I don't think they bought it.

On the weekends, when most teachers made an exodus from Cecil Plains, I would usually stay around to play football on Sunday. In my first year there I played at Pittsworth in the Too-woomba league, and the second year I played in the Dalby league for the Waratahs. I got payed a few bucks and a local business-man sponsored me by paying for my fuel to get to training. I really enjoyed playing in Dalby and we would travel as far as Goondiwindi (got flogged there 58–0 one Sunday), out to St George, Chinchilla and Tara. At my first game at Tara I recall running onto the field and it seemed the crowd was up me.

'Go, Sarra!'

'Get up there, Sarra!'

'Tackle 'em, Sarra!'

I was looking over to the crowd thinking, 'Gee, I don't even know anyone out this way!'

It wasn't until the second half I realised they weren't up me at all. They were singing out *Tara*: 'Go, Tara,' 'Get up there, Tara,' 'Tackle 'em, Tara!'

I loved the camaraderie of Rugby League. I loved training hard. I loved playing your guts out with the boys, and then sitting around having a laugh and a beer in the sheds afterwards. And, of course, there were the crazy nights at the Albion Hotel in Dalby on a Sunday after the game. There were some great guys in the team. A few worked in the Commonwealth Bank. One we called 'Horse', another was 'Sow', and another big tall guy we called 'Bird'. With those names it sounded more like they worked in a barnyard.

The Waratah Roosters was a great little club and we made it to the grand final only to get beaten in a game we should have won. I got sent off that day for ten minutes. Not my fault, of course. We were being hammered by the opposition, who had us on the ropes. I had just made the last tackle and with a quick play of the ball they would have almost certainly scored. I held the other guy down to give my guys some time to get back on side, but according to the ref it was a bit too long. As if I didn't know! They never did score from that penalty either. At the end of the season we contemplated our plans for our big trip away. After mad Monday the end-of-season trip has always been one of those occasions, and often monumentally notorious. Some clubs go to Hawaii, some to Fiji, others to Bali. We went to Jandowae!

It is a tiny little one-pub country town about an hour up the road from Dalby. It may not have boasted any sense of sun, surf or sand like some of those other exotic places, but after about fifteen beers we were all feeling pretty exotic in our own special way and the local ladies were all looking gorgeous.

After I'd been at Cecil Plains for almost two years I started to feel I could offer more by making a connection with larger Aboriginal communities. I loved the job, but making a difference to the lives of Aboriginal students was what I felt most passionate about. It had been playing on my mind for quite some time. I was home in Bundaberg when opportunity knocked. It was during one of the holidays and I was getting back into the usual things – going to Bargara, hanging out with my mum and sisters, and working my mojo at Krystals nightclub just up the road from our house. The whole nightclub ritual was somewhat crazy as most times we would not go out until eleven pm, and it would sometimes be five am before we stumbled home, unless some nice person offered a lift. One morning, Darryl the newspaperman had delivered our paper before I got home. The sun was coming up and I thought I'd have a quick look at the paper before I went to bed.

In the Positions Vacant section was a Commonwealth Department of Employment, Education and Training advertisement for Aboriginal Education Officers. This would not be teaching, but it would involve working with schools, setting up parent committees, and interacting directly with Aboriginal kids. I thought I could offer a fair bit in a job like this, especially lifting the consciousness of Aboriginal kids and parents about the importance of education and emphasising how crucial it was to know how to make the most of it. I wanted them to see the things I didn't see when I was at school. I figured that, if I applied for the job in Wide Bay region, I could work out of Bundaberg. I could play football with my old club, the Wanderers Tigers, and I would see more of Mum and Dad.

My brother Grant helped me write an application and he coached me for the interview. I left Cecil Plains with good memories, and some regret. I would miss those days with the kids and I would miss those long afternoons after school just hanging out chatting and laughing with Bill and his wife, Joan, Mick the groundsman, Mrs Olsen and Margaret Cook, the secretary that really ran the school.

In taking up the position with DEET I underwent six weeks of training in Brisbane before I moved home to Bundaberg, ready to start work. What struck me initially during training was just how undemanding it seemed to be. It felt nothing like the hard work of teaching, where you are on the go all day, not really stopping for lunch, and then being absolutely exhausted at the end of the day. Despite my misgivings during those weeks, what followed turned out to be a significant time in my life for another reason.

5

Finding the right path

'Mr Sarra, when we first found the shadow on your lungs we said
to you that we would need to run some tests to see if you might
have cancer. Now we've done the tests and we've found in fact
that you do have cancer.'

The doctor's words from that fateful afternoon at the Prince
Charles hospital at Chermside still burn in my mind. My father's
English was never good and so I doubt he took in much of the
explanation about what type of treatment was available for him
and what chances he had of getting better. The words he heard
and understood most readily were, *'You have cancer!'* I recall a look
of resignation on his face as he came to grips with what he had
just heard. He was sixty-six years old.

One of the tragedies was that he was planning to go on a long
holiday around Australia with Mum. My father never went on
holidays. Mum would growl because he would never take time
off and go away with her. He always worked and that's how it
was. When he finished his day's work for the council he would

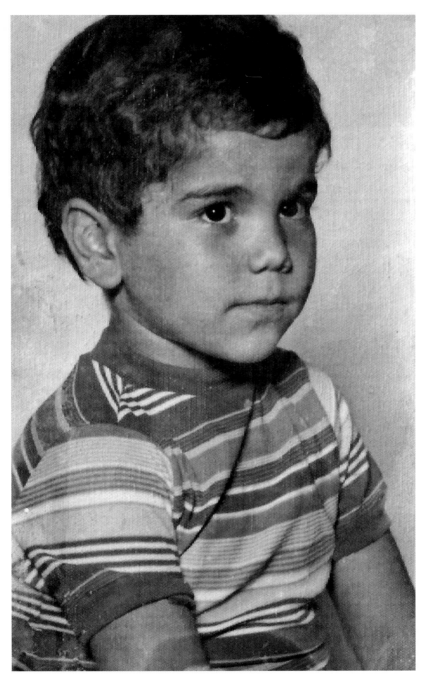

One of the few photos of me on my own as I was growing up.

Mum and Dad in their courting days getting set to rock the dance floors of Bundaberg.

From birth I was surrounded by my siblings. From right, me on my brother Cameron's shoulders, and Simon on Grant's shoulders.

We spent many family holidays at Berajondo during our childhood, running wild in the bush.

My brother Cameron was like a god to me when I was growing up. He would always take us to Bargara in his Valiant Pacer.

My first day of primary school in 1973 with (from left) my sisters Lieba and Tracie and brother Simon. Simon was born the year before me, but we started school in the same year.

My first day of high school in 1980 with my brother Simon (on the right).

Winning the Open Rugby League final in Year 12 was one of the highlights of my school years. From left to right: my brother Simon, Howard Currie and me. Simon scored three tries that day.

The SCG – Sarra's Cricket Ground. Hallowed turf for our family cricket and footy games.

Celebrating my 21st birthday with my parents under our house, which was the scene of many parties.

Arabinda the Boxing Goat was one of many of the Sarra family pets. She helped out as a 'curator' at our SCG, but sometimes we had differences of opinion (no animals were harmed in this photo).

The Sarra family on one of the rare occasions we could be gathered together as adults. My mum still growls me about wearing my sandshoes that day.

My Aunty Molly, who I lived with while I was at college. Every afternoon, there would be fresh pancakes and a game of cards waiting for me.

When I graduated with
a Bachelor of Education,
my sister Lieba was there
to share the day with me.
I owed a lot of my early
academic achievement to
her support.

Graduating with my
Diploma of Teaching
in 1988 with Clarrie
Diefenbach, one of the
pioneers of getting more
Aboriginal people qualified
as secondary school
teachers.

Uncle Michael Williams
has always been a
prominent figure in my
life, taking me 'out bush'
and teaching me what I
needed to know.

come home and work on our small farm down the back or go out to his mate's land where he share-farmed.

We were all in shock from the diagnosis and this would really test our family. I was twenty-three at the time, and at that age sixty-six seemed old, but it's not. I don't know that any of us were optimistic about his chances of beating it. I remembered once back in high school reading my PE theory notes to him about the effects of smoking: heart disease, clogged arteries, high blood pressure, lung cancer.

'I been smoking since I was ten years old!' he would reply, with a sense of defiance. He was a chronic smoker and it had really taken a hold on him. Even during his chemotherapy and radiation treatment he would sneak in a smoke when he could. I remember finding his stash of used butts hidden inside an old plastic bottle in the bathroom. I didn't have the heart to lecture him, or to tell anyone else about it. Such efforts would have been futile. This filthy habit had its claws on him and would not let go until the end.

We had to let his family in Abruzzo know the bad news. It must have been difficult for them. He had returned to see them only once after leaving in the 1950s. I remember that visit well as it was my final year of high school, 1984. He wanted to take me with him for a few weeks but Mum said I had better stay and focus on school. I was disappointed as I would have missed only three weeks of Year 12 and I reckoned I would have learned so much more on such a trip.

It was difficult for him. It was difficult for all of them I'm sure. There was no escaping the conversation about why he never came home to Italy to be a father to his three children and a husband to the wife he had married. Life is often complex and sometimes there are no easy or straightforward answers about why things happen in

the way they do, or why people make particular life choices. I guess
once he had started a family here it was always going to be difficult
to return. He reconnected with his brothers and sister, but sadly
it must now have felt all too brief. There was no way of knowing
then that would be the last time they were to meet. On his return
I remember him saying he loved Italy but he could never live there
again. Understandably, he must have grown too acculturated in the
new Australian way of life, and I suspect also that he returned to
his fatherland somehow expecting it to be very much like it was
when he left it. Many of his Italian friends would often say the same
thing. I suspect they might have returned expecting the country to
be like it was when they left, when in reality it had progressed and
changed dramatically in many ways, just as their individual lives
had. Australia was now their home.

I often wonder if Dad would have gone on for longer had he
taken that holiday with Mum and gone for the check-up on his
return. We'll never know. The chemotherapy dragged on and on,
and in his last few months he became very frail, losing the last of
what hair he had left. At one stage the doctor said he might hang
on for another two months. In some ways it seemed pretty good,
but when you start to break it down you realise that two months
is only eight weeks, less than a school term. Sixty days! Life is far
from infinite.

In mid November 1990 he took a bad turn during the night.
We rang the ambulance, and, when they came for him and started
taking him off the bed, he took off his watch to give to Dean and
the gold chain and crucifix that he had worn for years to give to
Tina. Tina fought back the tears we all shared, saying, 'No, no,
Dad, you hang on to them.' We had the same thought, 'Not yet,
Dad, please, not yet . . .'

For some weeks he lay in a bed in room four of the Mater Hospital in Bundaberg. Gradually he got weaker and weaker. We played cards with him when we could, but mostly we would just sit around and yarn about whatever we could, savouring every moment, every smile and laugh, and every word that left his lips, as we knew there would be so few of them left. While it would never be anything near what he was experiencing as he contemplated the ultimate moments of his life, I couldn't help feeling demoralised and helpless in our efforts to make him feel better. The best we could do was prop up his pillow, adjust him when he needed it, offer him water from time to time. Dean and Grant would give him a shave now and then. I took it upon myself to take his teeth out and give them the best damn clean and scrub I could. Making his mouth feel nice and fresh was just one little thing I could do to make him more comfortable.

In the early hours of the morning, on Monday 20 November, we gathered by his bedside at the hospital. It was still dark outside. There was so little we could do for him. I remember ringing Cameron, my eldest brother, who had just driven home from Bundaberg to Gladstone.

'You'd better come back straightaway. I don't think he will be around for much longer.' He got back in his car, having just got out of it, and returned. A few hours passed. We were all there except for Amanda, and Tracie who had gone to get her. We told Dad that Mandy was on the way, and that she would be here soon. His long-time Italian friend, Nicola, was also with us, encumbered by a grief that permeated the small room. Nicola was a portly little man who had been a friend of my father's for many years, ever since they had both came out from Italy.

'*Strenge a le mane*,' he was saying, as he fought back a man's tears, urging my father to squeeze his hand. He wanted him to fight on but by this stage I was feeling differently. I wanted him to let go. He had suffered for long enough. It was time. Somewhere in the chaos and sorrow of that early morning I had accepted that. I remember holding him close and saying quietly, 'It's okay if you want to go. We'll be okay. You don't have to fight anymore!'

Cameron returned looking exhausted. Mandy and Tracie arrived. It seemed as though he was waiting for all of us to be with him in the room. Not long after his chest rattled. He arched his back as he took his last breath, and then laid to rest. My father was gone.

We had no idea what our world would be like without him. I hugged him, not ever wanting to let go, and I remembered the feeling of holding his body and getting a sense that his spirit had already departed. Despite this, I am certain he lingered in the room with us in those most difficult moments of our deepest sadness.

Pantaleone Sarra was cremated in Bundaberg. Hundreds of people filled the hall and spilled out onto the crematorium gardens. This was a great testimony to the extent to which he was so well regarded by the many who knew him, worked with him and loved him. His ashes are placed in a wall at the Bundaberg crematorium.

The strange thing for me was that once he had passed I felt as if I could go straight back into work. I was pretty useless at work in the months leading up to his death, yet somehow it was fine now to get back on track. I guess I was moving beyond the trauma of watching him suffer in a way that must have been so demoralising for such a strong, proud, hard-working man.

★

My job as Aboriginal education officer for DEET was based in a Commonwealth Employment Services office. I worked on the delivery of Aboriginal education programs throughout the Wide Bay region and was teamed up with another Aboriginal guy, Robert Hill, who delivered Aboriginal employment programs. Robert and I became close colleagues and mates. He was large and effervescent and had dark brown skin. I used to think he had had his vibrant smile painted onto his big, round, bearded face because I hardly ever saw him without it. He had a good working relationship with the other people in the office because he had been there for some time prior to my arrival. As for me, I couldn't say I enjoyed such a positive vibe.

This was a time in my career when I really felt like I didn't belong. I wondered whether maybe it was because my position was newly created and I was housed with them, despite my work not being integral to the sort of things done conventionally around employment. I had built a small team around me, with Natasha Thompson and Graham Tanner, and the usual 'blacks out the back' phenomenon seemed to be applied. This is where you go into a school, a university, a hospital or any other institution, and if you are looking for the 'blacks', they will often be in some type of housing or office space that others would generally not tolerate, out the back. I have visited schools where Indigenous workers have been put in makeshift office space that were really broom closets right next to the toilets. When they made decisions about where to locate us in the CES office in Bundaberg we were never consulted. They just put the three of us down on the bottom floor at the back in the corner. I felt there was no use fighting it as, undoubtedly, there would have been some bureaucratic way to justify the decision – any explanation except racism. I am often amazed at how people can do such things with absolutely no idea about how offensive they are being.

It was not just my new office position that raised my hackles. They were also reluctant to share their resources with me. It was always a battle to get an office car. My role had provisions for a Z car – all Commonwealth car numberplates had a distinguishable large red 'Z' on them – but it would be some weeks before I could pick up the car dedicated to my job. In the meantime I had to talk to Frank, the guy in the office in charge of the car pool.

'Hey, Frank, I gotta visit some schools in the next few days, so what do I have to do to book a car?'

Immediately I got from him that grimacing face so many blackfullas would recognise. The one searching for a polite, yet bureaucratic way to say 'no', because they either don't trust you with it or somehow they don't believe you should have access to it.

'Yeah . . . look, I know you need a car for your role but . . . um . . . I can't really let you have one because . . . um . . . well, if I let you have use of one of our cars . . . um . . . then you won't be able to justify your need for a car.' In saying that, he seemed content he had found a suitable way to say no and his words from then on seemed to flow more confidently. 'You obviously have a need that is important but, you see, they will say your needs are already being met by having access to our resource, and so they will not provide you with a car for yourself,' he proclaimed.

In the end I just used my own car. By this stage I was driving a very reliable white Honda Civic hatch. Some weeks later my Z car arrived. I needed to drive hundreds of kilometres regularly to visit schools and communities as far south as Gympie, as far west as Cherbourg, Murgon, Kingaroy and Eidsvold, and as far north as Rockhampton. In the cassette player I still made room for The Boss, U2, Dire Straits and, of course, that old drunk, as Aunty Molly used to say, Bob Dylan, but I added The Cure, Hunters and Collectors and Paul Kelly to my collection. I had also taken a liking to some of the oldies but goodies so it was not unusual for me to be cruising along with Charley Pride and his 'Crystal Chandelier', or even the great Hank Williams who 'saw the light'. I was also known to cruise with that old blackfulla's favourite, Jim Reeves and his classic, 'I love you "big horse" you understand "me".'

The road trip I loved best was to Cherbourg because my crazy cousin Annette Rutherford was the Year 1 teacher there. She would let me take her kids for PE whenever I was in town. It was great to have this 'fix' because I really missed being around and teaching children. The Cherbourg children in Annette's class were always energetic and they certainly enjoyed their PE.

Finally having the Z car and a fuel card was great. Mind you, I did put it to good use travelling all those kilometres to spread the word about Aboriginal education, getting young Indigenous kids to see the things I didn't see while I was a student in school and setting up parent committees to work in partnerships with schools. Strangely enough, though, when I took carriage of my car, the other bureaucrats closed in on me and demanded to use this car as part of their resources.

'It's a Commonwealth car and it has to go into the car pool with all of the other cars so we can make use of it as well,' they would say to me. They seemed pretty determined to enforce this rule that somehow had just popped up in such an official-sounding way. I let them know what I thought of their bureaucratic hypocrisy. My mate Robert was a lot more affable and they sent him down to pacify me.

'Brother, what you getting wild with them fullas up there for?'

'It was good enough for them to let me use my own car and not their cars, and now they wanna take this one and use it too. That's bullshit!'

'Brother,' he would say in his own inimitable way, 'that's not your personal car. That's a government car. You gotta put it in the pool.'

'No, Robert. Fuck them!' I replied in the only way I knew how. 'What, they think I am some dumb little black bastard? I am black but I'm not stupid. You go back and tell them that if I let them have use of this car then they won't be able to justify the need for an additional car,' I said in my own smart-arse way. 'And you can tell them to get fucked . . . all of them!' I added for good measure.

There was a moment of silence, then Robert laughed. He got me laughing, too, even though I was so stirred up my blood was boiling. I felt bad for unleashing such a tirade on him, a man I greatly admired and respected, especially when it was others who were too gutless to come down themselves. I never did share that car.

While I was not so fussed on those in the office, I did meet some fantastic people out in the field. In Childers there was a young Aboriginal lad who was a whiz at maths. He just loved it. His teacher rang me especially to tell me about Dion Fewquandie and I just had to go and say 'g'day' to this kid and line up a tutor for him. I wanted to help him go from being a good B student to an exceptional A student. To me this was just as important as helping kids who were being left languishing a long way behind by teachers who had written them off.

I also met an older man who grew up in Cherbourg but now

lived in Murgon. He had worked as a counsellor at Murgon State High School for almost twenty years and all the children called him Pop John. He was one of those green-eyed blackfullas with a nuggetty build, and a heart that most certainly was built of solid gold. He had been a timber man for many years, planting more than his share in the forests that permeated the South Burnett. He was an old style of worker – a hard man yet so soft on the inside – a bit like my father in a sense. The kind they just don't make anymore. He was also the cricket coach and coached many children in boxing. Pop John had plenty of children of his own that he loved deeply, and all of the children he worked with at the school got to share and bask in his sense of love and passion for Aboriginal children. Sometime in those years of knowing and working with Pop John he would become like another father to me, and I felt very much like his son.

Pop John had grown up in the boys' dormitories of Cherbourg and would always have a soft spot for the place where he lived as a youngster. I remember organising a meeting to discuss Cherbourg State School with the Wide Bay regional director for the education department based in Maryborough in 1990. Pop John was not the least bit intimidated by this seemingly powerful middle-aged bureaucrat dressed in a business suit and tie.

'We are sick and tired of our children finishing at Cherbourg primary and going into grade eight in Murgon with years one and two literacy standards! They get in there and they can't cope. What is going on at the school in Cherbourg? Why can't Murgon High cater for their needs when they get there? You come with me to the Cherbourg cemetery and I will show you just how many of my young children I have had to put in a grave way before their time because, why? Because they have no decent education! This is what you're supposed to do, isn't it? Isn't it your job to make sure the schools can give our children an education? That's all we're asking for. We are sick and tired of being left at the foot of the mountain while all the others get the chance to climb to great heights. All we're asking for is that same chance!'

I am not certain the regional director knew how to respond. Looking back, I guess he had never been held to account for improving the quality of education for Aboriginal children. Even at that time many people in the education system just didn't seem to care about what was happening. From where I stood, along-side Pop John, it seemed the only real interest they showed in Aboriginal children was when they realised the Commonwealth government was starting to put money into this area. The more Aboriginal children in a school, the more money they got. All of a sudden it was worth making an effort to count the number of Aboriginal kids in their institution.

Pop John and I cared more deeply than this and, regardless of the apathy around us, we soldiered on doing whatever we could, both of us gaining tremendous satisfaction working more directly with the children, whether it was sitting in on homework groups or organising trips to visit tertiary institutions in Brisbane. We would do whatever we could to stretch the rules without break-ing them to get more support to the children and parents in his schools. We would occasionally laugh and wonder how we got away with some of the things we did, but we both knew that we always, absolutely always, had the interests of the children fore-most in our hearts and minds.

In between the long road trips to various schools and com-munities I started my Bachelor of Education degree to add to my diploma. I felt it was important that if I was telling children about the importance of education then I should at least be modelling a commitment to it.

As well as the study I was playing Rugby League for my old club, the Wanderers Tigers. I had been in the right frame of mind and was playing A grade again. I still so loved the game and the camaraderie. It was a setting where you didn't have to be so serious and could just laugh and have fun. One afternoon in the pre-season of 1990 we trained at Bargara Beach. For some reason there were many large jellyfish washed up on the beach. Not the stinging type, just the large jelly ones.

'Come on, boys, let's go for a run and show them the Tigers are back in town!' the coach yelled. As we took off, someone smacked me on the back of the head as he ran up front saying something smart. In the spirit of camaraderie there was only one thing to do. I picked up one of the jellyfish, caught up to him, grabbed the back of his shorts and dropped it in the back of his pants. Maybe he thought it was a stinging jellyfish because he picked up a few paces and we all laughed at the sight of him trying to run away while at the same time turning to get this big wobbly thing off his arse.

I always loved having a joke with the boys, whether it was at training, in the sheds or on the field. Some of our games were filmed and I was never one to miss out on being on camera. In the midst of playing A grade and trying to be serious, I would often run over when someone scored a try, not to pat them on the back, but rather to smile and wave at the camera because I knew that's where it would be focussed.

I was determined to have a good year and was going fine for the first few matches of the season, consistently winning points for best and fairest, and consistently being among the top one or two tacklers for our side. I was assuming things were going to plan until the coach, who worked up the road from my place, pulled me up on my way home.

He explained that he'd be dropping me instead of the other guy because I'd handle it and the guy would get sooky.

I sensed he was uncomfortable about having to speak to me about this but he was right. I was not the type to carry on and so I just took it on the chin.

'Mate, you're the coach. You have to do whatever you reckon is best. Up to you!'

I was a bit put out by it I have to confess. I didn't see why my form on the field at the time should be overlooked for some-one else's lack of emotional or interpersonal form. I never really dropped my bundle, but football became much less of a prior-ity for me. I focussed more on my work with kids and schools and finishing my Bachelor of Education. For the remainder of that year I was content just to captain the reserve-grade team. Our side went all the way to an epic hundred-minute grand final with two lots of extra time, only to be knocked off in the last moments when my cousin Clint Thompson scored a runaway try that broke my heart.

By mid 1990 I had been promoted to the role of manager of Aboriginal education and employment programs. The pay was pretty good but the work was becoming dissatisfying. I was fed up with the office politics inside the CES office and most of the Aboriginal parent committees for schools throughout Wide Bay had been set up and running. It was going pretty well but by now I was looking for a new challenge, although there were some per-sonal challenges going on.

Natasha had arranged for me to meet a lovely girl who became my girlfriend. In the early days of the relationship she seemed to be into it but I sensed something was not right. As it turned out she was facing some pressure from home. Her father was a decent hard-working and respectful guy. I admired him a great deal. Her mother, however, was putting the pressure on to make her choose between her family and me because she 'didn't want her daughter going out with a coon!' The relationship remained pretty solid for a while because as far as I was concerned the problem was not with the daughter but the mother, but it was pretty shocking and hurtful to find out what her mother thought. It was one of those times when I could have confronted the mother but I was determined not to fan any negative beliefs she might have had, but to work through the situation and make sure she got to see Aboriginal people in a way that was positive. Eventually she did, I suppose, and things were okay. But some things stay the same and some things change. For me it was time for a change.

An opportunity for a six-month secondment, working in the department of the prime minister and cabinet in Canberra, came up. Given my frustration with the DEET job, I decided to go for it as I thought it might give me some insights into the upper echelons of bureaucracy and government. I applied and was successfully appointed. The Council for Aboriginal Reconciliation was being set up and driven by PM&C at that time and so my timing enabled me to play a very small part in that. My involvement was at a very basic level, although I did find it worthwhile in many ways. For my part I got stuck into the laborious task of ministerial responses to correspondence to the prime minister. People would write all sorts of interesting, insightful and sometimes crazy letters. If there was anything relating to social policy they would come to our division and would usually end up on my desk because I was so enthusiastic about them.

I found myself yearning for that feeling of working hard, and the only way I could get this was by getting stuck into drafting the responses. Being an ex-English teacher I enjoyed the discipline of having to get every word, every sentence, every space and every bit of punctuation absolutely perfect or otherwise it would come back for re-drafting. Occasionally we'd get correspondence from other ministers making requests for extra dollars for their respective portfolios and so we'd have to do the preliminary research to find out whether or not this might be warranted. On other occasions I would have to draft PPQs – possible parliamentary questions. Before I arrived in Canberra I would watch Bob Hawke and be amazed at how he could be so knowledgeable during question time in the House, particularly when someone would ask even the most obscure questions. He always appeared to be across a whole range of matters. His secret: the PPQs.

The newspapers would have to be scoured daily for social policy issues. We'd try to predict what we thought the opposition might ask in the House, and we then had to draft the answers. All the various divisions would have to draft and finalise PPQs and answers and have them at the PM's office by eleven am sharp. I would often go up to Parliament House and sit in the Senate chamber or the House of Representatives and listen in on the discussion. In some ways I felt it was like sitting on top of a mountain. It was the place where policy and legislation was enabled and it was interesting to contemplate how such policy and legislation would play out in the real lives of your everyday people out on the street. I did get to meet Paul Keating on the run one day, not that he would have remembered. He was pretty fired up because he had just been ejected from the House after having a monumental blow-up with John Howard.

In my eyes Keating was a master and I enjoyed just watching him in action. I would often trawl through Hansard just to re-read and reflect on some of his oratory finesse. While many people came to despise Paul Keating I admired him for many reasons. He did not forget his working-class roots and I affectionately remember hearing him on some documentary talking about his days of working with cockroaches running up and down his legs. I also admired his shrewd intellect, his ruthless and relentless attacks on what he perceived as unjustness and, most of all, for having the courage to deliver the Redfern Speech: 'We took the land, we took the babies . . .' It was one of those speeches when, like many other people I suspect, I just had to stop and say to myself, 'Did I just hear our prime minister say that?'

Sometimes I wonder what might have been in terms of social policy if Keating had had the opportunity to do another term or two in a way that enabled him, and his kind of thinking and leadership, to be more influential. It was an influential moment in Australia's time, where I think we had the potential to be bold and courageous and step into what some might call a 'brand new day' on Indigenous affairs. Instead it seems we became crippled by our own fear and lack of vision, retreating to the confines of a mediocrity in which our relationship surrendered integrity yet again.

Influential, however, is not a word one would use to describe the type of work I was doing in PM&C at the time. There were moments when I thought I would have more enjoyment being back home picking watermelons and tobacco. I pondered the possibility of making a career in the public service in Canberra. Could I make a difference on a bigger scale if I worked my way up to executive level? I wasn't sure what to do. I ended up staying in Canberra after the secondment and worked in the head office of DEET. I landed a job in the section that looked after Aboriginal recruitment development programs, getting them up and running in various public service departments.

While I really enjoyed living in Canberra, I didn't enjoy the culture of Canberra's public service. I would often go out to see some live theatre or take off into the surrounding bush, or go up and check out the snow. It was great living in a city where there was such a range of different nationalities. But I became fed up with the never-ending 'what level are you on' conversations with every second person I met. I think I could have stayed and had a successful public service career, earning really good money, but what bothered me was being surrounded by many well-paid career public servants who had spent little time in the field but were formulating policy proposals that would eventually affect the nation. It was time for me to get back to the 'real world' and work more directly with people and communities.

I didn't want that feeling of going backwards to teaching and so I decided to train as a school career and guidance counsellor. In September 1992 I applied to do the year-long course as well as a Masters in School Guidance and Counselling in Brisbane. Before the courses started in 1993, I decided to spend three months travelling. I was still in my early twenties and travel was something I had to get out of my system. I had always flirted with the idea of living in England and getting by being a brickie's labourer or something, and playing in third-division Rugby League competition. Sadly, I never got the courage to play this out in reality and I would always regret it. In my head I was thinking there was so much to be done in Aboriginal education, but on reflection I could have easily taken a few years for myself and still had plenty to do on my return. I really enjoyed my three months away, though, and travelled to several countries.

My first stop was London, where I managed to get ripped off in a club in Soho, as so many gullible tourists do, I suppose. Then I went north to Scotland to tour the highlands. I found some truth in the old saying about the further north you go in the United Kingdom the friendlier people get. I met a local guy called Donny Gegan within the first three minutes of arriving.

'Mate, do you reckon there might be any rooms available in this pub?'

'No, you don't want to stay in that pub,' he said, with his rich Scottish accent. 'Come with me and I'll show this other pub where my team drinks.'

We had the usual conversation about where you from, what do you do, what's it like in Australia and all that. When we got to the pub Donny said, 'Chris, why don't you put your bags away and I'll take you for a few beers with my mates?' I was pretty tired but having a drink with the locals on their own turf was too good an opportunity to miss. I listened to their conversations with fascination, the way they spoke and laughed with each other.

'Aye, you had a really tough game last night. I thought he had you there in the last coupla minutes but you just got on top of him in the end.'

I thought they were talking about soccer or something but as it turned out it another 'tough' game: Dominoes! I wondered how the hell you have a tough game of dominoes as I got stuck into the beers and the match-day sandwiches made by Donny's missus, who was at home with a swag of kids. As the night unfolded I realised that I had probably chatted incidentally with more people in the first three hours in Scotland than I had the entire three weeks I had spent in England.

After touring the highlands with a lovely old couple, who were friends of my sister Lieba, I went to Glasgow, and from there I took the ferry across to Northern Ireland and down to County Wexford. I stayed in Wexford with Ivor Bradley, an old Irish friend of the family who had a sheep farm down in the south. From Ireland I took a large ferry to France, destination Cherbourg! I just had to send a postcard from there to Pop John. Cherbourg in France was the first place I encountered what it was like to be in a country where you do not speak the language. That initial feeling of disconnection is overwhelming. I approached a lady, trying to get directions to Paris, and we did not have one word in common. I can still see her face, wanting to communicate, wanting to help, but the both of us could only shrug and gesture. It was an amazing experience that I thought really tested my humanity. I think everyone should have this experience, to know what it feels like to be a minority in society. I suspect the entire world of an individual can be transformed as a result of such an experience.

After a few days in Paris I flew to Italy for three weeks. I sat on that plane from Paris to Rome feeling nervous and anxious. I was returning to the homeland of my father, meeting for the first time my eldest brother and my two eldest sisters. My sisters from home, Tracie and Lieba, had visited them a few years earlier. Tracie had even rung our Italian brother Guilio to let him know I was coming over and when I was arriving in Rome. He and his family had been very kind to Tracie and Lieba but I was still bursting with apprehension. Would they be resentful? They certainly had every right to – Dad had left them behind and started a new life without them, on the other side of the world. We got to have him as our father and, because of that, they had missed out. As the plane taxied to the terminal, I turned to an English-speaking Italian lady near me and said, 'Today I am meeting my brother for the first time!'

She couldn't believe it. I don't even know why I said that to her. I am usually too shy to talk to people next to me on the plane. By now, though, my feelings where overwhelming as I rambled anxiously through customs. I emerged from behind the customs doors to a sea of faces and a cacophony of noises of people eagerly anticipating their loved ones.

A slender, olive-skinned man in his forties, with a small but neat moustache and a receding hairline, held a piece of cardboard with 'SARRA' written on it. He didn't need the card, the blood and spiritual connection was obvious. Immediately he knew who I was, and immediately I knew him. I walked over to Guilio, dropped my bags, and he threw his arms around me. Both of us were overcome as we embraced and shed tears together. Why was I ever worried about this moment?

He introduced me to his sixteen-year-old son, Emiliano. My nephew. He kissed me on both sides of my face as men in Italy do – Tracie had explained this to me before I arrived so it would not be the basis of some form of culture shock. We then drove west from Fiumucino airport for three hours in Guilio's little car to his home in the village of Spoltore in Abruzzo, where my two sisters, Venere and Maria, and their husbands and children were waiting to meet me.

They lived not far away in the seaside town of Montesilvano. Spoltore and Montesilvano were also not that far from Miglianico, where Dad had been born. I met my sister-in-law, two brothers-in-law, aunts, uncles, nieces and nephews, and was accepted with open hearts and curious minds. There were many tears and kisses and looking, just looking at one another, with amazement at the family resemblances. Different ones said that I looked just like Dad when he left Italy. In fact, he had been the same age as I was, twenty-three. We spent hours talking, stumbling our way through broken yet priceless conversations. Emiliano could speak some English, and his little sister Serena was also learning English at school. We had fun laughing and making jokes. I taught her some English, although it was probably not the kind you would find in a regular English language curriculum. The best I could teach her to say was 'Come on, baby, light my fire!' She sounded fantastic as she said this with a real blackfullas' accent.

Despite the language difficulties, we had deep conversations along with deep silences. We connected. The connection was articulated perfectly by Guilio when in one conversation I tried to describe the nature of our relationship.

'We would be called half-brothers,' I explained. '*Mezzo frotelle!*'

'No. Not half-brother. Not *Mezzo frotelle!*' he replied. '*Tu sei meo frotello.* You are my brother!' In that perfect and beautiful moment I was mesmerised by the wisdom and love of my eldest brother.

I also met Dad's first wife, Emma, a number of times. She was a petite and dignified old lady who continued to wear black dresses after she had heard of the death of my father. She rarely spoke. Occasionally I would catch her fixed gaze on me, and her subtle look away to wipe tears from her eyes. I knew what she was thinking about. There were other little things I noticed about them, too. In the mornings everyone dipped their bread in their coffee, just like my father used to do! They cut the bread just as he did. Items were put in certain places, as he had done in our home in Bundaberg. The little quirks we had observed and remarked on over the years had not just been his personal oddities; they were glorious and beautiful little windows into his culture and his identity.

I met Dad's brother, Raffaelle, and he walked with me around the village of Miglianico, pointing out places of interest. Here is the church, St Pantaleone, your dad's name. This is where we lived when we were kids. See these holes in the wall – those are gunshot marks from the war. The Germans walked down here, and here, and here. Uncle Raffelle even showed me the place he'd been shot in the leg. We also visited the graves of my grandparents. I felt a strong and in many ways a spiritual connection with Miglianico. The feeling is one of those things that is hardly possible to explain, yet perfectly understood by many. I left Italy feeling that my identity, and my family, had been expanded and enriched by a new layer. I would forever feel different; somehow more whole, like I had located some of the very important pieces of my own sense of personal being.

I had always felt a strong sense of being Aboriginal. Now I was feeling just as strong in my sense of being Italian. There was no confusion here, just greater clarity. I have an equally strong sense of being Australian. Lots of people don't seem to get this. They will ask whether you see yourself as Italian, Aboriginal or Australian, like you should be just one.

From my perspective, identities will always be layered. On one level I will feel strong and proud about my Italian part, while on another I will feel strong and proud of my Aboriginality.

6

The Millaquin Mojo

Back in Australia I was living in Brisbane again, but this time on the south side at Yeronga. I was just across the river from the University of Queensland where I would start my Masters in Education, and only two train stations away from the Support Centre where I would complete my guidance officer training. As a young man I was never famous for getting out of bed early and I would take every moment of sleep I could before I did. I worked out I could get up at nineteen minutes to nine, have my shower, and walk into the centre a few minutes after nine without getting into trouble.

The guidance officer training was great. I met some really sharp people. Machelle Flowers was a feisty redhead who had just returned from the Gulf country. We enjoyed many conversations about life and working with Aboriginal kids. Peter Hosking was a deep thinker and genuinely nice guy whom I really enjoyed just sitting and yarning with. I also became mates with Bruce Muirhead, who was pretty savvy and knew what he had to get done in life to go places. He had the driest sense of humour and often I would think I could throw him in the river and he would still be dry.

I loved catching the Dutton Park ferry across the river to the university, and then making my way through the grounds and up the hill to the buildings. I loved being on campus and studying for my Masters. It was a rewarding time. Even coming home at night across the river was particularly nice, although, like any blackfulla, I was never too fussed walking past the Fairfield cemetery at night. I would usually make a brisk pace for that part of the walk home, even during the daytime.

After a year of studying I headed north to Cairns where I worked in several schools, including Trinity Bay State High School, Mossman State High School and Yarrabah State School. I like to think I was pretty good at being a career and guidance counsellor. The idea of being a champion for students was incredibly meaningful and I took it upon myself to advocate strongly for Aboriginal students and Torres Strait Islander students. My first few days at Trinity Bay High would signal just how important this was.

To make myself known to my new colleagues I went around to staffrooms to touch base and say, 'hi'. On the whole they were a great bunch of teachers. I did find the conversation with one of them a bit disturbing, though. This young female teacher had sized me up before I could say, 'High expectations!'

'G'day . . . Are you the new CEC?' CEC stands for Community Education Counsellor and these positions are usually Aboriginal or Torres Strait Islander para-professionals who are located in schools to support Indigenous children.

'No, I'm the new guidance officer,' I replied, not knowing how this would go down.

'Oh!' she said, with a very surprised tone and look. 'So you're like . . . a "real" guidance officer?'

'Yes. Yes, I am!' I said, doing my best to let my facial expression say, 'You have no idea just how offensive you are being right now!' Not that she would have realised.

'So . . . you've been a teacher?' she said, as though she was not quite convinced.

'Yes I'm a PE and English teacher,' I said, while thinking silently, 'and I have completed my Masters in Education so I am more academically qualified than you . . . and I get paid almost double your salary.' I would have liked to have said that last bit out loud but it was one of those situations of avoiding being pegged as a smart arse or a blackfulla with some kind of chip on his shoulder. It is not always easy to bite your tongue in these circumstances. It takes a great deal of strength to react in a way that is dignified and measured. I contemplated with some frustration the futility of trying to get her to understand just how insulting her comments were. Something just wasn't right for her. Here was an Aboriginal guy and he was a guidance officer, who had been a teacher. If I had been a less-qualified CEC she would have made sense of that.

'But you're not like a real Aboriginal, are you?' she followed. 'Look! My skin is nearly as dark as yours.' She put her arm up next to mine to compare our skin colours.

If I had been under a tree drunk or a CEC I would have fitted her understanding of 'Aboriginal'. Sadly, this is a view I have come to know well with lots of people struggling to make sense of Aboriginal people with relatively light-coloured skin, or in successful roles beyond the stereotypical. Even the fairest-skinned Aboriginal people don't have their identity questioned if they are staggering around drunk in a park. Yet the darkest-skinned Aboriginal will be questioned about their identity or their percentage of their heritage if they are successful and in a role beyond the negative image. The most disturbing thing about this particular circumstance was that there were many young, black students in the school. If she struggled to see someone like me as a guidance officer, then how was she going to see any of her black students as anything beyond the stifled and negative stereotypes she had?

Despite this encounter, I enjoyed working at Trinity Bay High with some fantastic teachers who were totally committed. Sandy Russo was my *paesano*, my Italian countryman, on staff. She is one of those teachers I still regard as one of the best I have ever met. She just got it. She understood the importance of relationships being the most fundamental aspect. She was not content to just 'teach to the middle'. She wanted all of the children in her classroom to be successful and she would venture way beyond the bounds of the classroom walls to make sure of it.

I loved the work, though. There was something special about being able to talk to a teenager who might have been crying or deeply disturbed and talking about suicidal thoughts, and then see them off laughing and smiling. This kind of contact made me realise that no race or class of people actually owned the tendency to feel hurt or disenchanted with the world. Everyone, no matter where they come from or how well off they are, is susceptible to the pain of neglect, hurt and dysfunction. It also made me realise just how good life was for me as a kid. While we may not have been financially loaded, we certainly were incredibly wealthy when it came to spiritual and familial wellbeing. On one occasion I remember having a pretty rough day counselling some kids who had endured some extremely challenging circumstances. Like all kids they were good kids who just needed love and guidance from parents who knew how to give a child love and a caring environment. When I got home that afternoon I rang my mum to say thanks for being a great mother, and thanks for being there for us, knowing that there were some really tough times for her.

Maryanne Crowe was the CEC in the school. She was a short, middle-aged Torres Strait Islander woman with beautiful black skin and the most gorgeous frizzy black hair, accentuating an ever-present smile. She had been in the school for many years and kids would often lob up in her office to sit down and have a yarn, or to grab a Vegemite sandwich or whatever was going. Maryanne helped me to become more enlightened about the differences and the conflicts between Aboriginal people and Torres Strait Islanders. It is an unfortunate dynamic that does not help our causes. Sometimes I have encountered conversations with people who have suggested Torres Strait Islanders are just a little better and, as I have heard on some occasions, 'more cultural' than Aboriginal people. I suspect Torres Strait Islanders might hear it the other way around. Either way, it is a destructive attitude that creates horizontal anger and disharmony that causes us to fight with each other. Like dogs, we end up scrapping over a bone that has been thrown at us instead of standing back, understanding what is going on, and fighting together so that each of us gets a decent bone. Unfortunately, I see this destructive phenomenon in a range of places. Some argue that it emerged with the native title claim, where we ended up fighting each other in utterly destructive ways rather than stepping back and realising where the real fights lay, and who or what is the real adversary.

As a guidance officer I had to drive two times a week up to Mossman High on the picturesque Cairns to Mossman road that runs past Port Douglas. No matter what the weather it was always a spectacular drive that slithers between the mountainous rainforests, which flowed down to the spectacular beaches that concealed the Great Barrier Reef.

Deborah Kachell was the principal of Mossman High. She had two deputies, with one standing out, almost regal-like, with a blazing turban sitting like a crown upon his impressively bearded head. Iqbal Singh was a few years older than me and he was an Indian–Australian and devout Sikh. I liked Iqbal and from those early days working together at Mossman we would become as close as brothers. He was quite slender in build with brown skin and eyes, with a hairy face and body. As I discovered he would not cut his hair for religious reasons. He was so different from anyone else I had worked with. He was so very decent with everyone around him, his family, colleagues and, especially, the students. He had a great sense of humour, although not as good as mine; and he always enjoyed sharing and having discussions about religion and culture.

On one occasion he came to work with the flashiest and reddest turban I had seen. It mesmerised me. At the end of the day, when the kids had gone home and we were sitting around yarning as we often did, I just couldn't help myself.

'Iqbal,' I said inquisitively, yet feeling safe to be so, 'is there any significance in the colour of the turban? Like . . . see how you have that really deep red one on today . . . is that kind of symbolic of anything in particular?'

He hesitated before he answered. I waited, anticipating some kind of very deep and spiritual insight like a devotee before his guru.

'Nah . . . not really,' he replied. 'I just felt like wearing red today!'

'Brother,' I said, 'you could have given me some flash exotic answer there. I was waiting for something deep!'

We both looked at each other and burst out laughing. We had plenty of good times together and we would often enjoy trying to catch the other one out whenever we could. I usually had his measure for practical jokes, particularly when it involved getting the students involved.

At Mossman they had a daybook as a way of communicating to each other. In the morning, staff and students would write notes that would be photocopied and distributed for reading out to the class. One morning I wrote in the daybook: 'Free puppies to give away. If anyone wants a free puppy please come and see me today. They are very cute. Mr Singh.' For the rest of the day Iqbal was hounded by students wanting a free puppy.

As well as Trinity Bay and Mossman I would also have to visit Yarrabah for one day a fortnight. It was a crazy arrangement, as they really should have had someone in the role full-time. The kids of Yarrabah were fantastic but it was clear that some were doing it really tough. I became good mates with Danny Murgha, one of the local guys working at the high school. Danny had a small physique and was talented with both a guitar and his fists. He was a gun boxer in his day and had fought Jeff Fenech, breaking his nose. He was well regarded by the kids yet it seemed the school leaders did very little to embrace the exceptional talent he had to offer. This was, and continues to be the case of many Aboriginal workers in schools who are paid very little, yet are expected to perform the role of a teacher aide, social worker, psychologist and general school dog's body, all with the pleasure of not really being able to 'clock off' within their own communities.

There were days at Yarrabah when Danny and I had to work

with the students to get them past their anger and determination to knuckle up against each other. On most occasions this seemed to be stuff brought into school from out in the community. Often it was a kind of intense anger and hate from some fight going on in another part of the family or community. Sometimes things just seemed to escalate to a point where many had actually forgotten where and why it started in the first place.

Given that I could only be there one day a fortnight in a community where building trust was fundamentally crucial, my efforts felt profoundly futile and there was little I could achieve. The best I felt I could do was work with the secondary kids and try to get them thinking about what might exist beyond Year 10. I wanted to also organise a bus trip for the years 9 and 10 so they could get some exposure to jobs in Cairns but the principal was not so keen on the idea.

'It's a waste of money,' she said. 'They won't turn up for something like that!' Despite her negativity I went ahead and arranged the trip so that we would visit a few local industries, particularly those where I knew there were Indigenous workers. I wasn't content to just sit back like others who threw their hands in the air. It would often drive me nuts to hear teachers and school leaders talk this way, as if there was no need to put in any effort. Yet they would turn up day in and day out without any sense of guilt about getting paid for being complicit in the delivery of an education that offered very little to the kids.

On the day *all* of the kids turned up. We cruised up over the 'Old Yarrabah Ranges', as the song used to say, and into Cairns for a fantastic day out. It was great to see the kids in a different context, where other adults had a genuine interest in what they were doing and what their plans for the future might include. It was really wonderful seeing the kids asking questions and taking it all in. I could not help but feel triumphant over low expectations, yet in some ways sad that, with more time, I might have made a real difference. I would have loved the opportunity to work full-time at Yarrabah.

There was one art teacher at the high school of Yarrabah who worked exceptionally hard to connect with the kids. She was funky in many ways with short-cropped hair and a nasal ring. The kids responded well to her, reaching out because they knew she was reaching out for them. Sadly, this teacher was just one ray of hope amid a blanket of darkness and the scourge of low expectations.

It would break my heart to see kids in Year 10 almost completely illiterate. As far as I was concerned there was no good reason for this to be the case. There are so many excuses but I knew that, if the relationship was respectful and right and the learning experiences made sense, these kids could certainly learn as well as any other. I would occasionally pull some kid out of class to work one-on-one with them. I had a young guy trying to read with me and I could tell he was feeling shame about his illiteracy. The more these kids felt shame in front of me the more I would feel incensed as I pondered how many teachers had just gone through the motions with them, not even trying to push their students, just simply assuming Aboriginal kids could not learn to read. With this kid, as with many others like him, I tried to explain that there was every chance it was not his fault that he could not read. I explained about how some teachers just didn't believe that Aboriginal kids could be up there with everyone else and so they just would play videos in the classroom and do colouring in and that sort of thing. I could tell he knew exactly what I was talking about.

'You don't have to be scared of big words,' I explained to him. This boy loved horses and I knew in his traditional language the word for horse is *yarraman*. I wrote *yarraman* on his piece of paper and said, 'What do you reckon this word says?'

'I dunno,' he replied.

'Big word, 'ay?' I said.

He nodded his head in agreement.

'Remember what I was telling you: don't be scared of them big words. If you wanna work them out just break them up. Like this. Look!' I said to him as I split the words on his paper: yarra / man. I then covered the first part of the word.

'What does this say?'

'That says man,' he replied.

'Good boy! Now, how did you know that said man?'

He looked at me and said, 'Well it's man. It just says man!'

'Okay, then. Have a look at this first part and what do you reckon it says?' I helped him as he sounded it out and after a bit of mouthing it he looked at me and said, 'Yarra!'

'Good boy! Now how did you know that said yarra?'

'It looks like that sign there when you come into Yarrabah and it's got the same letters.'

I was really proud of his response as he was obviously working hard with me and searching the confines of his knowledge to crack this one.

'Now. Put them together and tell me what word you reckon this one!'

He mouthed it slowly, getting it. For a second he seemed unsure, perhaps wondering if this really was one of 'his' words holding a valid place in a school classroom. He looked up and said sheepishly and with a soft, uncertain voice, '*Yarraman?*'

I smiled with exuberance for him, and I guess some pride for me, as I saw that light go on. This was that magical moment teachers live for, the moment when you have helped a young person to just get it. No amount of money can pay for what this moment is worth.

'Yeah. *Yarraman*. You got it!'

He smiled back, feeling proud, I'm sure, because he had cracked an eight-letter word, and even more so that it was one of 'his' words.

'And what's that now? What's *yarraman* mean?'

'*Yarraman* . . . That means 'orse!' He beamed.

We then moved on to a big long yarn about his horses and what he got up to on the weekends with them. I knew bugger all about horses but I was happy to let his enthusiasm flow in that wonderful conversation.

On the odd occasion I would have to go to a conference to listen in on whatever the latest thing was. I never liked going to conferences much. They were all right, as you got to meet people, but I never enjoyed watching others run amok in the evenings, getting smashed and then struggling to turn up or be with it the next day. My good mate Leigh Schelks and I would always say, 'You can play hard, but you gotta work hard too!' Leigh was a charismatic and chunky little white guy with a great passion for Indigenous education. He was also a great buddy of mine and we certainly knew how to play hard, but I always admired him for turning up the next morning ready to go.

Maybe I'm just a bit too square about such things, although I didn't mind checking out the women at such events. At this stage I was enjoying being young and single. I knew one day I would settle down and have children but at twenty-seven it wasn't really on my radar. There were a few boxes that needed to be ticked on the form filed in my head under 'the perfect woman', and I hadn't yet met anyone who completed it adequately.

In September of 1994 I went to an Indigenous education conference in Rockhampton. Leigh was attending, as was Michael Blackman, my cousin, who had just returned to Cairns after many years teaching in Aurukun. After flying in I lobbed up at the conference venue and the first person I saw was my crazy cousin Annette Rutherford, who was also there.

'Hey, my cuzz. How you doing?'

'Good,' she said, with her usual big smile.

I then asked the usual conversation suspects, like 'Why haven't you got a man yet?' and 'Do you want me to find one for you?' She laughed as always with that grand cackle of hers. At that moment I looked over to the pool and saw a gorgeous young black woman just standing, smiling momentarily at us, and then looking away. She was wearing a long t-shirt with flashy knee-length purple tights latching on to some very smooth brown legs.

I watched, mesmerised by this goddess teaching the torches to burn brightly. Annette smiled at me knowing exactly what was going on in my head. She knew me so well.

'That's our Grace!' she said. 'She's a new member of the NATSIEP team from Townsville.' NATSIEP was the National Aboriginal and Torres Strait Islander Education Program team, which was active across Queensland.

Later that night I caught up with Michael Blackman at the bar.

'You been working that mojo of yours,' he said, laughing out loud with his shiny silver front tooth well on display.

'No, I haven't really been taking much notice,' I replied as honestly as I could.

'Anyone around?' I asked him.

'So you haven't seen Dorothy Savage's daughter then, 'ay? She's the one everyone's talking about.'

'No, I haven't seen her. But if she's here I'll get her,' I said, not even knowing why I responded in a way that was so cocky. I knew Dorothy Savage reasonably well and she wasn't the kind of woman to mess with. She was an older woman whom I respected greatly as she had worked as a Community Education Counsellor in Townsville high schools for years, supporting young black kids to get through high school. In many ways she was very feisty and she reminded me a lot of my mum in her prime.

I didn't think too much more about the conversation until the next day when the conference was over. Annette dropped me at the airport and I went in to catch my plane. It was the north-bound 'milk run' that would stop in Mackay, Townsville and then finally Cairns. To my surprise, Dorothy Savage was waiting to catch the same plane and who should be beside her? That same black angel who I'm sure was missing from heaven.

My heart was going giddy-up and my body was tingly all over. I wasn't too subtle as I ambled over, making out that I wanted to say hello to Dorothy and ask how she enjoyed the conference. I wasn't really interested in her thoughts and I think she knew it.

'This is my daughter Grace,' she said, with a fairly firm tone that was kind of saying, 'This is my daughter but don't go looking too hard!'

We made small talk until it was time to get on the plane. As luck would have it I was seated next to Dorothy. She was tired but she found some energy to chat; in particular, to let me know that Grace was living with a boyfriend who was from a very big family. I got the message, but thought, 'Who knows what the universe can bring?'

The universe did indeed bring all kinds of opportunities, one being the invitation to sit on the Advisory Board for the Indigenous Education Support Centre in Townsville. There were some other great people on the board, but none greater than the very delightful Grace Savage. Her mother was not there to keep an eye on her nor was she out having drinks with us later that night, or sitting with us at McDonald's on Flinders Mall until five am talking about some very complex relationship problems. Grace was upset about what was going on in her life. Clearly I was a trained counsellor and by this stage a very good friend. What else could I do? I was going to counsel this poor girl right into my nest. I returned triumphantly to Cairns, telling Leigh Schelks and Michael Blackman that I had met the girl I would marry.

'Who?'

When I explained that it was Grace Savage from Townsville they all said with guarded surprise, 'Hasn't she got a boyfriend?'

'Yeah!' I said.

'Haven't they been going out for like eight years or something?'

'Yeah, that's her,' I said. And the rest, as they say, is history. It turns out Grace could not resist the Millaquin mojo after all.

While things were unexpectedly looking up on the personal front, the professional front was bringing new challenges. I took on an executive development role that had arisen in the Cairns District Office. They called it a 'shadowing' opportunity, and I basically followed the guy who was working as the Assistant Executive Director, Indigenous Education. The regional office was a change of scene and I enjoyed the opportunity to work closer to Steve Miller, the Executive Director. He was a pretty

shrewd operator and while he seemed quite firm there was something about his style that I really liked. I was less impressed by
some of the people around him, though, who would bow down
to him and talk so nicely to his face, but stab him in the back at
any opportunity when he wasn't around.

My mentor in the office was Paul Campbell, an ex-principal
with a very soft and gentle manner about him. My mates Leigh
Schelks and Don Andersen would often tease me about this
relationship. Leigh would call me the 'black shadow' or the 'the
black prince'. Don was less cruel and more insightful posing the
most obvious question, 'Have you ever noticed how shadows are
always black?' In retrospect the notion of shadowing never really
made much sense. You either have faith in someone, throwing
them into a role, or you don't. Simple as that!

I did get frustrated and this wasn't helped when my mentor
asked me to assist him in running a strategic planning session on
literacy for Cape York schools. I was not involved at all in the
development of the program, but on the day he had me running
around quite a bit. As they wrote their insights on butcher's
paper Paul would signal to me to come and get the paper and
Blu-Tack it to the walls. Leigh and I were looking at each other,
giggling like schoolboys at first, but after a while he could sense
my growing frustration and anger. It was just getting a bit too
silly.

'Fuck this!' I thought. The next time he asked to stick something to the wall I raced over to grab it off him and in my best
American deep southern accent I said, 'Yeah, boss. I go stick 'em
real good up on the wall there for you, boss. I go stick him right
here like this, boss. I go stick 'em up here right like this, boss!'

Leigh burst out laughing loudly above all of the other nervous and guarded giggles in the room. They weren't too sure how to respond and by this stage I really didn't give a shit.

The next day my mentor chipped me about it and said it had caused him some embarrassment.

'Good,' I said. 'Because you treated me like I was some dumb black nigger in there yesterday. All you did with me was make me stick the papers on the wall with Blu-Tack when I could have run that whole day for you!'

What followed was a pretty robust conversation and to be fair he got what I was talking about and apologised. He was overall a very decent man, and after that we developed a pretty good sense of respect for each other. In retrospect it was always going to be an awkward yet ineffective way to have a professional relationship.

After six months in this role I decided to have a crack at working in Central Office. This meant having to move back down to Brisbane, and I was sad to leave my really great friends in Cairns behind. Grace had already moved to Toowoomba to work with her Aunty, Gracelyn Smallwood, at the University of Southern Queensland, so it meant I would be closer to her. For the first few weeks I lived at Redbank Plains under my sister's house. This was always a temporary arrangement and the drive along the Ipswich to Brisbane road each day drove me crazy. I had to get a place in town. A mate of mine, Ken Riddiford, agreed to find a place with me to share. Once we found a place we liked Ken did all the talking to get things sorted. The prospective landlord sized him up.

'You guys Aboriginal, 'ay? I am a bit dubious about Aboriginal people in my properties!'

Needless to say we didn't get that place. There was no real surprise about what just went down. I'm always amazed when I hear politicians say there is no racism in our society. I'd rather they said something like, 'As a society we are certainly not perfect and we must accept that racism does exist. The challenge for all of us is to ensure this despicable phenomenon is dealt with rather than tolerated.'

The work in Central Office was nowhere near as enjoyable as in schools. Maybe I was just not cut out to be a bureaucrat. I was located on the lofty heights of the twenty-first floor at 30 Mary Street, working as an Executive Research Officer, all of which sounded impressive, I suppose. I bumped into my old guidance officer training mate, Bruce Muirhead, who was working on the eighteenth floor.

'How's it going, buddy?' he said.

'What the hell is this place?' I responded. 'Nothing happens here. It feels like we just do nothing that has anything to do with what goes on in schools!'

Sensing my frustration he said in his usual dry way, 'You don't worry about stuff like that in here. You just hang in there and after a few months you start to believe you really are making some kind of difference. The truth is you're still achieving nothing, but you actually think that you are!'

We looked at each other and I responded in the only way I knew how, 'I'm going to flog you in a minute, Bruce!'

We both laughed with a sense of futility and went our separate ways. I was never going to survive in this kind of environment and nor could Bruce. He eventually went on to bigger and brighter things. I was contracted for six months and honoured the arrangement. I was sent all around Queensland to do research and scoping work to inform the strategic directions on Indigenous education for the department. While this sounded influential, it didn't take too long to realise that the 'research' would be for appearances' sake only. Decisions were already made by one or two other figures higher up in the building.

Against that background I tailored my response to people in communities to protect my own credibility and reputation, which was very important to me. I would explain that I could guarantee their voice and concerns would be heard back in Central Office, but I couldn't guarantee the extent to which those in the house would be receptive. I think people understood and respected this. I felt sorry I could not offer more than this. The end of my contract in Central Office was approaching rapidly and I had to make a decision about my next move. I applied for two jobs up north. One was for the Band 7 classified deputy principal role at Mossman, which Iqbal had vacated when he moved south to take up a principal posting. The other was as the head of campus at Yarrabah's secondary school. It had a Band 5 classification, which I had been at for many years. Despite it being a sideways shift, I figured the Yarrabah job would be something I could get into. I was also considering a job offer from Gracelyn Smallwood to lecture at the University of Southern Queensland, with the prospect of starting my PhD.

Going to Yarrabah would mean having to lock horns with a principal with stifled perceptions, but going to Mossman again meant working with the very decent Deborah Kachell. As it turned out I would not have the luxury of making such a choice. I got a call from Yarrabah saying they didn't think I would be suitable for the job. A few days later I got a call from Jeff Umback, the other deputy principal at Mossman.

'Mate, we want you for the job! We reckon it would be really great for the school to have someone like you on board,' he said with sincerity.

I couldn't help thinking of how crazy it was that I could be offered a Band 7 job while being told I was not considered up for a Band 5 position, a level I had been working at for the past four years. I told Jeff I would get back to him with an answer after the weekend. I also had to consider the offer from USQ. I had completed my Masters in Education with some additional focus on psychology subjects and I knew I had to go all the way through to a PhD at some point. It was such a difficult decision.

That weekend I got in the car and just drove down the highway to do some thinking. I figured a good long drive would surely enable some thinking time. Driving out of Brisbane I decided I would not turn around until I made a decision. I got to Mullumbimby in New South Wales, not far from Byron Bay. There was not much there but I did manage to find a cafe, had a cup of coffee, and then headed back to Brisbane. The need to start my PhD was most prominent in my mind, which ultimately meant I was going to Toowoomba.

7

Lecturing and learning

I felt bad having to ring Jeff back and reject the Mossman offer, particularly as they had shown good faith in my ability while others clearly hadn't. It would always be one of those decisions I would reflect upon and think, 'What if?' But on that drive back to Brisbane I had to be content I had made the right decision. I had always planned to go for the highest award academia had to offer and now with the lecturing position it was probably the best time to do it.

It was always my intention to complete a PhD. When I started my first college diploma in 1985 I had no idea what a PhD was. My experiences at college and what I came to understand about low expectations made me determined to go all the way, whatever that meant. Looking back, I am not sure my logic was sound or pure, but it certainly was part of what motivated me on those long and lonely nights of writing. If a PhD was the top prize in education, then I was going to take it, even if just to prove wrong those who implied Aboriginal people had no rights or abilities in education. I wanted to show that the sacred PhD was not so untouchable.

Another part of what motivated me was to show other black-fullas that a PhD was within our reach. I understood that we live in a world where people seem to take more notice of you if have a 'Dr' in front of your name. The PhD would give me credibility and status and I would need this if I wanted to be influential in changing low expectations of Aboriginal children in schools. Undoubtedly, it would also be extremely hard work and I would need a lot of self-discipline, but I was not the least bit daunted. For me it was the same at some level as working in the tobacco fields. You just have to know what needs to be done and you just keep going until the job is finished. Anything I started I always finished.

For eighteen months I lectured at USQ, focusing on Indigenous education. It was an opportunity to read and clarify my own thinking and put forward some fresh ideas for students who were preparing to become teachers. Some of them were wonderful, committed to learning and ready to take up the challenge to go out and make a difference. Others were stuck in old ways of thinking. Pauline Hanson and her crazy ideas had a high profile at that time, especially in south-east Queensland, and that didn't help advance the Indigenous cause nor Australia's cause. I remember a prominent figure of the uni's student union coming out and saying, 'We do not have a position on Pauline Hanson or her policies.'

'How gutless!' I thought. Like many I tended to think of university student unionists as feisty renegades who will wave a flag or banner for almost anything. Not in Toowoomba it seemed. In his own blissful naivety I doubt this guy even realised that by not taking a position he was actually taking a position – a position of passive complicity in which one either believed in the unevolved trash being spewed out, or simply had the luxury of not having to care about those affected.

Despite this I didn't mind Toowoomba and I met some good people, although there were some elements that were not so pleasant. I was just one of many Aboriginal Rugby League players, I'm sure, that ran out on to the main field feeling uncomfortable and awkward upon seeing the sign on the grandstand.

'Shit! Does that sign up there really say, "Nigger"? What kind of place is this?' I was thinking. It just seemed so bizarre to be confronted by the sign and I was so glad that Stephen Hagan, who later became a good friend, took up the challenge to have it taken down. Stephen was the kind of guy who would never be passively complicit with such distasteful and offensive behaviour and I admired him for having the courage to engage this issue. At the same time I had nothing more than rigorous contempt for other blackfullas who somehow tried to suggest that it was fine. I found this even more bizarre than the actual sign. How could they be that screwed up?

Despite these circumstances in which it seemed some brains might have actually shrunk, there were, of course, opportunities to open my mind a little more. I commenced my PhD and got hooked up with a very sharp supervisor, Professor Mark Rapley. Mark was in his early forties at the time. He was a shrewd thinker who in some ways was the typical psychology academic, yet in many other ways he was quite atypical. What I liked most about him was that he would listen intently to what I had to say, and if he felt he needed to then he would simply say, 'I think you're talking shit there!' I respected this because it challenged me to be sharper in my thinking. In many ways I had become accustomed to people around me being very impressed that I had done so well, agreeing with me on everything I said, telling me how great I was, and not ever having the courage to challenge me in any serious way. All of this is nice, I suppose, for anyone's ego, but if I was ever going to write a PhD worth reading, and one that would be considered good because it was great, then I needed someone who was going to be completely honest with me. I didn't want a PhD where I did whatever it took to get me across the line because I was a blackfulla. My final thesis had to be earned and considered on its own merits.

Working with Gracelyn Smallwood was indeed a great opportunity. In many ways she was an old grassroots campaigner and I respected her for that. She was well connected to many Indigenous leaders throughout the country and she would often call on those contacts to come and lecture at the university. On one occasion she had arranged for Michael Mansell from Tasmania to speak at a conference. I bustled my way in to being the one to pick him up from Brisbane airport and take him to Toowoomba. It was a two-hour drive I will never forget.

Michael would never remember how I was hanging off every word he said. I asked him questions about the challenges he faced, what it was like engaging in so many Aboriginal political manoeuvres over the years, and what advice he might have for a young blackfulla like me. We talked about the colour of his skin and how people would probably never question his identity if he had not been so intellectually shrewd but had fitted the negative stereotype. He discussed at length with me his motives for going to Libya back in the 1980s, the stunts they pulled in London to bring attention to the need for repatriation of the bones of Aboriginal ancestors stored in their museums, and the logic behind the Aboriginal Provisional Government. I could have driven him around for another eight hours that day being inspired by what he had to say, and by the depth and clarity of his thinking. Even today I think of him as one of the smartest guys I have met.

Not long after, in September 1997, I was given the opportunity to travel abroad. Gracelyn was keen for me to go with her through South Africa, and then on to Trinidad and Tobago to represent her at a conference. It was a tough gig but someone had to do it! The trip was extraordinary and broadened my thinking even more.

We visited a university in Grahamstown in South Africa and stayed with other academics. Grahamstown was our base and from there we visited a number of universities, most notably, Fort Hare, famous for having Desmond Tutu and Nelson Mandela among illustrious and esteemed alumni. I met and chatted with some truly impressive young black students at the university. They were keen to hear about the challenges of Indigenous Australians. What really blew me away were our discussions about identity and blackness, and how they had been taught, whether explicitly or subliminally, to despise the colour of their skin. I knew how that felt.

Gracelyn and I also had the privilege of meeting with the premier of South Africa's Eastern Province, Makhenkesi Stofile. He seemed to be a popular figure, well protected by all of his minders and the prominently armed security personnel around him. He was highly engaging and interested in hearing about the plight of Indigenous Australians. It was no surprise to us that he asked about John Howard with a measure of distaste to match ours. He also spoke about Joh Bjelke-Petersen with the same measure of contempt and lamented that back then South Africa had sent representatives to Queensland to find out and learn from the way they treated 'their blacks'.

When we visited South Africa you could still drive through townships and suburbs and notice the conspicuous change in people's skin colour as you moved out from one suburb into another. For me it was somewhat unnerving. One minute you'd be driving through a shanty town and people had gorgeous jet-black skin, and then you'd cross the rail line into a less impoverished suburb and all of a sudden you'd see kids walking the streets with gorgeous dark-brown and caramel-coloured skin. It was easy to see how history had constructed this circumstance, yet it still remained difficult to get my head around just how human beings could be so 'categorised'.

Significantly, though, South Africa had just begun proceedings in the Truth and Reconciliation Commission. Mandela had not long been president and had established this powerful and profound process. In the evenings when we'd get home to stay with our hosts we'd all be huddled around the television, aghast at the things we were hearing coming out of the Commission.

Without a doubt the highlight of the trip to South Africa was the day Gracelyn and I went to East London for the unveiling of the Steve Biko statue by none other than President Mandela. It was a special day. I had heard Pop John way back in Cherbourg often refer to Steve Biko as his hero, loving to quote him: 'It is better to die for an idea that will live, than to live for an idea that will die.' I always loved hearing Pop John talk of his passion for Steve Biko and his ideals and here were Gracelyn and I, excited and nervous at the same time, amid a prolific sea of black faces just as exuberant as we were.

Helicopters were flying overhead in all directions and the crowd would occasionally break out into song in a way that just moved you right to your core. We had a good view of the stage and there were about thirty esteemed dignitaries seated, awaiting the arrival of the man himself. Premier Stofile was one of the dignitaries and another was a prominent activist, Kwame Terare. Gracelyn had met him on previous travels to Human Rights forums around the world. Kwame spotted Gracelyn in this massive crowd of black faces and signalled for her to join him on stage. The next thing we know some soldier with a gun singled her out in the crowd, offering to escort her closer to the stage. Gracelyn froze and said, 'No. No. It's okay. I will stay here with my friends!' She said she was worried about leaving me alone in the throng, but I think she was just too nervous to take off by herself. If it had been me, and I had the opportunity to be taken closer to President Mandela by an armed escort, I would have ditched Gracelyn, no sweat.

As we laughed about it, just two little Aboriginal faces adrift in that sea of over-exuberant South Africans, a helicopter landed and out stepped President Mandela, walking ever so statesmanlike onto stage about forty metres from where we sat. The moment was breathtaking and one that I would never forget. After the unveiling, President Mandela stepped back onto the helicopter and flew off into the sky, leaving behind that ocean of adoring fans and constituents. He really was the people's president and I got to see him in the flesh. This was a man.

If that wasn't momentous enough we somehow were invited to be special guests at a council reception afterwards. We met the famous author and journalist Donald Woods, a very prominent figure in the tragically short, yet important, life of Steve Biko. We also met Steve Biko's wife and sons. It was incredible. Gracelyn invited them to come back to Australia for a conference she was running. They agreed, and, while I never believed they would come, they actually did make the journey the following year. Some years later Premier Stofile would also come to Australia and visit me at Cherbourg School. I remember his visit so well as we all hugged and embraced him. I tried to explain to the others that if we had tried to embrace him like that in South Africa we could well have been shot.

After South Africa I continued on to Trinidad and Tobago to a conference called Harmony in Diversity. It wasn't a grand affair, with fewer than a hundred delegates, mostly from the suburbs of Port Elizabeth, but I was an internationally invited speaker along with another guy from New York, who talked about the Taíno, a group of people indigenous to the Bahamas, Greater Antilles and Lesser Antilles. There were also representatives who were descendants of the local indigenous people, the 'Caribs', as they called themselves.

The conference venue was more like a suburban community hall, where a bunch of locals had rocked up to check things out. Knowing that it wasn't a five-star occasion I threw on a tidy pair of Levis and, knowing that I was an international keynote speaker, a tie. The other international guest turned up decked out in a full native costume, feathers on his head, showing off some flesh, and making offerings of tobacco in every direction. It was mesmerising in many ways and the conference delegates were really taken in. Apparently there were some murmurings from people wondering about where the Australian Aborigine was. Maybe I should have ditched the shirt, Levis and tie, painted myself up and rocked up semi-naked with a lap-lap and spear. Showing my body off wouldn't have bothered me but I didn't ever dress up like that, and I wasn't about to start here.

I suspect they might have wondered why I wasn't any blacker and didn't look like the pictures they could have seen in textbooks or on TV about Australian Aborigines. It didn't bother me, as I was never going to be something that I wasn't. I am who I am. That's it. I wanted to be true and authentic to who I was and how I grew up. The guy from New York was a little different as I discovered. As we travelled around and visited various places we got to know each other better.

'So what was it like for you growing up as a Taíno in your country?' I asked inquisitively.

'Oh, I didn't grow up as a Taíno,' he replied in his broad yet squeaky Brooklyn accent. 'I always thought I was Puerto Rican. My brothers and sisters thought I was crazy but it was some old guys from the old smoke houses who identified me.'

'I reckon I know where this is going,' I thought. And I was right.

'They told me I was a Taíno and I said to them, "No, I'm Puerto Rican." And they said to me, "No, you're a Taíno. And you better find out about your people!"' Then his eyes got all misty and he said with a voice that was little more enchanting like, 'And it was like this huge hole inside me just filled up, like I was a whole person and I had never felt that complete in my whole life!'

As he explained about his big hole being filled he motioned with his arms in a circular movement around his abdomen. I just sat there, kind of unsurprised and thinking, 'I'd like to put a big hole in this Yank's neck if he doesn't stop talking and going on with all his exotic shit!' To be fair I really didn't know him that well, but I had seen this type of person before back home. I always found that authentic blackfullas never had to go on about their identity, or try to make themselves overly exotic, or cloak themselves in too much red, black and yellow, or traditional regalia. Blackfullas are blackfullas, and we've never felt the need to put on an act for anyone else to somehow prove who we were. I wore my identity on the inside.

There are some, though, who bugged me as much as this guy was doing, when they put it on. For me cultural identity is something that you have, the good and the bad of it, and it is not something that you can adopt or become when you wear some form of costume to show off to people. This is made much worse when you have known some of these people for a long time, and remember there was a time when they pretended they were not blackfullas. The man with the big, filled-up hole spent the next few days fascinating people with the exotic regalia and stories about his ancestors, none of whom he could speak about in any 'connected' way. The last I saw of him was at the airport in Miami, Florida, when I was catching a connection to Los Angeles to go home. He was heading back to New York and seemed intent on avoiding me as he made his way into the crowd, woofing down a hot dog with mustard and dressed in the New York regalia of bomber jacket and faded jeans.

Despite this niggling experience it was a fascinating few days in Trinidad and Tobago. The questions about identity featured prominently. As in South Africa, I was struck by the dynamic in which young black people learned somehow to despise the extent of their blackness and in some ways their sense of identity. I discovered this same dynamic in other countries I travelled to, including Mexico, India, New Zealand, England and Europe.

Whether it was a good thing or not, listening to other people describe the challenges they faced because they were indigenous or dark-skinned people made me feel as though I had never left home. They would talk about their young people being disconnected from their traditional cultural identity; about being too readily influenced by American gang culture and an apparent lack of respect for elders; about feeling alienated by the mainstream society that had descended upon them. This trip, in particular, got me thinking a lot about the power of white societies and the extent to which they could make indigenous peoples from all parts of the globe feel somehow inferior, despite our connections to such rich and sophisticated ancestries.

As part of my lecturing job, we would take students on field trips to Cherbourg, a couple of hours' drive north from Toowoomba. It was great to get back there and see people like Pop John again. Cherbourg had an extremely rich history with its origins as one of the infamous 'dumping grounds' for Aborigines who were rounded up from all over Queensland and northern New South Wales. It was started as Barambah Mission in the early 1900s and had grown over the years into a permanent town of disparate peoples whose languages and cultures were eroded by the destructive policies of white administrators over the decades. I had visited Cherbourg with Pop John a number of times previously and had got to know a few of the people who lived there. Despite the difficulties they faced, there were many Cherbourg residents who had a strong sense of community and who were working for change.

While it was great to reconnect with the people, I never really liked these field trips. The school was depressing, as there was rubbish everywhere, broken windows and kids ran all over the place, sometimes in highly dangerous areas. The principal and her staff would sit down with our teacher trainees and tell them why it was like this and how hard it was to teach the kids at Cherbourg, that it wasn't a normal school and that we had to have different expectations for these children because they were so different. Something was telling me that it didn't have to be this way. I knew from personal experience that if you have low expectations of people then they are most likely to deliver on that. Similarly, I knew from personal experience, that if we have high expectations, children respond to that, regardless of how impossible things might seem. Somewhere inside I was wrestling intellectually with the fact that these teachers had been here for a long time even though it seemed like they really cared for the kids. Some had been there for more than ten years. Maybe this was the best we could expect from them! If this was true, then it left me with a sense of despair and hopelessness.

We heard stories about children not even getting to the end of primary school. We saw a school in chaos and completely dis-engaged from the community. In the face of all of this it was easy to look at the attendance data and student performance data and believe that the Aboriginal people of Cherbourg did not value education. There was something paradoxical about this, particularly given our earlier conversations in the day when we met representatives of the Cherbourg Council. Men like Warren Collins, the CEO of the council, and Ken Bone, the mayor, both spoke passionately about the need for good-quality education as a means to a positive future. The real question to ask, I suppose, was what existed in the school that was of any value?

At the end of our stay we got back on the bus and headed

home. I was physically tired, and mentally exhausted from the immense complexity we had just encountered. Could this really be the best we could expect?

Back at the university the same tired old question continued to raise its head again and again with some of the undergraduates I taught: 'Are you a qualified lecturer?' For my part, the tired old questions were: 'Is this worth it? Am I really achieving anything? Surely I could be doing something more effective than this?' Most of the students were pretty good, and I particularly enjoyed working with some of the mature-aged students who had been out in the world and had decided they could make a difference by becoming a teacher. For me there was something nice about that. I also enjoyed working with the younger students as well, and it was always fascinating to see their reactions when you opened up their minds to new perspectives on Indigenous matters.

On the whole, though, the lecturing was great but seemed a bit too easygoing for me. I would get home in the evenings, knowing that I was getting paid well but not feeling like I was working that hard. Maybe it was a hang-up from my old days working on farms, but for me when I knocked off at the end of the day I enjoyed the feeling of being exhausted after putting in a good effort. Walking off the footy field was the same, too. It was like you knew you were tired because you gave everything. Of course, the world of academia means a different kind of giving, but for me it didn't feel like I was giving everything and I certainly didn't feel like I was giving my best.

During this period in my life a sense of complacency had found its way into my existence. Looking back, I was probably at my lowest, yet my ego was letting me think I was riding high. On the work front I was thinking I was the 'big-time' lecturer, having just returned from a world tour, yet I was feeling completely dissatisfied with what I was doing. On the personal front I was spiralling out of control.

I was well into my late twenties by now, yet still foolish in many ways. My inflated ego would countenance a sense of arrogance and recklessness. It was a deadly cocktail for any young man and it would see me into some of the darkest days of my life. Grace and I never really got to a point where we were seriously on or seriously off. Given our complex circumstances I had become involved with another woman who was also in the middle of her own tricky circumstances. It was a tangled time and there were moments when I almost lacked the courage to deal with what was going on. On some days I'd fly down the road in my car, the needle well to the right of a hundred kilometres per hour, not even caring if I ran off the side and into oblivion.

There have been lots of times when I've looked back on those dark days of my own recklessness with a deep sense of despair and disappointment in myself. After years of beating myself up quite a bit, though, I've become more forgiving and accept that what happened, happened. It was a matter of looking deep inside myself and talking honestly to the right people to realise that, on balance, I was a good person.

What emerged was the gift of two beautiful sons from the two different relationships. Looking back, I now know I gained some extremely valuable lessons about life, but right then I was thinking about how to escape it all. I applied for a job at Edith Cowan University in Perth as a lecturer, on the other side of the country. I sent off the application ready to walk away from it all. With my big ego I just assumed I would win the job in Perth and I could walk away from Queensland and my family and somehow just start again. It was crazy thinking, and in many ways, as I look back, somewhat cowardly.

The universe was letting me know that I was not the 'big man' I thought I was. I heard nothing at all from Edith Cowan University, not even a letter to say they received my application. Not that this mattered, and in fact it was probably a blessing in disguise. This was not the time to run. This was the time to face up to all of the challenges in front of me, to do the best that I could do and to be as honourable as I could be.

Grace and I finally settled into a lasting relationship and awaited the arrival of our first child. The best and most honourable thing I could do for my other son when he arrived was to ensure I always paid child support to his mother. She has since married and had more children and it is so comforting to know he is growing up in a supportive and loving family and he knows I'm here for him. Once I had reached this point in my mind where I was not going to give up or run, but rather face up to my challenges, a new opportunity emerged.

One fateful day in July 1998 I turned up for work and there was a message on my desk to ring a guy called Reg from Central Office at the education department. I just assumed it was something to do with sorting out the extended leave that had enabled me to work at the university.

'Chris, thanks for calling me back,' he said. 'We're looking for a principal at Cherbourg and there is a bit of feeling around that it would be great if we could find an Indigenous person with the skill and potential to lead there.'

This was a conversation that had literally come out of the blue for me, and one that presented an opportunity to reflect again upon where I was in my career. It would be a seminal point in my life and in my career.

'Okay,' I replied, not sure whether I was surprised or stunned at the arrival of such an opportunity. 'It sounds like a great opportunity, but you realise I haven't ever run a school before?'

'Yeah, we know that,' he replied, not deterred. 'And we would have to put some support around you to make sure you can give it a good go.'

'Yeah, okay,' I said, as my mind was racing. I was trying to think about why this was such a great opportunity, and at the same time trying not to be spooked by all of the challenges it would bring. I had never run a school before, but I had seen plenty of school principals with what I considered much less talent than I had to offer. I was pretty young compared with others running schools of this size. I had been subjected to and achieved beyond low expectations before but on this occasion was I the only one guilty of having low expectations of myself?

Grace was pregnant, but Cherbourg was only two hours drive away. I'd done a lot of talking about how to improve schools and classrooms for Indigenous children, but I had never seriously been given the opportunity to make real decisions about how things could be done. This would be the time to put up or shut up! If I put up and failed, what then? Like many other academics I could have a great career talking about what to do without ever having done anything substantial.

'Hey, Reg,' I said, somewhere in our conversation and in the middle of my mind racing in all directions around these very complex questions, 'I really like the sound of this opportunity. And I really appreciate that you guys have gone out of your way to ring me especially. But can you give me a few days to think it over and have a chat with some people around me?'

He was very cool with that idea, and he also suggested I take a drive up to Kingaroy and have a yarn with Lyn Healy, the district director, and Mike Primmer, the district personnel officer. I promised I would but first I wanted to chat with my old intellectual mentor, Gary MacLennan, to find out what he thought.

'Don't do it!' he said. 'You would be mad! Cherbourg School is a basket case and you will be throwing away a very good academic career!' He was right, in one sense. The school was a mess and, as for the notion of my academic career, I couldn't help feeling that there was still something inauthentic about me as an educator, in the same way that I felt there was something inauthentic about those 'expert' senior policy people in Canberra all those years ago. I felt like I had been someone talking about what should be done, rather than getting in and doing what needed to be done. At the same time I was frustrated by the idiotic questions about whether or not I was academically qualified when I had already completed a Diploma, a Bachelor of Education and a Masters in Education. If I was this qualified and people were still questioning me, then perhaps I would be better off not bothering to help them along their journey but getting on with my journey with my people.

I drove to Kingaroy to meet with Lyn Healy and Mike Primmer. They asked me what I believed were the key challenges in Indigenous education. Given my experience to date, the lecturing I had been doing, and the reading I had been doing for my PhD thesis, I told them we had to create schools and classrooms that could 'untrick' Aboriginal kids so that they didn't believe that being Aboriginal meant being on the bottom. We had to get them to understand that they could be high academic achievers as much as anyone else. We had to get children to feel good and positive about being Aboriginal and not conform to some kind of negative stereotype to somehow prove they were 'Aboriginal'. I also said that we had to challenge teachers to see Aboriginal students more positively and with potential, we had to challenge teachers to see themselves differently and with the capacity to make a difference in the lives of their Aboriginal students.

It was always my belief that teachers generally knew what they had to know. In conversations about strategies to get the best out of Indigenous children they always know what those strategies are. They also know what type of teacher can get the best out of Indigenous children. But somewhere in these circumstance we get spooked by the cultural differences and the complexity of Aboriginal children, and we become professionally crippled, forgetting that at some level they are just children, like any other, hungry to learn things from us if we can engage and excite them enough.

The conversation was going well, so well I was confident enough to engage in some dialogue about local politics, knowing that Kingaroy had just voted in its first One Nation candidate.

'Look, I know very well that this is One Nation-type country, but I want you to know that I am not the kind of person to just sit back and let our people get trampled on. If I see injustices or read racist trash in the paper I will respond to it, and I wouldn't want to be restricted in my role as a principal in the education department. If I am going to be an Aboriginal person in Cherbourg in a leadership position such as this one, then I can't be seen to be sitting back and saying nothing while my people are getting treated like dirt. It's not something that I do!'

It was a bit like stating my terms and inviting them to take it or leave it. I was determined in this regard and I meant what I said. I am quite certain they had not had such a conversation before. But both Lyn and Mike were not too fazed by it, although I suspect the first part of our conversation about matters relating to Aboriginal students was easier to digest than the second part about matters relating to Aboriginal people politically. As far as I was concerned it was all a part of just one complex, yet interconnected, issue.

We got past the serious talk and Lyn had to go, leaving Mike and me to talk about Rugby League. He was mad about the St George Dragons and loved Anthony Mundine. I was crazy about the Cowboys ever since a sacred night of smooching up with my brown-eyed girl, Grace, behind the Dairy Farmers stadium. All of this was insignificant banter. What was important was what Mike said to me as he shook hands and saw me out the door.

'Mate, I reckon you can do this. We really need someone like you up here.'

His words featured prominently in my mind the whole two-hour drive back to Toowoomba. He believed I could do the job. It was time for me to believe that I could do it.

8

Time to walk my talk

I spoke with Gracelyn Smallwood about the job offer that was firmly on the table. She was reluctant to see me leave the university, yet understood what an opportunity this was. After what had been a challenging time, Grace and I were rebuilding our relationship and agreed to give it a go. On 1 July 1998 when Grace went into labour, her mother was in the delivery room while I waited outside. One of the doctors made his way outside the room with what I thought was a bundle of dirty towels to throw in some wash basket somewhere, but he walked up to me.

'Are you the father?'

'Yes,' I replied nervously.

Then he handed over this bundle of 'dirty towels' and in it was the most gorgeous little package I had ever seen. As I looked down at my baby son it was almost as if he was staring straight into my eyes. It was a moment of connection I will never forget. Strangely enough I remember thinking he looked like a little alien, all greyish and wrinkled, tenderly wriggling about in my arms. We called him Ezra.

I had picked the name at least ten years prior to his birth. Back in the days when Pop John and I would take school students on camps to motivate them to complete school and go on to positive careers, there was a young guy from Cherbourg named Ezra. He was quite charismatic in his own way, yet I just thought the name Ezra was pretty cool. When I told my mum his name she said, 'Ezra! That's from the bible.'

'Yeah, Mum, I know. That's where I got it from!' I replied, waiting to get struck down by lightning. I don't think she believed me anyway.

With the arrival of Ezra and settling down with Grace, I had to think about making my way to Cherbourg and the challenge of becoming the school's very first Aboriginal principal. We decided that Grace and Ezra would stay in Toowoomba initially and I would head to Cherbourg, driving back on weekends. There were a few things I had to round up with the university to honour my commitments before departing, and this meant I could not start at the school until late August. Gail, the departing principal, had to be out the door at the end of July and so there was a need for someone to hold the fort for three weeks until I arrived. A guy called Leigh Barker agreed to act as principal for this interim period and the three of us agreed to meet at some stage to discuss aspects of the handover. Once I took over from Leigh I would also only be appointed as acting principal and if they considered me good enough I would be appointed permanently.

I drove up to Cherbourg on the morning of our meeting and we sat in Gail's office. I was feeling reasonably confident with the challenges ahead of me and the three-way conversation was going well. At about five minutes past ten a gorgeous little black face appeared in the doorway.

''ere, Miss Gail. What you doin'?' It was Paddy Alberts from the grade five classroom down the hallway, through the staffroom and along the verandah.

'Good morning, Paddy,' Miss Gail said politely. 'One of these men is going to be the new principal of the school. Can you guess which one?'

Paddy sized us up before shooting his jet-black arm in Leigh's direction and shouting, ''im!' All I could think was, 'What? You don't think a blackfulla can be a school principal?' I guess he probably didn't. Why would he? He had never seen one in that role.

Miss Gail smiled. Leigh and I smiled with her. I couldn't help looking at the clock and wondering why this kid wasn't in class as it was prime learning time.

'Well, Mr Leigh will be here for three weeks, and then Mr —'

'Mr Sarra!' I interjected.

'Mr Sarra will be the new principal after that. He is taking over from me.'

I'm not sure whether he had a look of surprise on his face or whether it was just that natural sense of exuberance, enthusiasm and effervescence that you see on the faces of so many young children. He strode into the office at Miss Gail's invitation to shake hands blackfulla's way. Moments later he disappeared down the long dark corridor towards his class and we got back into our discussion about the annual operational plan.

A few minutes later, that same little black face reappeared in the doorway, only this time with four other little black faces that should really have been staring at their teacher rather than at me.

''ere, that's that new principal there! 'e black, too!' I heard Paddy telling them. They all mooched up to the door and were welcomed in by Miss Gail. We did the handshakes and all and moments later they disappeared again, down the hallway, through the staffroom and along the verandah to their classroom. We made small talk about how nice it was that they would come down to say, 'hi,' to us, and then the same black face reappeared again, only this time with another eight black faces. They all wanted to say hello and check out the new principal.

'Das 'im there, la!' he was saying. Feeling very pleased with themselves they all came in to shake hands and say 'g'day'. As I did the special handshake with each one of them I was thinking, 'You boys better enjoy this freedom of running around during class time because as soon as I get here it will be all over!'

Clearly it was going to be a tough job with many challenges, the likes of which I had never confronted before. I had been in and around plenty of schools during my career and been part of the processes of attending to such challenges. The difference now would be that I would ultimately be the person accountable for dealing with such challenges. The buck would stop with me and this was daunting. All the while, though, this felt like something I had to do.

In the weeks leading up to my first day at school I had visited Murgon to find accommodation. I checked out the schoolhouse at the corner of the grounds at Cherbourg and felt it was a bit too close for my liking. I chatted to Cherbourg's mayor, Ken Bone, and other local councillors to check how they felt about me not living on Cherbourg. I was conscious of how this might be perceived. I explained that I felt the schoolhouse was a bit too close as when I knocked off from work I wanted to have my own space without running into kids or parents from school. I also explained that while I might live away from Cherbourg for my own privacy, the community would certainly get a good few pounds of flesh from me while I was working. They respected my wishes and I think they appreciated that we had a conversation about it in the first place.

I was on the lookout for some kind of farmhouse or worker's cottage that might be a bit out of town. I went to one of the local real estate agents as I thought they might be helpful in that friendly country way, but on reflection I should have shaved my three-day growth before turning up at their door. Maybe I should have worn shoes, too.

'Hello. Do you have any places for rent?' I asked the young blonde girl behind the counter.

'Mmm. No, not really,' she stammered, as she sized me up and down. I may have looked unshaven and barefooted, but I knew I was somewhat respectable and tidy, even in a t-shirt and shorts.

'Nothing at all?'

'No, we don't have anything here, sorry!' she replied more confidently.

Something wasn't right about this. I walked across the road to the phone box and called a guy I worked with at the university in Toowoomba.

'Hey, Mick. I just been in this real estate office and they told me they got nothing to rent. Can you give them a ring and ask them if they got something? I want to see what they say.' Mick was a decent white guy and as we chatted he realised what was going on. He rang them and as soon as he got through they said, 'Yeah, mate. We got a dozen places. What are you looking for?'

It was one of those situations I had come to despise vehemently but it is even more despicable when people try to say this is something other than racism. I do not want to be confronted by something like this without there being some kind of consequence. So I called my old mate Stephen Hagan, who suggested I talk to Tony Koch, a journalist from the *Courier-Mail*. I had met Tony the previous year while I was in Toowoomba. He was good friends with Gracelyn, who would have been a handy contact for him, but I felt I was insignificant at the time and unsure if he would want to talk to me. Stephen organised for Tony to ring me and at the same time offered some words of wisdom about opening up a can of worms. He knew what he was talking about as he had waged a campaign to have the 'Nigger' sign on the football grandstand in Toowoomba taken down. He also warned me there might be some rough consequences for me to deal with going down this road, but I remained headstrong and wanted to proceed.

The *Sunday-Mail* headline read, 'Principal caught in Race Row'. It sounded a bit dramatic to me, but it was enough to show people that I wasn't prepared to tolerate such behaviour. As I discovered from the number of people saying, 'Good on you!' the agent had been doing the same thing to so many other black-fullas from Cherbourg and Murgon and got away with it. Many signalled their approval at how had I handled the situation. They also knew they were getting someone who was strong enough to stand up for himself, and for his people.

Eventually I found a place to live in a small worker's cottage on a property out of town. It was modest, just how I liked it, and best of all the sky was huge at night and bursting with stars.

My first day as principal of Cherbourg State School was freezing and windy. I decided to wear a tie, thinking, 'If kids at other schools see their principal wearing a tie, then these kids deserve to see their principal dressed up nice, too.' I have always hated wearing a tie and it didn't take long for me to stop wearing them. Every now and then, though, I would throw one on just to signal I thought they deserved to be surrounded by people dressed as they would in other schools.

I parked my car in the designated spot and took in a few breaths, sizing up the situation that I was in charge of now. There were some kids sitting around in the sun trying to get warm, while others were running around and playing kanga cricket. During the game they would sometimes hit the ball up on the roof of A Block, a predictable double-storey school building. As soon as the ball was on the roof at least two or three kids would shimmy up the drainpipe at the side of the building and run along the top of the building to get the ball.

'Holy shit!' I thought. 'I will be in deep if any kid falls off there!'

I was also struck by the unbelievable amount of rubbish lying around on the ground. The place was filthy. Amid this chaotic scene a young guy drove in the school gate in a bomb of a car, pulled up at the front of the children's play castle and sandpit, flung the door open to ditch his kids, and then planted his foot to do a complete lap of the play equipment, spinning the wheels a bit for good measure. This seemed to excite the kids who were playing in and around the sandpit. The worn car track around the equipment made me realise this was a regular route for many parents dropping their kids off by car.

The teachers greeted me in the car park and made me feel welcome. It was very nice of them, yet they seemed oblivious to the mayhem surrounding them. This would never happen in a 'normal' school. Upon reflection, what I was witnessing was somehow 'normal' if other Aboriginal schools I have visited in my travels were to go by. But I was in the position of authority now. From the outset, even before I moved beyond the car park on that first day, it was clear that with this authority I would have to choose whether I would be complicit in such chaos or I would challenge it. There was no real question that there were low expectations at play. I knew very well what it was like to be an Aboriginal student subjected to low expectations. I also knew that things could be much better than this.

I made my way up the stairs to my new office, armed with a fist full of keys. I selected the key for my office and tried to open the door. No luck. I knew there was a box with all of the school keys in the admin office so I walked there to say good morning to Michal Purcell, whom I had met on previous visits to the school. Michal was shorter than me with caramel skin and frizzy hair kept well under control with a few hard-working hair ties. She exuded a sense of confidence and professionalism that I admired. Like so many other administrative assistants at the front offices of schools throughout the world, she was obviously the go-to person for anyone who wanted to know anything about the school. This morning was no exception as there were so many things happening at once.

'Miss . . . Band-Aid!' demanded one little grade one child who had fallen.

''ere, Miss Shale . . . them kids gettin' cheeky to me!' another complained.

'Excuse me, Michal, can I get the key for the library?' asked one of the Aboriginal teacher aides.

''ere, Miss Shale!' another bright little face hollered. 'Miss t'ing told me to come up and get that t'ing for that t'ing. You know?'

I watched in awe as 'Miss Shale' seemed to know precisely about what 't'ing' for which 't'ing'. She also knew who 'Miss t'ing' was as well. She was definitely one worth valuing and keeping on side. Not wanting to disturb her I stared vaguely at the key box in the back room hoping that somehow the right key would jump out at me.

'What are you after?' asked Michal politely, as she reached across me to grab the library key from the same box. I held up my office key helplessly, explaining that I couldn't get it to work and stared with hope into the key box, still not wanting to disturb her.

'None of those will work, 'ay mate?' she said ever so calmly. 'Here give it to me and I'll have a go.'

She grabbed the key from me, told the kids she would be back in a sec, handed the library key on the way out to the teacher aide and walked over to my office door a few metres away. With a special kind of jiggle that I obviously knew nothing about, she opened my door. With me sorted she got back to business at the front office.

I had arranged for an assembly of the whole school on the morning of my first day. The bell rang and the teachers gathered together their classes to meet me. Their excitement and curiosity seemed to match my nervousness and anxiety. I am always fascinated at how so many kids can settle down and be quiet in anticipation of whatever words will be spoken to them at school assembly. At the moment of complete quiet, I raised my voice.

'My name is Mr Sarra!' I explained. 'You will refer to me as Mr Sarra!' I had to get this point across first as teachers were letting themselves be referred to as Miss and whatever was their first name. This was not something I could live with in a school as I harboured a belief in a sense of professional distance in a teacher–student relationship. To me, addressing teachers by their title was a marker of that. As well, if it didn't happen in a regular school I didn't want it happening in this school. I wanted this school to be a regular school.

'Good morning, everybody?' I said with my strong, brand-new school principal voice.

'Goooood mooorning, Mr Sarrrr . . .' they replied, with their voices tapering away with what I guess was a sense of apprehension about getting my last name right.

'Let's try that again! My name is Mr Sarra! When I say good morning to you I am acknowledging you and being respectful. I want you to be the same with me. So when I say, "Good morning, everybody?" I want you to say, "Good morning, Mr Sarra",' I explained, with my voice tapering upwards for clarity.

'Good morning, everybody?' I hollered.

'GOOD MORNING, MR SARRA!' they replied uniformly and in a way that was much firmer and more respectful. It may have been a bit pedantic but I felt I just had to get some of these little things absolutely right from the outset. Once this was established I wanted to get on to the main message. I took a deep breath and cast my eyes across a sea of curious black faces.

'The most important thing that you will learn from me is that you can be Aboriginal . . . and you can be successful. I want you to understand that I feel it is a great privilege to have this chance to work with you. I am here to work very hard, and I want you to work very hard with me. I will say this again. The most important thing you will learn from me is that you can be Aboriginal, and you can be successful. Just because we are blackfullas, that doesn't mean we have to be on the bottom.'

As I scanned the room I could tell they had never heard anything like this before. I doubt the teachers had heard anything like it before either. I was deadly serious, though. Mrs Langton, one of the four Aboriginal teachers on staff, was bursting with pride. Her face was beaming. She was considered an elder by many in the community and I have always thought of her as a strong and exceptional person. In many ways I think this was because she reminded me so much of my mum. She had started her career in education as a teacher aide and, like many other Aboriginal teacher aides, watched with frustration as young white teachers would come and go without ever acknowledging or honouring their tremendous skills and knowledge. Fortunately for the many Aboriginal children she decided not to be a slave to such frustration, and studied to become a teacher. There was no way of knowing on my first day at the school just how powerful Mrs Langton's presence would be in the school and, indeed, in our entire effort to change the tide of low expectations of Indigenous children in Australian schools.

School assembly was my first big event and I managed to get through it okay. The next hurdle would be the staff meeting. Some weeks earlier I had bumped into Bill Brazier, my old boss from Cecil Plains, at a principals' conference in Hervey Bay, where I was presenting a paper. His advice was to make it clear with the staff from the outset that I was interested in effective learning and teaching. It was good advice. Before making the point, though, I outlined where I had come from. In part I wanted them to know that while this was my first school as principal, I had in fact been around for a while and felt more than qualified to lead. By now I was truly sick of having my qualifications challenged and so I felt compelled to get my credentials out before anyone bothered to question them.

It is hard to imagine what they might have been expecting or thinking. I had known before going in that many key people in the Cherbourg community had been outraged at some of the behaviour of the school staff. I had been hearing concerns about them getting drunk with members of the local community and crashing to sleep wherever they landed. I had never witnessed this behaviour myself but it was a concern I was hearing from a number of sources. What outraged the people sharing this concern with me was that sometimes they would be crashing at houses where some of the students lived. It was hard to imagine how a teacher could maintain a respectful relationship in these circumstances. Against this background, an espoused focus on effective learning and teaching would be paramount.

Having articulated my focus I explained I wanted to visit every classroom just to sit in and get a sense of what was going on around the school. The thought of me visiting and sitting in classrooms to observe lessons seemed to unsettle some of them.

'So . . . what will be your plan of attack with all of this?' one of the senior teachers asked.

Looking back, I'm not sure why I had such clarity at this moment, but I responded by saying, 'I'm not here to attack you. I'm here to work with you to offer a good education to the kids of Cherbourg. If we are going to work together then I feel like I should be spending some time in classrooms.' It was a difficult point to argue with, even in a school where every teacher was a strident member of the Queensland Teachers' Union. That early moment of uneasiness would be a sign of things to come. A good relationship with the teachers would be important, and so would a good relationship with the kids.

Coming from a guidance and counselling background I felt

confident about building a connection with the students. I again made use of an emotional bank account with each and every one of them. Every explicit exchange I had with a child could either be positive or negative. I set about racking up as much emotional credit with them as I could because clearly there were going to be times when I had to discipline them quite firmly. I'm surprised so many teachers I come across do not get this very simple notion. For me it means throwing hoops with the kids on the basketball court at morning tea and lunch times. It also means visiting them in their classroom, having a look at their work and going out of my way to notice even the smallest ways they may have been improving.

In an emotional and psychological sense I had to be quite entre-preneurial to build some healthy credit with each of the children because inevitably I had to challenge them about their behaviour and the extent to which they were just as complicit in the failure, dysfunction and toxicity in which we were all located. Of course, one thing was clear: while the relationship between the teachers and children appeared to me at least to be quite dysfunctional and toxic, the children were not getting paid to be in the relationship. I was, and so were other people around me.

In the early days it was clear that little was done in terms of discipline in the school. I wanted the children to understand that there would most certainly be consequences for bad behav-iour, yet at the same time there would be consequences for good behaviour. It was going to be difficult to establish a sense of order and discipline in a place where it had clearly not existed. From the outset I knew that I had to get elders and parents involved in the process of getting on top of this poor behaviour that at times seemed quite wild. When a particular child played up or did something wrong I would find out the best person to get in touch with to have a yarn. From there I would either go around to see them or have them picked up and brought to the school. Usually the conversation with parents would start with, 'How's it going? What have you been up to? Are you happy with how things are going for your kids at the school?' Then we would move on to the more serious topics.

I would take time to explain that we were trying to take the school in a different direction and that we wanted the children to leave our school and be able to survive in high school. All of the parents agreed with this. This is what they wanted too. Then we would get on to their child's behaviour. Sometimes the behaviour warranted a suspension, but I was never too fond of this idea. It didn't make sense to me to exclude kids from a learning environment in which they obviously needed to spend more time, not less. Usually, if I could come to some arrangement with parents to deliver a consequence at home, then the child could continue with their schooling, as long as they understood the connection between their poor behaviour at school and the consequence they got at home. To me this seemed like a good partnership to have and once the children got to see that we were on the same page and both shared the same aspiration it was difficult to play one against the other.

Sometimes it meant I would simply 'growl' the kids at school – sometimes in my office, sometimes with their parents in the room, and sometimes in front of the other kids. Growing up as a blackfulla I knew that being growled was a strategy that worked for me. When we played up at home, the old people would growl us and we would pull ourselves back into line. Growling the kids from time to time simply meant raising my voice in front of them and trying to make the point in a louder voice than usual. I had a pretty loud voice and some kids were a bit shocked when pulled up suddenly for behaviour that was ignored in the past. I would growl kids for swearing at the teacher or at other kids in class. I would growl them for not being in class when they were supposed to be in class. Sometimes I would bang my fist on the desk or on the wall just to increase the theatre of it all. In many ways that's all it was, theatre.

On most occasions I was growling kids in such a thunder-ous and theatrical way so it would be a deterrent for the other kids watching on. I wanted them to be thinking, 'I don't want Mr Sarra talking to me like that!' I really hated growling the kids, but I felt it was something that had to be done. One of my unbreakable rules was that for every child I had to growl, I had to make sure I followed up with a quiet conversation. It always worked.

'I'm really sorry that I had to make you feel shame like that in front of all the other kids. But you understand I can't let you swear at the teacher like that and let everyone think you can get away with it, 'ay?'

There was a lot to like about the children of Cherbourg. What I liked most about them was their sense of honesty. You usually always got what you saw with them. In fact, I think this is true of many Aboriginal children I have seen across the country. When they are happy and cheerful they laugh loudest and with the brightest faces. When they are curious about you they will prod you, poke you, play with your hair, tug at your clothes, grab your jewellery and check it out, and in the same exchange they will ask you without inhibition the most intimate and incisive questions.

'How many kids you got?'

'You got a woman?'

'You a Christian, 'ay?'

It was always so funny watching the reaction of new people to the school when confronted by such inquisitiveness anchored by both curiosity and innocence. When they were sad or hurting they would cry, and pull in really tight when you offered them a much-needed hug. When they were angry they would tell you to fuck off with a palpable sense of passion and fire. This never bothered me so much when I knew kids were hurting or angry and confused. Some of them had very complex lives and in many ways had good reason to feel this way. I was certain the hurt I felt about being told to fuck off was nowhere near comparable to some of the hurt they must have felt sometimes as children in complex circumstances. At least they were honest with me and I loved them for that. What I saw was what I got.

This is not to say I was content in an environment where children were telling the teachers to get fucked and throwing chairs around the room, or climbing out the windows of the classrooms if they even bothered to walk in through the door. In many ways their behaviour was terrible, but again I thought it was only because we allowed it to be, rather than expecting behaviour from them that was much more positive. It seemed to me they were screaming out to know where the boundaries were, given that some of them were in a home context that was often volatile and unpredictable.

Regardless of the complexities of the homes of some of them I was still paid to be the principal in the community, and part of what any principal is paid to do is to connect with the children and their parents, regardless of what judgements we might make. For me, I thought it would be a good strategy to sit back and make some sort of assessment of those I believed were the leaders and power brokers in the school and in the community. If I could forge a positive relationship with such key figures I figured I could be much more successful in my role. In such relationships I had to understand that in some ways this would make my role so much easier, but in other ways it would make it so much harder. The mistake many leaders sent to Aboriginal communities make is to think that engaging Aboriginal leadership means bringing Aboriginal people to the table so that they can explain what great plans they have, and what they are going to do to them and their community. True engagement to me has always been about bringing people to the table so we can have an authentic conversation about what our respective priorities are, what our common ground is, what we think the problems are, and what we can achieve together and how.

In my earlier years as a guidance counsellor I led some work designing policies and processes to get elders from communities involved in schools. In part it was the result of reflecting on where I thought the power sat in communities and from where we as school people could get some leverage in complex circumstances. Another part came from reflecting on the day Mum made us walk all the way home after fighting in the back of the car. She didn't need a psychology lecture to make her understand the importance of drawing a line in the sand and making sure there were consequences if it was crossed. Barry Riddiford, a prominent Aboriginal senior bureaucrat at the time, saw the merit in this idea and backed its development. The end result was a very nice policy document that sat on the shelves of Central Office in Mary Street. In my role as principal it was the perfect opportunity to put one of my ideas into practice. It was one of the things I loved about the job. I had real authority to make decisions and I had people around me who trusted me to make good decisions.

On the school grounds we had a classic old one-classroom school building. It was brought here from Redgate, which is several kilometres away, where it had had a vibrant life as the Redgate school. These days it was just a storeroom for some of the junk that had been hoarded over the years. Some of the elders were very fond of the building as it was their school building during their early years. We cleared out all of the junk, had it repainted and decked out with some decent furniture and tea, coffee and biscuits on hand. It became the elders' room in the school. It was to be a place where they could come and sit and have a yarn whenever they felt like it.

To enhance their presence and sense of welcome we had a special ceremony at which I presented a symbolic gift to all of the elders in the community. Vince Conlon, the groundsman, was an exceptional artist and so I asked him to paint some pieces of wood that would be symbolic of traditional 'message sticks'. Attached to the message stick was a key that I had painted in gold. The symbolism was about traditional and contemporary methods of ensuring access. The message stick was our traditional artefact that enabled access to places, while the key was the contemporary artefact for enabling access.

In a neat twist of fate a friend of mine with whom I had worked at the University of Southern Queensland, Teresa Mullins, was now working for Dean Wells, who at the time was the minister for education. I was explaining to her the importance of having elders involved in the school and we talked about the symbolism offer enabling access. We also talked about that beautiful policy document sitting on the shelves in Central Office. Like all ministers, Wells was ever on the lookout for a good story in his portfolio and so it was decided to dig the documents up for him to launch at our school, as well as to present the elders with the symbolic gifts we had made specially. He also announced to the community that I would be permanently appointed to the job as principal and would be staying on for quite a while. I still remember the cheer from the children and the look on Mrs Langton's face as she jumped for joy at the news. It was a very special moment for me.

In fact, it was a great day all around with some really positive media coverage. Old Mr Button, one of Cherbourg's most prominent elders, got a great write-up in the *Courier-Mail* along with a great photo of him with the children sitting at his feet hanging off every word he said. A real sense of change was in the air and people were starting to know it. The weather was warming up, and so was the community appetite for change.

Zona Hussey-Smith was the community participation officer from District Office in Kingaroy. She had a soft spot for the Cherbourg community and worked tirelessly with me to enhance the sense of connectedness between the school and the community. In particular, she worked tirelessly with the elders and would do whatever it took to get them up into the school for a yarn. Most people thought Zona had a bit of Aboriginal blood in her, and given the way she looked and related to people I would not have been the least bit surprised to learn that somewhere back in her family tree someone had 'jumped the fence'. She worked in an excellent partnership with Mum Rae, who had worked at the school as a teacher aide for years.

Mum Rae had a gorgeous face that told many stories of tough times. She would often sit back, say very little, but her eyes let on that her mind was racing. Mum Rae was also a well-regarded elder in the community. Tragically, she was frustrated by demands that she fill in her timesheets in the morning and account for every minute she spent inside the school gate, while at the same time there was little recognition that she had no luxury of clocking off outside the school gate. She was well connected to most of the families in Cherbourg. To me it was obvious she had so much to offer the school with her tremendous sense of power and influence, yet inside the school any sense of power she possessed was rendered futile by those who could not recognise what was before them. I would watch on with dismay as she was ordered back and forth.

'Mum Rae, photocopy this!'

'Colour this in for me!'

'Take this kid home for me!'

I was not about to endure such disrespect. Mum Rae may not have had a flash university degree, but she was certainly well qualified in life and, more specifically, life on a mission, being controlled by others. Mum Rae became my right-hand woman, helping me out with all kinds of complex matters. She knew exactly who I should be talking to about particular students. She knew exactly when was the right time to visit people and when was the right time to stay away. There were times when she would mosey in to school and let me know if there was trouble brewing that might escalate. On such occasions we would jump into the car together and visit whomever Mum Rae said we needed to in order to sort things out before they blew up in the school.

My right-hand man was Hooper. I first met him at the school late one night. In the first few months I often worked back late in my office, until at least after ten o'clock most nights. In the afternoons after school a few kids would drift in to see if they could borrow a basketball to shoot some hoops. I never usually minded because they would keep an eye on the place for all of us. As it got dark they would head home, and then it was time for the drifters to cruise past. Some would come in drunk and sit down wanting to tell me their life story. At no stage did I feel threatened by any of them as I felt I could look after myself if I needed to mix it. I always hated talking with people when they were drunk, though, especially if they were totally smashed, as some were. The conversation would go around and around, and usually I had heard it the week before. I'd try my best to be polite and most times they would mosey on into the night. If they lingered too long I would leave them in my office to go into the admin office to ring the police. Sometimes I would get Cyril Fisher, or 'Blimps', as most people knew him. He was a local and greatly respected elder who worked as a police liaison officer. It was not an enviable job but he did it very well.

'How's it going, Mr Fisher? Chris here, from up the school. I got this lad up here and he's charged up, not making much sense.'

'Is he giving you a hard time?' he'd ask.

'No, he's just looking for people to feel sorry for him, that's all. But I'm trying to get some work done and he just won't go!'

'All right, my boy. I'll be up there d'reccly.'

Without fail he and the troops would be up the stairs, sharing a laugh and a joke with me and my vagrant friend. At the right moment they would say, 'Come on, now. Get along. This fulla gotta work, you know!' With that they would coax him down the stairs and send them off into the darkness of the Cherbourg night. Sometimes they would come back to share the same old stories over again, but this was usually a sign that I had to get myself home.

One of these vagabond friends was Hooper Coleman. He was such a rogue, with the blackest skin wrapped around a stocky yet reasonably muscular body. Every scar on his face and body had its own story about fights he had gotten into, police he had run from in his younger days, but most were about some lady he had loved and forsaken. He had a lot of scars!

Hooper would sometimes stumble in, telling me that he had been drinking metho, and it would be clear from the smell he was talking straight with me. Hooper never bothered me in the same way that others did, though, because I was often so intrigued by the things he would tell me about. He grew up on the Cherbourg mission and hated it so much that he ran away when he was fourteen to live on the streets in Brisbane. He also talked about knocking around with guys like Lionel Fogarty, a notable activist and poet from Cherbourg, and Dennis Walker, also an activist and the son of the famous poet, author and activist Oodgeroo Noonuccal, also known as Kath Walker. I was fascinated by Hooper's stories. He told me about all the rallies and protest marches in Brisbane when Joh Bjelke-Petersen was still premier.

'All these big-noting leaders would come around to pick up us drones at Musgrave Park and fill us full of grog. We'd love it 'cause it was a free charge, and then they'd take us to the rallies and put us right up the front while they stayed back because the cops would get to us first and flog the hell out of us. But it was okay 'cause we didn't feel anything . . . and we had to make a stand!'

To many, Hooper might have seemed like just some old drunk, but he was offering me an amazing insight into the challenges of Aboriginal people in the 1960s and '70s. This was different from what I had learned or experienced myself. This was the story of people from the mission. Through Hooper's rich stories, and the stories of others, I realised the challenges faced by Aboriginal people who had grown up on missions were quite different from those who hadn't. This is not to say it was easier, harder or more complex than living off the missions. It was just different. Their lives were more controlled. The policy saw them rounded up from as far north as Cape York and as far west as Cunnamulla and Quilpie, espoused in a rhetoric about 'protection' that was really more about 'control'.

I was blown away by Hooper's stories of the cruel treatment he received as a small child growing up in the Cherbourg boys' dormitory. The fact that he decided to escape spoke volumes to me about what type of man he was, and the strength of his spirit. He would not be assimilated in accordance with the policy intent of the time. Despite such cruelty Hooper remained true to his sense of self, true to his people, and true to his spirit.

Our yarns weren't always serious, though. We would often sit and laugh until we almost busted ourselves. He was most famous around Cherbourg for once being thrown in jail for dressing up as the Hunchback of Notre Dame and scaring the old people as they came out of the old picture theatre in Cherbourg. The more we talked, the more I got to realise that not only did he have a rich personal history to reflect on, he had also read many, many books. Sometimes he'd talk about ancient civilisations from other parts of the world, and sometimes he'd talk about the history of other world-renowned rebels like Che Guevara or the Black Panthers. He even mentioned that he and some others had met with the Black Panthers in Brisbane at some stage.

Hooper was obviously intelligent and well read, yet it seemed in a conventional context, he had little to show for it. In part I guess it may have been because he didn't step up into the right places at the right times. Conversely, I am also certain it was partly because the people he encountered simply didn't have the capacity to embrace the leadership skills he had to offer. Maybe this was because he didn't come in the conventional 'leadership package'. Maybe it was because it was easier to oppress and contain him rather than engage him in some type of authentic dialogue in which all would be challenged and, as a result, be better. Whatever it was, I was not going to make the same mistake of missing out on what he had to offer.

'Hey, brother, you ever thought about coming to work here at the school with me? I got nearly all females on staff and I need some strong males in the place.'

'What . . . you looking for a new groundsman or something?'

'No, no. I need you in the classroom. These kids have gotta see you in action and they need to hear the things you got to say.'

'Oh, yeah. I reckon I could give that a crack,' he replied, as I edged closer to cutting a deal with him. As he thought about it he became even more animated. 'You know, these kids are really smart but they just gotta be given a chance. They got hard lives some of them but they just need someone to kick 'em along and keep telling them they can do it. It was bad enough all the shit I had to go through when I was a kid and I don't want to see them end up like me. They got a lot of opportunities now and if they can just step up and get that little bit of a kick along they can really go places. Not like me. That's what I want them to do!'

It was an awesome soliloquy. I watched on in silence, mesmerised. A flicker of light was emerging from the darkness of his life. In this one conversation Hooper had shifted from being just some old drunk whom most people didn't take too seriously, to a man committed to changing the lives of the children of Cherbourg and ensuring they were projected into a future that was better than his past. I have always been amazed at the leadership you can see, when you give it a place to be.

Hooper and Mum Rae were great at rallying elders and parents to come and sit down in the school for a yarn. I really loved those times when we would sit for hours and listen to their stories, and what they thought I should be doing with the school. Clearly they loved telling their stories as much as I loved hearing them. It was such a rich, vibrant and authentic exchange that was much more than talking about stuff. This was something real, listening to Mrs Gambrill, Mr and Mrs Broome, Ralph Chambers, Old Roy Fisher, Victor Bond senior, or 'Dimedum' as he was better known. Uncle Joe Button would growl me occasionally for saying 'kids' instead of 'children'. Cecil Sullivan, who was better known as 'Gunboat', would tell us his stories about his dancing days. Uncle Paddy Alberts, who had been the janitor/groundsman at the school for so many years, enjoyed the opportunity to reconnect. Occasionally, when he was not so busy, Mayor Ken Bone would turn up to see how things were going, having to endure stories about how old Pop Sam Murray senior and his gracious silver-haired wife would discipline this 'would-be mayor' as a child. Sometimes Mrs Leedie and Mrs Bond, whose daughter Sylvia worked as teacher aide at the school, would come along, as would Jenny Thompson, Mrs Jacobs, Mrs Clevens, Mrs Morgan and Aunty Ada Simpson as well. I remembered Aunty Ada well from the days when I had visited the school some years earlier. Uncle Swampy Fisher was another who was always good for a funny yarn.

Sitting there, listening to these wise voices, I recalled the meeting with the regional director of education and Pop John, when Pop John demanded with frustrated dignity that something be done about Cherbourg School. He passionately pleaded with the director to change the despicable circumstance in which children were leaving Cherbourg in Year 8 with Year 1 or 2 literacy standards. Yet here we were, eight years later, and the children were still leaving Cherbourg with low literacy standards. It was as though the people responsible for changing this circumstance were colluding with endemic failure, while at the same time finding it easy to explain that this was the best we could expect for Aboriginal children and that somehow this was fine and it should be accepted. This attitude I experienced in a chilling exchange I had with the performance measurement person from District Office, who told me I would be wasting my time focussing on performance targets for comparison with state averages.

'In your operational plan you have to set targets for comparison with like schools, and for comparison with the state averages. But you wouldn't want to be worried about state averages here. You're better off just focussing on like schools.'

'Well, actually, I do want to focus on the comparisons to state averages because I think our kids should be up there, too,' I replied, to her obvious surprise.

Pop John knew back then they should be up there, too. He knew I was now here for them and he knew that at last the winds of change had blown in. He knew that we could do this if we worked together and he was determined to do whatever he could to see our energies aligned and moving in the right direction. In my first meeting with the elders, Pop John stood up for me in a way that made my role in the relationship so much easier.

'I've known this boy for a long time now. He's a hard worker and he will do whatever he can to make things right for our children. One thing I know about this boy is he loves his people! We need to get behind him now and do what we can to help build a better future for our children!'

It was a tremendously humbling endorsement from one whom I consider to be so great. He read me right. I was never afraid to work hard. I was prepared to do whatever it took. I did love my people.

With my priorities focussed primarily on delivering an excellent education in which children could have academic outcomes comparable to any other child in Queensland, and a strong and positive sense of their Aboriginal identity, I felt confident about finding some common ground. I was under no illusions, though; even with the enthusiastic buy-in from the elders, parents and the children, there was always going to be lots and lots of hard work to do, and many challenges to confront. We were, after all, contemplating a different reality well beyond the convenient and watered-down status quo, which most people, particularly teachers, were comfortable with and which remained unchallenged. Inevitably, there would be kickback from some parents, teachers and students.

On one occasion I visited the Year 7 room. In my effort to engage with those I considered were the leaders and power brokers, I wanted to talk to Billy. He was one of the biggest and toughest kids in the school and he wielded a sense of power over the other kids, and it is fair to say he even had control over the teacher in many ways. When he was in the classroom he set the tone. On the days he was around, the other children and the teacher would watch him and almost wait to see what type of mood he was in or what type of scene he was prepared to set. I knew if I connected with him then I had a better chance of connecting with the other kids.

I walked over to Billy, who became nervous in my presence. He was quite a handsome young man, much bigger than the other kids in his class and no doubt had seen things in his life that a thirteen-year-old should not. As I approached him, he was displaying the form of bravado that had obviously got him places. This transformed quite quickly to a sense of anxiety and nervousness, which even made me uncomfortable. I hated doing this to him. I hated making anyone feel this way, especially in front of their mates. But if I was going to get through to the other kids in the school, I had to get to him.

'Hey, Billy. I want to hear you read.'

He resisted by dismissing me as if I was joking, while at the same time checking out how the other kids were reading this situation. The more he protested, the more I insisted, and he knew I would not let up.

'Come on. Let's go over in this corner where no one can hear us,' I said, as I grabbed a book off the shelf.

'I'm not reading that!' he protested.

'Okay, you grab a book then,' I pressed.

With that he grabbed a book and ambled over to the corner of the room. By now he seemed less concerned about what the other kids were thinking or doing, and more about how he was going to get out of this situation. He was clearly very uncomfortable. I wasn't doing this to hurt him, I just wanted him to know that maybe he was not the big man he thought he was, and that it wouldn't hurt for him to be a child sometimes. I wanted to let him know he had great leadership skills, and if he used this positively then he and I could work together to get the rest of the kids heading in a new and more constructive direction.

We sat down and he started to 'read' to me the story of the

three little pigs. Clearly his discomfort was building as he wasn't reading the book but rather retelling it from memory, in the same way that a three- or four-year-old might. My discomfort was building; in fact, I was quite outraged. I had a feeling he would not be able to read yet I didn't think he would be this far behind. As I watched this charade I became more and more incensed, wondering about all of the teachers who had let him slip through, letting him call the shots in his own way and not learning beyond the level of a seven-year-old. He wasn't the only one.

'There. I'm going back to class now!' he insisted, as he moved to get up.

'No, hang on a second!' I said, wanting to push him just a little more, knowing where this could probably lead. 'I want to hear you read another book. But this time I'm gonna pick the book!'

With this he became more agitated and more animated. It was like he knew the only way he could get out of this was to make a scene. He got to his feet, kicked over his chair and screamed at me.

'Fuck off, you cunt! I told you I'm not going to fucking read anymore!' He stormed out of the classroom, kicking the fridge and breaking one of the door's components. He was too angry and so there was no point chasing after him to calm him down. He needed some space and so did I.

I was angry, but not at him. It never bothered me that he swore at me or attacked furniture on the way out. What bothered me most was here was the biggest, toughest kid in the whole school and he found it easier to make a scene, telling me, the principal, to fuck off, rather than admit he just couldn't read. Of course, he would be embarrassed that he could not read. Of course, he would be hurting and angry about it and probably so many other things. He had a right to feel this way, but not so much at me – more at those who had pretended to be his teachers and let him slip through year by year, without ever taking seriously their responsibility to help him to become literate. I was angry because I knew it wasn't his fault.

On his return the following week I caught up with him as I always did whenever I had a run-in with a child. We had a serious and quiet conversation about what had happened. I explained how I felt hurt and angry, too, about how he couldn't read at his age.

'It's not your fault!' I explained to him.

He got exactly what I was talking about. I explained that if we worked together we could try to at least do something about it before he went to high school. From then on we had a great relationship. He was never the perfect student, but then I never expected him to be an angel. But he did have a go, and there were times when I was able to engage his charisma, maturity and leadership to bring the other kids into line at times. I often wonder about what could have been if I had been able to connect with Billy much earlier in his life.

I still really enjoy those moments with kids when you just know you are getting through and connecting. To me it is something that seems quite straightforward as long as you work hard at building your relationship with them and in the process rack up substantial amounts of emotional credit. The relationship with the staff, though, was not so straightforward.

I really struggled to build a positive relationship with the team I inherited. More specifically, I struggled with the non-Indigenous teachers. In my mind I wondered if they were finding it hard to work for an Aboriginal person. Ultimately, this didn't matter and I could not let myself get too hung up or sidetracked by it. Regardless of what they thought, I was only in control of what I did and I had to be content I was doing *my* best to forge a positive foundation that would ultimately be good for the kids and the community.

In the past, when the stakes were low, I had been guilty of keeping the 'peace' by being polite and not engaging seriously with questions of racism or deficit thinking about Aboriginal people, particularly in the assumption that something is wrong with 'them'. In this circumstance, however, the stakes were too high and I had to lead the school out of its toxic status quo, towards a more productive direction that offered integrity.

After six months in the job, having sat back and observed for long enough, I was feeling a little more comfortable about challenging them. My colleagues clearly did not like this. We entered mediation discussions with District Office people and the union representative for Wide Bay, and the teachers would accuse me of not valuing them and the work they did. My relationship with most of them was strained, and they were right in some ways about what I thought of their methods.

I could not and would not feign appreciation for their efforts in a school where children in Year 7 could not read. One senior teacher described innovation as having a liberal classroom in which students were set two literacy tasks, a numeracy task and a fun task. The students could choose whichever one they wanted to work on and if they finished all the tasks by lunchtime then they got free time in the afternoon. This was certainly an incentive to complete the tasks, but on my calculation it meant that if a child completed four tasks every morning they would get five hours of free time in the week. In a school where the data screamed out for the need to maximise every second of learning time, I could not value it.

I also despised watching on as each non-Indigenous teacher had the latest and greatest computers in their classrooms while the Aboriginal teachers had the old computers, or no computers. It was clear that as the new computers came in, they went to the white teachers who always had some way to explain how this was appropriate. I could not value a situation in which senior teachers on staff either had little or no serious lesson, term or semester planning for their classes or, if they did, it was usually the same folder with the same photocopies of work that I had observed the year before. This didn't make sense to me, particularly as the year before had delivered poor student outcomes with plenty of data proving how ineffective the planning was.

On challenging teachers about why the data on student performance or attendance was so poor they would often lay the blame on parents, whom they said did not value education, or the home life of the children because it was just so complex, or the community for being so dysfunctional, or the tests for not being relevant, or the District Office for not understanding how tough it was for them. The list of people or things to blame went on and on, but there was no point where we could put up a mirror and ask: What needs to be changed? How might we be contributing to the endemic failure?

It was obvious to me we had very little or no control over any of the things they listed. We controlled only what we did inside our school, inside our classrooms, and inside our relationships with the children. In those relationships we had to be hardworking, innovative and excellent. We had to be something worth valuing. This is the point I made to Greg Purches, the Queensland Teachers' Union rep.

Greg was a decent and fair. He visited the school several times. In our first meeting he said he remembered me as a kid playing football for Kepnock High against North Bundaberg High, where he was teaching. He was a huge man, whom I got along with well, despite having some firm conversations. He quite rightly pulled me up on occasions because there were some things I could have done better in terms of the relationship with teachers. My inexperience as a principal showed. I respected the way he went about his business, though, and it felt like he respected me and the complicated role I was in, as well as my difficult challenge of trying to deliver a quality education in complex circumstances. Greg knew very well of my respect for our Teachers' Union, of which I was a member. My respect for unions is borne out of memories of my father and the challenges he encountered in his workplace, with limited English skills, as well as a working-class work ethic that could be exploited easily if others with good negotiation skills had not looked out for him. Greg and I reached a new level in our negotiations once we established a common understanding.

We shared a common view that the Teachers' Union existed to protect the integrity of our profession, and not to protect lazy and incompetent teachers. It also existed, like many other unions, to stick up for the underdogs. In this circumstance the underdogs were not teachers being paid a decent salary to play videos or hand out photocopied worksheets and colouring-in sheets. The underdogs were the children at the school, who had so much potential but not enough people around to believe in them, and the parents, who were being told the school was going great when in fact it was disastrous. It was not all disastrous, though. There were a few little pockets of hope that existed like flickering candles in the darkness.

Martina Jacobs was a local woman who had run the kindergarten in Cherbourg for more than twenty years. She worked in a magical sort of harmony with her sister Sophie and together they engaged and excited children about coming to school and learning. Their gentle yet firm way was always great to watch. It was clear the kids were getting a good start at school with Martina and Sophie, and I always loved visiting their classroom and having a good belly laugh with their students. The other uplifting place was Mrs Langton's classroom, which was an oasis amid a sea of chaos.

On days when I was feeling downtrodden, feeling as though my efforts were futile, I would sit at the back of Mrs Langton's classroom and just watch in awe at how she conducted herself, how the children behaved, and how remarkably functional their classroom was. Children would sit at their desk and take instructions from their wonderful teacher. If Mrs Langton asked a question they would shoot their hands up enthusiastically and wait until they were invited to speak. If they had to move around the classroom they would ask, 'Excuse me, Mrs Langton . . .' Some would call her Aunty Beryl or Nana Beryl.

Other teachers had said to me that we couldn't expect better from some kids because of their home life. In Mrs Langton's classroom there were kids who lived in the same house as some of those other kids, and that home life was not an issue in this classroom because there was something dramatically right about the relationship with the teacher and children. The teacher was nice, she had high expectations of them and they knew what they were, she would pull them up if they played up and praise them when they did good things. She visited their parents to tell them about the good things and the things that could be better, and she believed in the children and made them feel special and loved. It was not rocket science, as you'd say.

It may not have seemed so remarkable to others but what made it special for me was that it gave me hope. It enabled me to believe we really could make a difference. If it could happen in Mrs Langton's classroom then we could get it happening in every classroom.

Mrs Langton didn't only pull the kids up when they were slack, she would often pull me up when I was feeling slack.

'What's the matter, boy? Why you looking so slack today?' she would ask with genuine concern.

I'd explain how I was feeling tired or run-down, or most times I would explain how frustrated I was that things did not seem like they were changing. In spite of this doubt, there was never a time when I felt like giving up. I used to think about the people who believed in me, like Mrs Langton and Pop John, and this helped me to keep believing in the children. There was something right about me being in this place, as difficult as it was.

My relationship with the Cherbourg community was excellent. I was loving the challenge of developing and putting all of my people skills to the test when I was yarning with the elders; sitting in front of the Cherbourg Council getting grilled; being a guest on Radio Us Mob, the local radio station; visiting parents to talk about their children for good things as well as the challenging. I even had a go at calling the bingo numbers on bingo night at the Cherbourg community hall. As a bingo caller, I made a great school principal.

9

Starting a ripple

I grew to love and admire the people of Cherbourg. Being brought up on a mission was something that I was never going to fully understand as it had not been my experience, but I know that it was different, and respected that. Paradoxically, a clear sense of closeness and some unbreakable bonds were established among those who had been brought up in these often harsh and cruel circumstances. In fairness, some people reflect quite fondly on aspects of mission life. While many white Australians argue it was the result of policies with good intention, the scars left from taking children away from their families have clearly cut across generations. In spite of this, many of the people of Cherbourg emerged with a sense of pride, tenacity and resilience. Cherbourg blackfullas had something that no other Australians had, not even other blackfullas. I knew I could never be a part of whatever they had, but I was happy just to sit at the edges where I could simply observe and enjoy it and harness the positive energy from it.

Prior to my arrival, the relationship between the school and the council had not been good. Over the years the Cherbourg Council had developed a range of enterprises – some successful, some not so. They enjoyed some great outcomes with a few of their building enterprises, with spectacular homes going up in a newly established subdivision, colloquially known by the locals as 'Snob Hill'. It was made flash by the large and palatial designer homes built by teams working for the Cherbourg Council, a defiant departure from the usual mission-type homes of several decades earlier. Those mission-type designs existed all over Queensland, from Thursday Island to Aurukun, Palm Island and Woorabinda. They all looked the same. Whoever made the decision on the design was probably more concerned about dollars and less bothered that in summer they would be sweltering and in winter be freezing.

The council, though, had turned its back on Cherbourg School. Dissatisfied with how things were being done, they provided a daily bus for those parents wanting to pursue a better education for their children in Murgon, and it was impossible to blame them. But like many Australian country towns in the vicinity of Aboriginal communities, within Murgon there is often a sense of racism that is usually denied. People say stuff like, 'We don't have a problem with the blacks in this town. Everyone gets along just fine.' But when you speak to 'the blacks', as they are so often described flippantly, it is usually a different story. Sometimes it seems that the racist behaviour is endemic, that people simply become acculturated into treating Aboriginal people as inferior, without anyone, including some Aboriginal people, realising what is going on.

I had already had my run-in with the local real estate agent, but I was amazed and at the same time incensed at how palpable racist behaviour could be so prominent, yet denied or ignored. By now I had developed a pretty good nose for it and there were some occasions in which the stench was putrid. I recall trying to book our children in at the Murgon swimming pool for their PE lessons for the upcoming summer season. When I went to book them in I was told I was too late, all the days were filled, and as a result we had to send our kids to the town pool in Goomeri, a further fifteen kilometres away. In my determination to get them booked in at the Murgon pool to save some school time and hassle, I fronted up two months early.

'No, you're too early!' I was told. 'We don't take school bookings for another six weeks.'

Five weeks later I fronted up at the pool again, still determined to book them in.

'No, sorry, you're too late,' they said, with what I perceived as a feigned sense of concern on their face. 'All the other schools are already booked in. Have you tried Goomeri or Wondai? They might be able to book you in!'

I took a deep breath. My being a school principal counted for nothing as they did not bother to contain their racist behaviour. But I had to control my sense of frustration and outrage as I thought of Charles Perkins and the Freedom Rides to Moree. On that famous ride they made the attendants who tried to prevent them entering the pool feel so ashamed that they had to let them in. However, I was just one blackfulla on my own. As I stood there I thought about mobilising the kids and community to re-enact that glorious victory from several decades earlier, but I wasn't so sure about whether this would serve any purpose. There would always be a way to rationalise the situation, a way to explain it away. I called this rationalising with 'rational lies'. In the end I decided not to bother. I breathed deeply and walked out the door, harbouring enough anger that made me want to smash something. Clearly that was not the answer. My energies were better spent focussing on doing my best and being the best I could be with the kids and the community at Cherbourg.

Of course, not everyone in Murgon was like that and it was important to keep this in some perspective. I could easily be making the same mistake as so many white people if I assumed all the white people in Murgon were like that. Clearly this was not the case but I do wish some in Murgon could afford the people of Cherbourg similar respect. Part of my challenge was to get those parents who sent their kids to Murgon to believe Cherbourg School now offered an education that would be considered good for their children. Another part of my challenge was restoring the relationship with the council.

Vandalism at the school was an incessant problem. It was endemic at times and I felt like I was living in a war zone, having to out-think the enemy. It took so much strength and patience on my part to not to see those young and destructive vandals in this way. While they caused much damage and much heartache – not only for me, but also for the kids, the community, the teachers and other staff members – I had to think about why they did what they did. I made sense of their behaviour by reflecting on myself as a kid, recalling those days when I was so angry and felt like smashing something because of a situation that had nurtured a sense of rage, which was anchored by a self-perceived sense of powerlessness. I remembered that day in the classroom when the teacher and kids were all asking me to explain everything about the complexities of Aboriginal communities. For the kids at Cherbourg I realised it was really a way of saying, 'I hate this fucking school! I hate this world! I hate what is happening to me!' I realised how many of them felt disenchanted, dispirited and disempowered.

Many of the students had good reason to hate school, the world and what was happening to them. They were illiterate and innumerate for no good reason as far as I was concerned. The school had delivered little to them. Vandalism, graffiti and smashing up the buildings must have seemed the only way to have a voice and exert a sense of power, and it didn't matter how many times the cops told them it was their school they were destroying. The challenge was to get them to understand and believe that, in spite of their shitty experiences, they could have a sense of power that was positive and untouchable. I had to understand and believe this was possible, too. Together we had to get to a point where we could unveil an authentic sense of power that resided in their basic humanity and was embellished by their cultural identity.

This is not to suggest for one moment that I found such behaviour tolerable or excusable. I truly felt like giving them a good kick in the arse as much as the next person. That would certainly work for some, but for others it would probably just make them angrier and more alienated. The challenge here was to get them to understand that if they continued down this path, eventually the system would close in around them to the extent that they would inevitably be locked up in a small cell somewhere, where someone else controlled every aspect of their life, just like in the mission days under the Protection Act. I wanted them to understand they could transcend the shackles of their past and feel strengthened by a positive sense of power and cultural identity, coupled with a degree of intellect that enabled them to constructively challenge the world around them. Of course, empowering young Aboriginal kids to take on Australian society is one thing, developing the capacity of Australian society to embrace powerful young Aboriginal men and women is another, and often the latter is more complex than the former.

I had to get the balance right. Like everybody else, I was wary of having kids locked away in juvenile detention centres without taking into account their extraordinarily troubled lives, but there had to be consequences for inappropriate behaviour. The police worked hard with me to try to get on top of the challenges of vandalism, but their frustration was that once they got the kids before the courts the magistrate would give them a tap on the back of the wrist, so to speak. In some ways it felt like we had to endure such adolescent antisocial behaviour in a way that would never be tolerated in other communities. It seemed that if it was only blackfullas involved, then what was the problem?

I invited the local magistrate to visit the school. As she walked around with me she shook her head at the senseless vandalism and graffiti that was prolifically on display.

'Chris, we just can't send Aboriginal kids to jail for stuff like this,' she said, signalling her own sense of frustration and limited ability to offer any real solution. She was right, yet there had to be some deterrent to discourage kids from such destructive behaviour. Some elders in the community wanted them to be flogged and publicly shamed. I'm not so sure that was the answer either.

As we walked under the library I showed her the computer cabling that had been severed just for fun, three times in the last three nights. It was no fun in a school where we were going hard at computer excellence.

'What would you want done if this type of attack was

happening on your home?' I asked her. She didn't have an answer, but I think that is where the solution might have lain. To me it seemed rational that she should just forget this was an Aboriginal community and consider what she would expect to happen if someone, anyone, consistently violated her property.

For me, in order to come to grips with the challenge I had to reflect on which behaviour was more malicious and evil than others. Was it smashing windows and defacing walls with a range of profanities, or was it giving them a school with teachers who did not believe they could amount to anything truly special and powerful? Against this background I could leave my ego on the shelf and not feel so personally inflicted or attacked. It became just one of those things I had to deal with. On Monday mornings one of my first jobs was to walk around the school and count the number of smashed windows or louvres, or identify where any doors had been forced open or vandalised. Michal would hear me trudging up the two flights of stairs towards the big sliding glass doors of the reception area.

'How many today?' The record was sixty-four.

She'd duly make a note and then send a fax off to QBuild, the government contractors, who in turn would send a fax to an expectant Wayne, the local cabinet-maker in Murgon. Almost religiously Wayne would rock up ready to go.

Wayne was quite a decent guy in many ways. At least he was one of those white guys in Murgon who had the courage to actually come out to Cherbourg rather than preach a negative view about the town and its people without ever having been there. He'd get stuck into the job with half a fag in his mouth, sometimes whistling as he worked.

'Any bloody wonder you whistle while you work!' I'd think.

We were spending tens of thousands of dollars on Wayne's services, knowing he'd be back again the following week to do more of the same. It made no sense to me that all of this money was going into Murgon while the Cherbourg Council was building such flash and palatial houses just metres from the school. This was a no-brainer. Surely it would have made sense to get local Aboriginal people to do the maintenance at the school. Clearly they were more than capable. The money would then stay in the community. If the kids saw their own people, perhaps even their father or uncle, fixing the doors, walls and windows, surely they would be less likely to perpetuate such vandalism. And if they did cause damage and their dad or uncle found out then it was likely they would usually get that kick in the arse that they sometimes deserved.

Fortunately for me the department's facilities manager for my region was Terry Aldridge, a very smooth ex-plumber who knew how to wear good trousers and a shirt and tie properly. Terry was made even more slick by his silver hair with eyebrows to match. We connected well, not just because we both swore quite a bit, but because we shared a genuine interest in fixing the problem without seeing young kids locked away or attacked by vicious security dogs. The department rulebook said we had to get QBuild to do all our school maintenance. Terry and I weren't the kind to break the rules, but we were both prepared to stretch them to accommodate a complex set of challenges.

With Terry's decency, support and ability to be innovative, we managed to establish a process in which the Cherbourg Council became the preferred provider on all maintenance matters at the school. This would see vandalism diminish significantly from a time when we would average more than twenty broken windows each week, to fewer than twenty in a year.

Changing the maintenance contract to employ local Aboriginal people from the Cherbourg Council was more than just about arresting the problems of endemic vandalism at the school, and more than just about keeping many thousands of dollars in the Cherbourg community. As the school's leader representing the education department, and in some ways representing the government, I wanted to send a clear message: 'I believe in the people of Cherbourg!'

Signalling such a message in a way the community had probably never encountered before from the school or government people was an important way of reaching out to key leaders to engage them as equal and valid partners in a very important function: capturing the interest of children in school in a meaningful and purposeful way. In my travels I had seen plenty of people mouth such words in a patronising way. It was like bringing Aboriginal people to the table under the banner of 'consultation', but in practice was more about 'letting you have a say and then explaining what we are going to do to you!' I wanted people at the table with me as an equal and valid partner with real authority and a tangible role to play in terms of turning things around.

Adjusting the maintenance contract for the school, making room for an extra signature block for the elected Aboriginal mayor on the school's operational and strategic documents, and meeting regularly with the council to keep them up to date were just some ways of reaching out and building relationships in the community. They then realised I was serious about working with them as a partner. Before long they were reaching out to the school to establish ways of supporting us. Together we negotiated a circumstance in which workers on the Community Development Employment Project (CDEP) could come and work in the school. CDEP was a work-for-the-dole type of government program started in the early 1990s after the first major review into Aboriginal employment and training. Historically it became known as the Miller Report because it was chaired by one of Australia's Aboriginal stalwarts, Mick Miller, a man I had the honour of once meeting when I worked in Cairns. It still amazes me that the notion of working for the dole actually started with Aboriginal people. They put their hands up to signal a strong interest in being productive despite limited access to employment opportunities, in spite of the dominant perception that Aboriginal people were lazy and did not want to work.

At Cherbourg some CDEP workers were employed on the school grounds while others had much more to offer inside classrooms. Unlike in a few other communities, I was determined not to accept the CDEP workers as free labour. Their involvement in the school, especially when working with children, had to be purposeful. The arrangements we negotiated saw the council pay them for fifteen hours, and I would find money out of the school's budget to top their wages up so they worked twenty-five hours per week. This meant they would have the dignity of working every day.

I also committed to restoring the Remote Area Teacher Education Program (RATEP) and covered the costs of their training and professional development. The RATEP program enabled Aboriginal people to study teaching without having to leave their community. This arrangement also meant they could work in the mornings and study in the afternoon. Effectively, someone could come off a work-for-the-dole program and commence work and study that would see them on a meaningful career path. It was also an effective way of attracting more local

Aboriginal men to come and work in the school. On my arrival in August 1998 there were only two men on staff, out of thirty-five: me and Vince, the groundsman. Vince had an uphill battle trying to keep the grounds clean and tidy as many people used the school as a thoroughfare on the weekends and during school time. We got the grounds under control pretty easily but it was inside our classrooms that had to be conquered. There was one guy I knew who could help me, Fred Cobbo.

Fred and I had met way back in high school. He was billeted with us in Bundaberg when he came over from Cherbourg to play in the Wide Bay under-fifteens. It was a time we both look back on and smile, when we were young and innocent with skinny bodies and big Afro hairdos, quite the thing in 1982. By the time I came to Cherbourg, Fred was an electrician working for the local council. He was taller and chunkier than me, and we had both lost our Afros. Today we laugh when we recall the time I recruited him. It was a long shot as he was already in a great job and there was no way I could match what he was getting paid as an electrician.

'Hey, brother, how's it going?'

'Yeah, good, brother! What you up to?'

'Yeah, I'm all right, just a bit slack from some of these hard-head kids giving me a hard time. They smart but they run amok on me and make me wild. I don't want to suspend them 'cause they'll just end up in no place. They're good kids underneath, you know, brother, but they just so bloody stubborn!'

Fred knew exactly what I was talking about. He was genuinely concerned because we had talked about the school plenty of other times before and he would let me know what people were thinking. He'd tell me about different sets of parents whom I should be having a yarn to, but he'd also let me know there was an overwhelming sense of satisfaction about the school, how it was changing, and how some of the teachers were finally being taken in a serious way. I handed him a folder with a list of names.

'Here, this them strong head lads, now! What do you notice?'

Fred took the folder and checked it out. A strained kind of smile, or maybe a grimace, forced its way onto his face.

'Yeah, I know these lads, brother,' he said, with genuine familiarity. 'That's all my family, these lads. That's all my nephews right there!'

I had a feeling he might recognise them, thanks to some good advice from Mum Rae.

'Brother, be great to have you on deck with us . . . help me get these fullas back on deck! We're going okay but it would be great to firm things up a bit with you around . . . specially for these lads here!'

'Let me have a think about it. I'll come and have a yarn with you about it in a coupla days.'

As I walked away I had a feeling he knew what I was up to. Fred had a bit of a reputation for being prickly from time to time, not suffering fools lightly, and I knew at his core he was a decent man. This was obvious in our subsequent encounter when he came to let me know he would quit his well-paid job as an electrician and come and work with me to get his nephews and nieces, and so many other children, back on track. These days Fred is almost a qualified teacher himself and I have always admired and respected him for that very important and selfless decision.

Despite many people telling me that Cherbourg, like other Aboriginal communities, had no real sense of human resources to draw upon, I found this to be quite unfounded once I got to know people beyond initial impressions. For me it seemed that once you signalled a belief that something good existed in people, regardless of how run-down they seemed, something good would emerge. One of the things I liked about running the school was that I could give people a go if I thought they had something to offer.

Hooper was already going like a champion with the kids. They really took to him in a way that was different from how they might have engaged with him on the street. They took him more seriously, and clearly he had taken his life and his new role much more seriously as well. The kids would hang off his words when he told them all sorts of things about his life. He had a new spark that would ensure he remained solid. He never gave up drinking completely, but he drank a lot less these days, and he became pretty cautious about letting the kids see him while he was on the drink.

Barry Fisher was an Aboriginal guy living locally with Elvie, his missus, who was from Cherbourg. Although he had a bit of a larrikin streak he was softly spoken and chose his words carefully. He'd been out of work for a while and when we gave him a start he turned out to be extraordinarily solid. He had many challenges, having led a pretty tough life, but he was determined to ensure his kids had better than he did. I remember well his words when we were chatting late one afternoon after school.

'I've lived a pretty tough life, you know . . . been involved with drugs and all that. I know what it's like to grow up without family close around you and I just want to make sure we stick together so my kids get to have what I didn't.'

Llew Conlon was another local guy who was short and nuggetty with a moustache that would make any old walrus proud. He had grown up with white parents in Kingaroy. We'd talk about this occasionally, and it was interesting to hear him reflect on the things that were good about it, and not so good. The children loved Llew, in part I think because he was the same size as them. It was clear he had much to offer as a teacher aide in the Year 2 classroom, a role he embraced with a real sense of love and enthusiasm. As a teacher aide he could offer a greater contribution to Cherbourg and the world compared with his previous role as a fence builder.

Frank Malone was an iconic Cherbourg man who had worked a few days for the council and was then on the charge a bit with his mates in his spare time. Lots of people thought of Frank as the 'black Wally Lewis'. On the football field he was legendary. Those who know him know that, if he had been prepared to leave his family and Cherbourg behind, he could have easily cut a successful Rugby League career on a great contract in Brisbane or Sydney. What a contrast that would have been, but clearly it was not a priority for him. Frank worked as a teacher aide in the senior classrooms. Today, as a qualified teacher at the school, Frank is a living example of success, from being on the dole through CDEP and working and studying at the school to becoming a teacher at the school.

With guys like Fred, Hooper, Barry, Llew, Frank, Pop John and the others the vibe of the school changed quite dramatically. Their presence was well matched by the strong Aboriginal women I had already working as teachers and teacher aides in the school. I was also well supported by some solid Aboriginal local women, Bethyl, Dori, zany Serena and quiet Karen, who worked as cleaners and would always be at school by quarter to five in the morning. Together we got the school humming with a sense of seriousness and of, 'We are here for business!'

I recall one day my mate Don Andersen coming to visit me. Don was a highly experienced school principal, particularly in community schools in Cape York and throughout the Torres Strait Islands. He stood with me after school assembly one day and said, 'Yeah, this feels like a good school. It feels like a school that's buzzing and going in the right direction, with the blackfullas in charge!' For me that was significant. Even though the school was essentially a white institution, somehow it had been reclaimed by Aboriginal people, and it was progressing positively . . . on our terms!

With so many strong and positive local people working in the school, I didn't have to bring in any flash sporting star or someone the kids might have seen on TV. The strong and smart were right in front of them. Not only that, these role models were there in a way that was 'touchable'. A big-time superstar can get kids fired up, buzzing with a glow of enthusiasm, but after a few days that glow and euphoria diminish. A few weeks later they tend to disappear completely. This is not to say that such role models are not useful or effective, but I think it is better when role models and their stories are on hand more consistently. I like to think our school offered day-to-day role models. There was something powerful and touching about seeing an Aboriginal man or woman turning up for work in the school regularly. Even more powerful was the notion that the role model may have been related to the children. Their stories were more touchable when the children saw them turning up day in day out, and emerging from a house with a kitchen, lounge, bedroom and yard that looked very much like their own.

It was great having so many Aboriginal people working in the school, but being Aboriginal wasn't simply enough. They had to have high expectations for the kids and for themselves. While most of my staff embraced the new high-expectations agenda, there were some who needed to be challenged on their attitudes. The conversations I had to have with them were never easy, but as the person leading the school I could not shy away from such matters, even if I wanted to. I found individual conversations were made easier by collective conversations. Sometimes we as the Aboriginal staff would just meet up, which I suppose may have been peculiar to the non-Aboriginal staff and perhaps made them feel left out. I had to work with them to help them see the importance of our meetings, how sometimes as blackfullas we just had to talk straight with each other in a way that may never occur when others were in the room. I'm pretty sure they got this.

In our conversations as blackfullas we'd talk about walking the talk. It was obvious that we couldn't talk one way and then be seen in the community doing something else. This meant a whole range of things had to be done, like turning up for work five days a week, being professional and tidy rather than dishevelled, and staying well above the often vicious 'community politics', as difficult as this was, as we were in the school for all the children, not a few. Any allegiance to particular factions or family groups had no place in the school. I know this was really difficult for some but the strength shown in relation to this particular challenge was amazing. Elsewhere these might seem quite basic ways of being, but here, like in many other Aboriginal communities, factional community politics could be agonisingly complex and difficult. As Aboriginal people working in the school they were up to such challenges in the community as well as in the classrooms.

I'd say to the teacher aides, 'When I bring a visitor to the classroom I don't want them to be able to tell who the teacher is and who the teacher aide is.' This was a challenge, but they rose to it. There were days when I'd walk into a classroom and see the teacher at the back of the room working with one or two children, one teacher aide taking a small group for focussed reading activities, and the other teacher aide at the whiteboard at the front leading the remainder of the class. Even today it is one of those wonderful memories I reflect upon.

There were also occasions when I had to challenge the abilities of some Aboriginal teachers. I recall asking one teacher if she felt confident enough to teach in a mainstream school, such as in Brisbane, Bundaberg or Toowoomba. It became quite a heated conversation as she resented being questioned. I watched her really struggle at times and it was not serving the best interests of the children in her classroom, or herself, to pretend things were fine. Eventually she confessed she didn't feel confident enough to teach in a mainstream school and it was clear the very thought of it scared the hell out of her. She was a teacher who tried her best, but unfortunately had been told by too many of her colleagues that she was doing great when in fact she was struggling. The obvious question was, 'If you don't feel like you are a good enough teacher to work in a mainstream school, then why should you be considered good enough to teach here at Cherbourg?'

In some ways this is a cruel question, but it must be asked. The same questions were asked of non-Indigenous teachers, too. When a white first-year teacher on a short-term contract arrived I assigned her to what I thought was the most settled class in the school to make her transition easier. Once, they had been a pretty boisterous cohort of children but over the years they had gelled quite nicely into a beautiful class. Within a short space of time, however, it seemed the little monsters in them had not been completely purged. When I say some of them were climbing the walls I mean, literally, out the window and down the wall to get away from their new teacher. I tried lots of ways to support the teacher and develop her capacity to be successful. I'd sent her to professional development activities to broaden her repertoire of behaviour management skills and on visits to other classrooms in the school and in the district to watch and learn from other more experienced teachers. Eventually we had to have a frank discussion.

'Look, I'm doing my best!' she pleaded with me, as she was keen to see her contract extended. Unfortunately, my reply was not the one she wanted to hear.

'I'm sorry, but if this is your best than you have to understand your best is not good enough for the children in your classroom. The parents and the children of Cherbourg deserve better than what your best is!' Her contract was not extended.

I felt cruel having to be so honest. Intervening in such a clinical way was not something I was accustomed to, but I guess it was what I was paid to do. I don't think it was something I ever got good at, but a colleague of mine described the skill of those hard conversations like our muscles. The more you exercise them, the stronger and more efficient they become. It made sense but I realised that before I ever got to such a conversation I had to be content I had done as much as I could as the leader to ensure my colleagues had every opportunity to be the best they could be.

The one thing that did make such difficult conversations easier was wondering about whether I would put up with such a teacher for my own children. If the answer to that question was no, and I did not consider a teacher good enough for my own child, then there was no way I would ever expect the parents of Cherbourg to tolerate such incompetence either. It was as simple, and as complex, as that!

Most of the parents were really great. For me it was always important to make time to listen to what the parents had to say. It was even more crucial to make time to listen to those parents who had complaints about the school. I always went by the rule if there were negative perceptions of the school that were matched by reality then there was a problem; if there were negative perceptions about the school and they were not matched by the reality then there was still a problem. The only way we could get on top of such problems was to make the time to hear about them, understand them, and together work out ways to get past them.

When people were angry the main thing was to acknowledge their anger and do my best to understand it. On every occasion we were able to work things out, mainly because I think people recognised that I was genuinely concerned about hearing them. Prior to such meetings, I would always stop for a moment and imagine how I would want my mother or sister treated if they were in front of me. I had seen plenty of school principals treat parents and their views as insignificant. I really hated that kind of smugness coming from a position of unjust power imbalance and I was determined to be something different and fairer, not to mention more effective.

On one occasion it was clear there were quite a few parents that were quite unhappy with how things were going. There was a bit of murmuring going on in the community, and rather than let it fester unchecked I was more inclined to bring it in and stare it in the face so we could deal with whatever concerns together. I asked Mum Rae and Hooper to let me know who had an axe to grind and among the three of us we would get them all together to 'have it out' so to speak. To me it seemed important to give them the chance to meet as a group as it would have enabled them to be more powerful in a way, thus paving the way for a more honest conversation.

About twelve parents assembled and, unsurprisingly, they were all the parents of children that we really struggled with. The meeting was tense to start with. When I sat down, Mum Rae sat beside me. She didn't have to but she did. I invited them to open both barrels and let me have it. Certainly, there was a sense of intense anger, but once we acknowledged that, and its source, then we moved on to a really constructive conversation about how we could work together to get the very best for their children. Beyond the anger it was the usual kind of school principal and parent conversation. They mainly talked about the way I was being too firm with their children.

One parent became quite animated as she complained about how I growled her kids or manhandled them on some occasions. It was a fair criticism and she had every right to raise it with me. She went on, though, to accuse me in a way that seemed a little unfair to me.

'If you're rough like this with the kids then I'd hate to see what you do with your women when you're at home then.'

I let out an uncomfortable laugh, but I was hurt by this comment. Domestic violence is an issue I had taken on at the school by working in partnership with the women's group in Cherbourg. During domestic violence week we would take the entire school on a march around the community, chanting 'No More Violence!' I could live with and reflect on the criticism about being too firm with the children but I was not going to sit there and be accused of abusing my woman. But it was more important I left my ego hanging at the door because it would surely get in the way if I let it.

The meeting concluded some two and a half hours later. Despite the tense beginnings we finished with a good laugh about a whole lot of things, and also discovering how my family tree had connected in some ways to some of theirs. It took time but they got what I was about, not only as the principal, but also as another blackfulla. I wasn't going to let their children think they could come to school and throw things around, or swear at the teachers or stop other kids from learning. Of course I got what they were about, too. They were parents that loved their kids. They didn't want to see them manhandled in a way that was unfair. That was fair enough and I had some reflecting to do also.

Some days later I visited the lady who accused me of belting my woman and explained how I was hurt and offended by her comments. She apologised and explained that she didn't mean to hurt my feelings and that it was all said in the heat of the moment, which it was. We both moved on together.

I often wonder how many other Aboriginal parents had such frustrations ignored by principals and teachers or were told not to worry. I'm sure there would have been times when some had the police called in on them for being animated about their concerns and frustrations with principals or teachers who had no idea about or no real interest in connecting with them. Only on one occasion did I call in the police to speak with a parent, and even then I was reluctant to do so.

It happened one morning after we drove in the school gate. I'd given Grace a kiss goodbye and as I headed up the stairs I noticed one of the parents standing there, a young guy in his late twenties. He had a fairly agitated look on his face and I didn't think too much of it. As I had done hundreds of times before I walked past the front office, said good morning to Michal, and headed on into my office. I put my briefcase on the ground and turned to walk out again to check in with my colleagues and the guy stormed into my office, shut the door and then grabbed me by the throat. It was one of those surreal moments in which time seemed to stop still.

'Come on, you cunt!' he screamed at me. 'You fucking grab my kid by the throat, now let's see how you fucking like it!'

'What the . . . what are you talking about?' I yelled back, trying to match his tone.

'You fucking grab my kid by the throat and I'll fucking grab you by the throat, you cunt! 'Come on . . . let's see what kind of big man you are now!'

He had his fist cocked ready to go and I had my hand out and open telling him to calm down. Despite the drama and chaos of the moment I still recall a strange sense of clarity in my thinking. I recall summing up the situation. He was about the same size as me and his fist was clenched and held low. I could drop just one punch straight and hard on his chin and knock him out cold on my office floor. I spent some moments wondering about how that might play out. At the same time I could hear the kids playing and having a good time outside, blissfully unaware of the drama that was unfolding in my office.

'Strong and smart!' I kept thinking. 'If I knock this guy out then I will lose these kids forever.' Somehow I had time to imagine that sea of unconvinced and sceptical black faces on school assembly as I tried to explain that after all of my pious ranting about having more strength to walk away from a fight, it was somehow okay for me to punch someone. It just didn't make sense.

'Fucking calm down!' I said. 'I got no idea what you're fucking talking about, or who your kid is!' Matching his language and tone I was trying to get to the same level as him so that I could bring him down. 'What's your kid's name?' I asked.

When he told me I said, 'Well, get your kid and bring him up here so we can sort this shit out properly!'

He stormed out of the room and grabbed his kid who was standing just outside. With one hand on the boy's shoulder he shoved him into my office and shut the door again. As I glanced out the door I noticed Hooper and Dion Fewquandie standing by with a look signalling they were there for back-up. I gestured to them with my hand and eyebrows to let them know I thought I had this under control, but it was good to know they were there so readily.

With his boy in front of me I recalled having growled him for playing up the day before. I did grab the front of his shirt as I was raising my voice at him, but I knew I had never grabbed him by the throat.

'Now listen here, boy,' I said, 'you better come clean here now. I growled you yesterday for playing up and not being in class when the other kids were inside. Now, you show your dad where I grabbed you.'

With his own right hand he grabbed his shirt as it sat above his chest. At that moment I really appreciated his honesty. His father watched on and by now I sensed he was feeling not so good.

'That's not your fucking throat! You told me he grabbed your fucking throat!'

'No. Here, Dad! He grabbed me here!' and he again raised his hand to his chest.

The situation became awkward. I looked at the boy and his dad as they both seemed unsure where to go with this.

'Look,' I said to the boy, 'you go outside and get ready for class and leave me and Dad to sort this out. Thanks for being honest, 'ay!' He walked out the door, hoping, I'm sure, for a normal day after such a crazy and dramatic start.

I closed the door behind him and turned to the father. With a bruised and sore throat I said to him, 'Brother, what the fuck are you doing? This is fucking crazy! Sit down and calm down and let's talk about this, 'ay?'

With his head in his hands he sat down on one of my office chairs and I sat down adjacent to him. As he sat there still looking down I reached out and put my hand on his shoulder.

'Brother, I can see you must be under a lot of pressure. People just don't do shit like this so you must have a lot of things going on. But I'm not going to be your fucking punching bag. There is a better way to sort this shit out.'

With that he opened up and started explaining to me that he was having dramas with his woman. He was having serious diffi-culty trying to cope with his kids. He was having serious trouble just trying to cope with the pressures of life. As he opened up he started to cry. It was a moment of raw honesty and human authenticity. I felt a deep sense of hurt for him. My sore throat was insignificant next to the pain and hurt that had descended like a black cloud upon him. We ended up yarning there for about half an hour in my office, and even found some things to share a laugh about. As we wrapped up our yarn I explained to him that while I didn't want to, I probably had to call the police and have a yarn to them about what went on that morning. I explained I was not interested in pressing charges or anything like that, given that we had worked things out, but the main reason was that the other staff had to see that when things like this happened then I would take them seriously and call in the police. He understood what I was talking about and we left each other on good terms.

Reluctantly I did call the police and the sergeant came up to the school. He checked out the bruises on my neck and I explained to him what had gone on.

'Look, this guy's under a lot of pressure and we did work things out,' I said to the sergeant. 'But I don't really want him to be charged or make more pressure for him. Maybe just go and visit him and let him know you've been up here. People are gonna know what went on here so I suppose if you check on him then they will see it has been dealt with officially.'

The sergeant was pretty good and he seemed to get what I was talking about.

Some weeks later I was really rocked by the news that the father had committed suicide. I was hurting for him and for the two lovely children he had in our school. At times it seems you can connect at a deeper level somehow, and still have absolutely no idea about what sorts of pressures are making their fragile lives so complex.

There is no doubting that while life growing up and living in a discrete Aboriginal community has tremendous riches, it also has inconceivable complexities. I reckon it must drive some Aboriginal people to the brink when they are judged by those from the 'outside' with absolutely no idea of the day-to-day realities of life on a community. I was absolutely clear about being something of an outsider to the community, but for my part I just wanted to be the best I could be in the role. I didn't want to somehow try to trade off the fact that I was another blackfulla who was also the principal. In some ways this would work for me but in other ways it could work against me. I am not so sure that guy would have come and grabbed me by the throat if I had been a white principal. In other ways some Aboriginal people, just like some white people, would question whether or not I was actually a 'qualified' principal, or whether or not I was just there because it was a black school.

On one occasion a mother sat down in my office with me and Felicity, our Year 1 teacher, to explain that she was angry about her child coming home upset from school. She was very dark with quite a large and very intimidating frame. Felicity was the antithesis of this with very white skin and quite a petite frame. Together, Felicity and I sat with disbelief and perhaps a touch of fear as we were confronted by a sense of rage fired from the loaded black finger she was pointing in our faces.

'If my boy comes home from school tomorrow and he's cry-ing . . . I'm going to come up to this school and I'm going to bash you! Do you hear what I'm saying? I will come up to this school and I will bash you!'

She certainly said it in a way that was believable and made Felicity's back straighten up.

'Hang on a minute!' I said to the mother, who was surprisingly calm given the words that had just left her mouth.

'This young girl works really hard in the school, you know, because she wants the very best for your child, too. If any child plays up in class then I expect her to jump on their behaviour and she will do it, because I expect it from her. And also because she desperately wants them to read and write before they leave for grade two. You've probably seen teachers come and go from here who don't give a shit, but not this one. She's like me. We want what you want for them. We want them to be strong and smart. We don't want them to be fourteen years old and sniffing petrol or glue because they couldn't survive in high school. But she can't give her best if you're making threats to come and bash her like that if something goes wrong. I can see you're wild about your boy coming home upset but you have to understand the whole story about what happened with him in class.'

With Felicity's help we then went on to explain how he had run amok in the classroom and thrown things around, while being disrespectful to the teacher, the Aboriginal teacher aides and to the other kids. After this the mother became more conciliatory.

'What do you want us to do when he carries on like this?' I asked her.

We then moved on to a really good conversation about how we could work together to get on top of her boy's challenging behaviours. The mum apologised to Felicity and they went on to have a reasonably good teacher–parent relationship.

After that particular meeting I sat down with Felicity to talk it through. For her it must have been quite traumatic and another teacher might have taken some time off for stress leave. Felicity was fine, though. In our conversation we reflected on the mum's behaviour and tried to get below all the bravado on display. Underneath it and the threats we could see that this was a mum who just loved her child. We could also see that this kind of lashing out and making threats was possibly the only way she knew how to deal with conflict. Against this background we couldn't help wondering just how many times this lady must have had the door slammed in her face, or the police called in because people could not get past her frustration to really hear what she was concerned about and find a way to work together on possible solutions.

This is not to suggest for one moment that I would condone such attacks on teachers or other school staff. As I reflected earlier, though, I think it is worth understanding that often we start the relationship with many Aboriginal parents from a point of deficit, and we should commit to some effort to restore relationships rather than just shut them down or call in the police every time it gets a little bit hard or complex. What I found over time is that in any incident like these will always have the potential to pop up, but it will happen less frequently or indeed is less likely to occur if we can get the culture and the relationship right with kids and their parents.

As long as we were determined to get the relationship positive and right it didn't really cost too much. If we put the time in and made an effort to invest positively in our relationships with kids and parents then we'd inevitably be in a situation where of course some things might have gone wrong, but, because the relationship was good, we might have been excused for making the odd mistake here and there. People got to know that we wanted the best for their children and so they were prepared to work with us when we needed to understand things better. The alternative was to have a poor relationship and have things blow up every time as they so often did in other places where there was not the same level of investment in positive relationships.

What struck me about building positive relationships was just how easy and enjoyable it was. This really did become one of the best parts of the job. I think the reason it struck me so prominently was that I had watched so many other principals and teachers become crippled with fear about having to deal with Aboriginal parents. While some would make excuses about time and resources restricting their ability to connect, there was no sound basis for this fear and anxiety.

It cost nothing in terms of time or money to be at the front gate in the morning to say 'hi' to parents and ask them how their day was going. It cost nothing bail up a parent at the supermarket and make some small yarn about what funny thing their kids did at school that week. On some days I would really love to turn up at someone's house with the express purpose of telling them something really positive about their child. On one occasion it occurred to me that the only time I was having any contact with a particular parent was to tell him about how his child was playing up.

His child was in grade four and had come to us from the school in Murgon, which had given up and expelled him. I remember the first day I laid eyes on him. After hearing the horror stories about his behaviour I was struck by just how tiny this little guy was. It seemed his file was bigger than him. He strolled into my office quite meekly and was even meeker as he listened in on my conversation with his father about how he needed more discipline and to be in a school where someone was going to be firm with him. He was still a handful in many ways but eventually we got him back on track. Late one afternoon I pulled up at his house to talk to his dad, who was in the front yard potting around doing some work. By the look of him he had already put in a pretty hard day's work with the council.

As I walked towards him armed with his child's school exercise books, he looked up with a well-practised yet almost resigned sense of exasperation. He initiated our conversation with a huge sigh.

'What the fuck has he done now?' he said.

'No, mate, it's all good. I just wanted to drop by and let you know that your boy is going really well lately. He's working hard. Here look!'

I opened the exercise books and drew his attention to his child's writing in the early pages, and then compared with the work he had done most recently. He gazed down upon the schoolbook and his look of confusion and exasperation turned into one of joy. I watched him with a sense of awe as he filled his chest with pride and his entire body took on a new and unfamiliar demeanour. With tears starting to well in his eyes he looked up at me.

'No one has ever shown me anything like this before!'

I believed him absolutely. It was obvious to me that he had become so unfairly accustomed to school people turning up to tell him how bad his kid was.

'He's really smart, you know. I mean really smart!' I said to him as I held his gaze, trying at the same time to somehow signal that it was okay to be feeling emotional about this. He remained very silent almost as if he was in a state of shock or disbelief.

'Yeah, well, okay then. Thanks for that!' he replied. He looked down at the books again and it caused him to smile with a renewed sense of pride. His hand reached out for mine and very firmly we shook hands in a way we had never done before. With that I jumped in the car and headed home, feeling pretty happy about how deeply authentic that exchange felt to me and to him. He remained standing in his front yard and waved to me as I drove off. It was a precious moment that cost nothing, yet was worth so much.

From the very outset I had made it clear that I believed in high expectations. I went into the job remembering what it was like to be an Aboriginal student, and as a college student I had read all of the Indigenous education reports. In 1998 they were saying the same type of things they had been saying fifteen years earlier. Aboriginal parents wanted their children to be as smart as the white kids and able to get jobs in the community like the white kids. But, while they wanted their children to be as clever as white kids, they didn't want them to be 'like' white kids. They wanted them to retain their sense of Aboriginal cultural identity.

The question of Aboriginal cultural identity is complex, yet crucial. This was a matter I had given very deep thought and to which I would dedicate a large section of my PhD research. In my work I was able to quantify, to some extent, that mainstream Australia held a negative stereotypical perspective about Aboriginal people. To add to this, it was also clear that many young Aboriginal people were also somehow 'tricked' into subscribing to this view. I would see young black kids drag other young black kids down for trying their very best.

'You think you're too good for us!'

'You're trying to be a white boy!'

'You're a coconut!' meaning, being black on the outside and white on the inside.

I watched these sorts of attitudes and behaviours unfold in our school and indeed in other schools throughout Australia. For me it seemed they thought that by running amok in their school and community, or displaying antisocial behaviour, they were somehow 'reinforcing' their sense of cultural identity. The challenge, as I understood it and stated in my interview for the role, was to 'un-trick' them and get them to realise that they were not reinforcing their cultural identity, they were simply reinforcing a negative stereotype. They had to understand what it really meant to be Aboriginal. As I said to them on the very first day, I wanted them to know they could be Aboriginal *and* successful!

Having read just about every review into Aboriginal education, I used this knowledge as the basis for crafting a new vision for the school. Clearly the aim was twofold as Aboriginal people wanted their children to be well educated, but not at the expense of their cultural identity. I took to the council, parents, elders and staff that aim articulated as follows:

> The aim at Cherbourg State School is to deliver academic outcomes that are comparable to any school in Queensland, and to nurture a strong and positive sense of being Aboriginal in a contemporary society.

It was well received, but now I had to get the kids to buy in.

It was one of those situations I would ponder on my long drives to Toowoomba to see Grace and Ezra, when swimming laps in the pool, or in moments of meditation. My favourite spot for pondering such quandaries was in my backyard while I was mowing the grass. I did some great thinking out there. In fact, the solution stuck me in the backyard pushing the mower. My head was buzzing just as much as my second-hand two-stroke, but with good precision and clarity.

The school aim was good, but it was too much of a mouthful to sell to the kids. I had to sharpen it to really catch them. 'Academic outcomes that are comparable to any other school in Queensland': Smart! 'Nurture a strong and positive sense of being Aboriginal in a contemporary society': Strong!

'Smart! Strong!' I said to myself. 'No, wait a minute,' I thought, 'it sounds better the other way around: Strong and Smart!'

That was it. Like most great thoughts, I had write it down immediately. I didn't even turn the mower off, leaving it to whirl unmanned as I raced inside to grab a pen and paper. It was a good feeling and I was so excited I couldn't wait to get to school on the Monday morning. I walked around to every class to talk about this really cool new school motto I had been thinking about and it certainly wasn't hard to be cooler than the one painted in the front of the school: 'Footsteps to the future.' Whoop de doo! No wonder no one took notice of it. Strong and smart, though, was much more solid.

The kids took to it. They got what it was about. On school parades I would take them on with this new school motto: 'When we leave this school what are we gonna be?'

'Strong and smart!' they would scream out from somewhere deep inside their gut.

Initially some of them were embarrassed about screaming out such a mantra, but they came to understand in their own way that this was much more than just jingoistic ranting. I am not so sure that I would have appreciated the complexity and power that went with the strong and smart philosophy had I not encountered my own experiences with the toxicity of stereotyping and low expectations and come to personal revelations. If I hadn't, I might have been more ineffectual as a principal. If I had been more accustomed to a school environment where everything was nice, it is hard to imagine how I would have had any idea about what it is truly like to be in a school and a community that was continually subjected, explicitly or implicitly, to the debilitating stench of low expectations. Almost feeling a bit like some kind of zealous preacher, and I was a zealot when it came to things like this, I would explain to the children, their parents and the elders: 'This is about power!'

'Education is about power!'

'When we learn to read we get power!'

'When we learn to write we get even more power!'

'In the past people tried to take power away from us as

Aborigines, but they couldn't take it all. We had it in a way that it can't be taken. We have our own power because we are the only Australians that can say we are related to the very first Australians.'

'This *is* about power!' I'd reiterate, knowing that they knew exactly what I was talking about. Even the six-year-olds.

'School is not just about learning to read and write. It is the place where we bring out our power. This is not the kind of power that white people "give" us. It comes from inside us. From our hearts! From our spirit! From our land! This is our power! Nobody gives it to us and nobody can take it away from us! Not unless we let them. So don't let anyone take it away from you!'

It was so exciting to be able to speak to them in this way, energised by their silence and the steely look in their eyes as they locked on to mine. On some days I would say, 'Hands up if you're Aborigines!' Their hands would shoot up immediately.

'Keep your hands up if you think that's great. Keep it up if you are really proud to be Aboriginal!' Some would try to push their hands in the air even more.

I would stare back at them, with my hand held high also, and simply say, 'You better be proud to be Aboriginal!'

There was something euphoric and spiritual about the connections we made in those sacred moments. They were not intimidated by my challenges when I'd say, 'This has to be more than words coming out of your mouth! You can't scream back to me that you want to be "strong and smart", and then go missing from school because you feel slack! You can't say "strong and smart" and then play up in class for your teacher! You can't say "strong and smart" and then just throw your papers on the ground so that our school looks like a rubbish dump! That's not strong and smart! That's not about who we truly are!'

Then we'd talk about what it meant to be strong and smart, and their hands held high matched my enthusiasm. Their eyes lit up with their gorgeous black faces beaming as they yelled out their answers.

'Coming to school every day!'

'Being nice to the teacher!'

'Respecting our elders!'

'Working hard for the teacher!'

'Putting our rubbish in the bin!'

'Being nice to our parents!'

There were moments when I could have cried with joy at what I was hearing. It was so different from what I was seeing and hearing in the past. The strong and smart mantra not only helped shape the thinking and attitudes of the kids, it was a message that permeated every aspect of our school culture and way out into the community. It meant the groundsman had to keep the school looking strong and smart; the tuckshop lady had to speak to the kids in a way that was strong and smart; teachers and teacher aides had to turn up to work looking strong and smart; classrooms had to look strong and smart. I had to be strong and smart!

The Aboriginal people on staff locked on to the new mantra with enthusiasm, as did the young white teachers. We made time to discuss the important dynamics of what was going on and they got it. They absolutely got it and I was really proud of them. They understood that while this was about raising our status and sense of blackness, it was not about putting down white people. Understanding and embracing one's power is never about putting others down. In fact, by putting others down we put ourselves down. We also understood that if we didn't get kids to understand that being Aboriginal meant they could be strong and smart, then the society we lived in would somehow imply to them that they were inferior. We all got that our children were much more than this. This was about offering a way of being that was different from our sense of being in the past. It was a more honourable way of being with more integrity. It was a way of being that was more authentic and closer to the truth about who we are as Aborigines, Australia's first people who carried the blood of the oldest human existence on our planet.

It would disappoint me greatly to see the children tearing each other apart at school and trying their best to drag each other down.

'There are enough people around ready to kick you in the guts and put you down without you having to do it to yourselves! We have to stick together,' I would say at school assemblies. Easy enough to say, but I wondered if there was a way to truly pull them together. I thought about my days playing football and wondered what the special ingredients were to create team cohesion. Strangely enough, the time when I felt most at one with the team was in the sheds after the game, when we'd sing our team song.

Clunk! The penny dropped. We had to have a school song!

The Wanderers Tigers of Bundaberg had a great team song made up by the local club legend, Paddy Gerrard, who went on to become a big-time DJ around Australia: 'Jingle Bells, Jingle Bells, Wanderer boys are here . . .' The rest of the song is way too bawdy to be repeated outside a Rugby League dressing shed, but it was so good I had adapted the words so we could sing it at Waratahs in Dalby.

'Surely I can somehow adapt the words for Cherbourg,' I thought.

As I was driving towards Toowoomba one Friday night the words were coming quite easily. Instead of 'Wanderer boys are here' we could say, 'Cherbourg School is here'. Instead of the line about the other team's girlfriends and Fourex beer we could say, 'We're young and black and deadly, so come and hear us cheer'.

The last line would be easy enough: 'We're from Cherbourg State School, and you know we're the best! Hey!' But the ones in the middle were trickier. How do you adapt 'Bring out your best players and we'll put 'em to the test. We're the boys from Wanderers', followed by a line to assert we were the best with a swear word delicately placed for jingoistic pace and rhythm. It took me ages to crack the final piece to fit in but as I meandered down the Cooyar range towards Toowoomba there was another clunk!

'Bring on every challenge, put us to the test!'

Again it was one of those nice moments of inspiration that I never take for granted, so I had to write it down before it disappeared. It was impossible to pull over on the winding road. I slowed down and reached into my bag for a pen and paper, then start writing as I was driving – not the safest thing to do, but I felt a higher sense of purpose about this and I had to get it down, especially the second last line. At the bottom of the range I pulled over and made sure I had it right.

Jingle bells, jingle bells, Cherbourg School is here.
We're young and black and deadly, so come and hear us cheer.
Bring on every challenge. Put us to the test.
We're from Cherbourg State School, and you know we're the best!
best!
Hey!

There it was, our new school song. Even though it was Friday afternoon I couldn't wait to get back to school on Monday morning to let the children in on the new song. At first they were shy and quiet about as they recited it in a polite manner. But this was not a song to be polite about. It had to be sung with the same gusto as in a dressing shed. It had to be loud, and we had to be as one on this.

'You can't sing words like "We're young and black and deadly", and then look down and cover your mouth and act all shame like you're not young and black and deadly. The words have to match your voice and your body. So if you're gonna say it, lift your chest and your face, look black and deadly, and sing black and deadly like you really are.'

After a few goes they got it and loved it. They practised singing it with such enthusiasm. It was truly awesome hearing the whole school singing our school song as one. I made it clear that nobody else had a song like ours. It really was a deadly song. They knew it was deadly and they felt deadly singing it.

The new school song did so much more than just unite the kids and make them feel solid, it gave me room to challenge them to lift the bar even higher in a range of ways. Given that they'd sing the song with such gusto and passion, I had the leverage now to really take them on.

'If we are going to sing "Bring on every challenge", then this means we have to work harder in the classroom; it means we have work harder at getting stronger and smarter; it means if I growl you about playing up then you get yourself back on track rather than being sooky and swearing and carrying on.' It was such a positive message, and we sang it loud.

It was becoming increasingly clear to me that we could lift the school, but only if we had enough people on the team believing it. After about a year in the role, I decided I had to start making firm decisions about what was the right thing to do for the school.

Instinctively, I had held off from making judgements about those staff members who still seemed to collude with low expectations. It was necessary for me to spend that twelve months to sniff the breeze, so to speak, and to make a determined effort to think about what was good and worth keeping or building upon rather than bowling in and casting aspersions without having an authentic sense of what was going on. I think this is a mistake lots of school principals make.

Senior teachers were now trying to explain to me that it was necessary for us to adjust our expectations. When the District Office sent out a skills checklist for students in the region I was keen to see this executed across the whole school. I sent the checklist to a few teams I had established, only to have it sent back with a note attached saying, 'We think this is too advanced for our children and so we are working on another checklist that is more suitable.' It was so frustrating to see such toxic trash coming from those who were supposed to be the experienced leaders in the school. What kept me going, though, were the moments when Pop John, Mrs Langton or Mum Rae would pull me up and say, 'Keep going boy! You're on the right track. We can do this!' I kept asking the hard questions with a genuine interest in what people thought the answers were. I'd ask why we had to endure failure and such endemic disengagement; the answers coming back were not good.

'The kids come from really rough home lives.'

'There's a lot of domestic violence and alcoholism in the community.'

'The council doesn't support us!'

'District Office doesn't support us!'

'The tests are not culturally relevant!'

'The parents don't value education!'

All the things I had heard from them pointed the finger of blame at someone or something else. My long and deep analysis was contrary. How could you value an education where children worked with photocopied sheets for much of the day? How could a child value an education offered by teachers who think that mainstream schoolwork is 'too advanced' for them? How could anyone value education offered by a teacher who was given a job in an Aboriginal community school because no other mainstream school would take them? How could you value an education from a teacher who had been seen around the community in a drunken state?

The Cherbourg community was rallying around the school, which made a lie of the perceptions that Aboriginal parents did not value education. In my time as principal I did not find one parent who said they did not want their child to have a good education. It was one of those things that was easy for people, especially teachers, to say in a way that inflicted a sense of blame on parents and the community. Having seen and heard enough I had a good sense of what was going on. Having grown in confidence as a school leader, it was time for me to articulate what I believed to be a firm direction for us as a school and as a team. It was time to stop pointing the finger away from us, and have a long hard look at the things we could do to provide a better quality education.

There was a sombre mood in the staffroom on the afternoon I called a meeting. I was beginning to dread staff meetings, as I am sure the staff did, too. I had to think of the faces of the children in the classrooms and remind myself that I owed it to them to stick up for their rights. While it was going to be tough, this was what

I was paid taxpayers' money to do, and I do not like seeing tax-payers' dollars wasted in Aboriginal communities, and I certainly didn't want it wasted on me if I was not doing my job. I thought about myself as a student, and what would have happened if people like Clarrie Diefenbach, Stu Pow and Gary MacLennan had not persisted with the hard conversations to engage and transform apathy about Aboriginal students. I owed it to them as much as the children to purge my own discomfort and to have the hard conversations. I took a deep breath and steadied myself to articulate to my colleagues what I thought was a more honour-able direction for us as a team and a school.

'What I believe, what the parents and elders believe, and what we should let our children believe . . .'

I paused and took another deep breath.

'. . . is that our children can leave our school with academic outcomes that are comparable to any other child in any other Queensland school. They should also leave here with a very strong and very positive belief and understanding about who they are as Aboriginal people!'

I took pause again because in the silence I wanted them to focus so that they would be crystal clear about what I had to say next.

'If you don't believe this . . . then you shouldn't be here!'

There was an audible gasp from a senior teacher, but every-one else was silent. As I glanced around the room to take in the response to my assertions, I noticed Hooper's chest seemed to be filled with pride. I assumed it was because another blackfulla was able to say such a thing in this space, with such authority. I wasn't necessarily espousing my views as a blackfulla, though. I was being a leader who wanted to lead with integrity and honour.

Mum Rae wore something of a guarded smile, exposed in part by her shining eyes, as if she was submissive and nervous about the reactions from the other teachers and exuberant about the prospect of a positive future for the children at last. Mrs Langton was not the least bit coy or concerned about her colleagues as she beamed with pride and confidence, and I guess a sense of relief that at last it had been made clear. Enough was enough. There would be no more collusion with low expectations.

There was little need to say anything more after that. Having noticed the response from people around the room, I have to say I wasn't overly interested in their response. I'd made the time to listen and see what was good. I'd spent enough time considering what we had as a team that was worth building upon. This was a time to assert a new position. I truly believed in what I had articulated, and I wasn't going to back down!

The response was reasonably swift. Most of the Aboriginal teachers and teacher aides were excited. Some white teachers beamed as well because they finally had a sense of direction that would be anchored by integrity and professionalism. Other white teachers and some Aboriginal teachers and teacher aides appeared to be left with a sense of bewilderment on their faces about what this meant for them.

Within the next three weeks, six of the twelve teachers on staff applied for a transfer out of the school. For a moment this felt daunting and I have to confess I questioned whether or not I had done the right thing by challenging them to the extent that they were prepared to move on. There were some I would have preferred had stayed, as I think they might have taken to the new directions and thrived. Ultimately, though, they made their own decisions and I had to take this seriously. I went back to that question as always, 'Would I like my own children to be taught by any of the other teachers?' What right did I have to expect the people of Cherbourg to tolerate these teachers if I wouldn't? As difficult as it was, this was the right thing to do.

10

Making waves

Over the next few months I travelled to and from the District Office in Kingaroy to sit down with Mike Primmer, the Senior Personnel Officer who had recommended me for the job as principal. With his help I was able to headhunt a few people I knew and some other excellent candidates. The new recruits included my partner Grace, who was an outstanding teacher. Her academic career at the University of Southern Queensland was on the up at the time, and so in some ways she let her career take a back seat in coming to Cherbourg. It was an excellent move as far as I was concerned, as it would mean there was another strong and experienced Indigenous teacher on staff, not to mention the fact that a man can get lonely out there in the bush!

I also appointed Rob Blatchford, who turned out to be an exceptional teacher as well. The kids grew to love Rob and his Canadian accent. He had a nice way with them and I think they really appreciated having a teacher that ran his classroom like a 'normal' classroom, and acted like a 'normal' teacher. The same could be said for the other new teachers who came on board, Tammy Hebblewhite, Nicole Pollard and Melissa Orthman. Once I had been notified the appointments were confirmed I rang all of them to offer my congratulations. I also explained that Cherbourg would probably be like no other school they had worked in, that they had to come to the job with high expectations of the children and be prepared to work really hard. These were honest conversations as I felt it was necessary to make my expectations and the challenges they faced clear.

'If you don't think you are up for this, or if you have any apprehensions about working with Aboriginal children and within an Aboriginal community, then it is probably best you don't come in the first place,' I'd say.

'I'm really keen but I've never even met any Aboriginal people, so I can't really say I'm an expert on Aboriginal culture or anything like that,' one of the teachers said, with a degree of apprehension yet honesty that I really admired.

'Yeah, look,' I replied, 'in a school like this you really just need to be an expert teacher. I don't really need experts on Aboriginal culture. I am surrounded by an entire community of experts in Aboriginal ways. What is most important is that you are an expert teacher. That said, I do expect you to get out and about and meet people and find out more about where your kids are coming from, you know. Be ready to make time to drop around and have a yarn with the parents and get some sense of what they want for their kids. And don't worry about getting out and about in the community. There's a lot of talk about how rough some places are, but with such an important job in the community you can't afford to let yourself be crippled by such unfounded fears. There are some very good and solid Aboriginal people on staff here who will look after you and get you settled in, though. You'll be fine if you come to work hard, and you come with high expectations.'

That kind of conversation always seemed to relax them. Nobody I asked ever refused to come. I wanted the teachers to appreciate the role of the Aboriginal teacher aides as well, as it was so tremendously infuriating to see Aboriginal teacher aides in any school being treated like second-rate citizens, as they had been when I arrived at Cherbourg.

'With two Aboriginal teacher aides in the room,' I'd say to the teachers, 'I want you to give some serious thought as to how to maximise their time to get the best outcomes from your kids.' In a more direct tone I made a point of saying, 'These guys may not have a flash degree like you, but they have life experience and knowledge of the community and the kids, and that will some-times be much more valuable than a degree. Don't use them just to photocopy worksheets; they are also not your crowd control-lers if you lose control of the class. They have much more to offer than that. Don't treat them like "niggers"! I want you to work with them respectfully and embrace them as co-educators in the classroom.'

It was a pretty blunt way of getting my point across, but I felt I had to be on this matter. If the teachers got this relationship right, there would be exponential benefits. When children see white teachers embrace Aboriginal teacher aides with respect, they usu-ally respected the teacher more, as did the parents. The children would also be more inclined to better behaviour. A teacher aide who once had a reputation for going missing in action from work would start turning up five days a week and stay well beyond three pm to do help plan the lessons with the teacher who dis-played such simple respect.

The teacher aides would also play a vital role in getting the new teachers settled in and I'd say to the new teachers, 'You'll also have one or two Aboriginal teacher aides working with you as well and they are locals so they will tag along and make it easy for you to get connected to the right people.'

It was wonderful to see the teacher aides take this important responsibility so seriously.

'Now, look after them!' I'd say to them. 'And when they get here you watch their eyes come real big when I tell them they have to get out and mix it with people in the community.' They'd all smile, as they knew that wide-eyed look I was talking about. They also knew precisely how important it was to help them. They appreciated the important job the teachers had to do.

We assembled an exciting new team with a really good blend of Aboriginal and non-Aboriginal teachers, and experienced teachers alongside some fired-up young rookies. Lots of principals complained about the rookies but not me. I was always excited to work with them, as their enthusiasm was palpable. What always bugged me was when long-serving teachers thought they were experts just because they had 'survived' in an Aboriginal community. What bugged me even more was those who said things like, 'My life has been transformed by working in an Aboriginal community,' when clearly nothing about the lives of those children they taught had been transformed. My advice to young rookie teachers was to always be cautious about the senior teachers they would look to for advice and direction.

Simon Kelly, one of our young first-year rookies, had no experience working with Aboriginal people but was prepared to give it a real go. The kids thought he was pretty cool with his long surfie hair. While they presented him with many challenges, he knew they deserved a good-quality education. He was looking to other more senior teachers for guidance and direction and my advice to him was to take advice only from those who were getting results and working with kids in a way that had integrity. I never liked teachers who just assumed they should be respected because they had been in the job a long time. The first key questions when looking to other teachers for guidance are: 'Does this teacher love the job as much as I do?' and, 'Do they get results?' Fortunately, we now had relatively senior teachers and teacher aides on staff who loved the job, got results, and were certainly worth listening to. Our new school team believed we could make a difference and make a difference we did.

Things were now going really well at school and I was able to turn my attention to my home life with Grace. In 2000 we decided it was time to get married. I really loved the thought of making plans with a partner for the next ten, twenty, thirty and fifty years, rather than just one or two years ahead. Ezra was almost two years old, and, while many others had got by without marriage, I wanted to be more serious and committed to our relationship and the family we would build together. Once we agreed to get married, we discovered our second child was on the way and would be at the wedding as well, although in the womb.

We got married in Townsville on 8 July 2000. Grace and I had chatted romantically about having a small intimate occasion with just a few family and close friends. That was never going to happen as she was the first in her family to have a wedding, and I was the youngest child in mine. The numbers of both Grace's family and mine alone also buried that idea. We hired a school hall to fit everyone invited to the reception. It was a great day. On one occasion I found myself holding someone's hand, and I leaned over and whispered into Grace's ear, 'Who's this one here, from your family?'

She casually glanced around to see and with a polite voice whispered back, 'I don't know. I thought that was your family!'

We also seemed to have a few ring-ins because the NAIDOC ball was held on the same night, but there were also lots of people we didn't know but who were family. When we had done the wedding invitations Grace's mum and my mum were both saying, 'You gotta invite this one! You gotta invite that one!' In the end we printed off sheets and sheets of blank invites and gave them to our mums, saying, 'Here, you invite whoever you got to invite!' It was the only way to do it respectfully and we didn't really mind. At the end of the night, as we made our way out of the hall to the limo, we hugged and kissed everyone, saying our goodbyes to our wonderful family and friends and felt truly blessed.

At the wedding, during the speeches, Hooper had got up on the stage to make an announcement. I had just been named NAIDOC Cherbourg Community Person of the Year. It was a great honour and a sign that the community was really getting on board and excited about the work happening at the school. As a team of dedicated teachers working in partnership with parents and the community we reduced unexplained absenteeism quite substantially within eighteen months. Real attendance was to jump from sixty-three per cent in 1998 to ninety-four per cent in 2004. Student enrolments for Years 1 to 7 increased from eighty-nine when I first arrived up to one hundred and sixty-five in 2004. In a turnaround, parents from Murgon and further afar were now sending their children to Cherbourg.

Literacy and numeracy performance of the children surged as well. Clearly, as the children's attendance improved and expectations rose, their academic performance was destined to improve. Year 2 literacy improved sixty-two per cent within two years. For the Year 7 reading diagnostic test in 1998, all children were rock bottom. By 2004, seventeen of the twenty-one children in Year 7 would be within the state average and the remaining four children were just below average.

A few months after being married I received an invitation to attend a Human Values in Education conference in India. My old mate from Mossman, Iqbal Singh, had put in a good word for me in the right places and before we knew it we were both on a plane with his mother to an Ashram of Sai Baba's, one of the most followed gurus. It was a fascinating experience for us, although I worried about leaving Grace while she was pregnant. I loved India, though. Iqbal, of course, had been there many times as he had family in the north. We travelled south, having landed at Bangalore, in a crazy three-hour taxi ride that cost about twenty dollars. I'm sure the driver was doing just fine but for me it was a crazy kaleidoscope of new images to take in, not to mention the elephants, monkeys and cows sharing the road, or the thousands of people and cars honking and buzzing their way through as they negotiated this chaotic, yet amazing world.

As I watched the people in India I couldn't help but notice that despite severe levels of poverty, the children were always dressed immaculately for school. I wondered how some of them could turn out in a clean and well-pressed school uniform when they lived in what was little more than a shack. Obviously, they really valued education. I could not help wondering also about how sometimes, as blackfullas back in Australia, we thought we were poor yet even some of the most rundown Aboriginal communities might have seemed wealthy compared with the extent of

With Grace on
our wedding day
in July 2000.

With our three
precious children
(from left), Talia,
Marcellus and Ezra.

At an Indigenous peoples' conference in Trinidad and Tobago. While others saw the need to dress in traditional costume, I didn't need to dress up to prove who I was.

Travelling to South Africa gave me cause to reflect that the challenges faced by Aboriginal Australians were universal.

School assembly at Cherbourg was often fun but sometimes serious. There were times when I'd challenge them to think about whether 'strong and smart' was something we just said, or something we lived.

Aunty Ada Simpson was one of the Cherbourg elders who had grown up on the Mission and, despite the injustices of that early life, she managed to retain her dignity and cultural identity.

By 2002, amidst a sea of chaos in Indigenous education, the media had begun to appreciate the power of a positive story of a school on the move.

It was impossible to be everywhere. On this occasion I'm using Skype to share knowledge and wisdom about the stronger smarter approach with educators from the Kimberley region.

As the Director of the Stronger Smarter Institute, I missed the close connection with the students, so I always enjoyed any opportunity to visit classrooms on my travels. Here I am with a class of students of Mt Margaret Remote Aboriginal School, WA.

With former Queensland premier Anna Bligh on the day I received my Queensland Australian of the Year Award, 2010.

I never did get to play representative rugby league at Suncorp Stadium, but with my appointment to the ARL commission I did smash a glass ceiling for Aboriginal people at the highest echelons of Australian sports administration.

Two prominent men in my life are Pop John (centre) and journalist Jeff McMullen (left). When times are tough, I've always been able to turn to them.

With Gary MacLennan, one of the greatest teachers in my life. My mum had kindled a fire in my belly and Gary came along and threw petrol on it.

An important day for me in 2012 when my doctoral thesis was published and launched by former Queensland premier Peter Beattie.

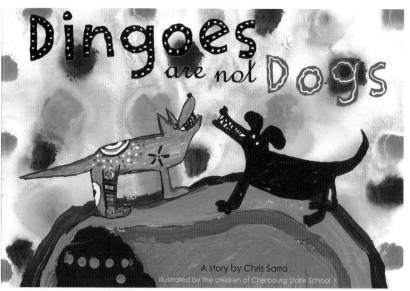

My children's book (published in 2011) contained messages just as important as those in my thesis: in some ways we're the same and in some ways we're different, but we all belong to the same mob.

poverty in India. In many ways I guess it is relative to what exists within our own context, and on the question of education it is always worth pushing hard so we make sure what we offer is worth valuing.

The entire trip to India was fascinating, including the opportunity to come face to face with the great Sai Baba. Many of his devotees lined up faithfully for years, sometimes decades, just to enjoy such proximity to their great guru. They could not believe Iqbal and me when we told them of our experience and that he had actually spoken to Iqbal. The conference was fantastic, too. It opened my eyes to the potential for growth in our school with a really good human values program.

The exceptional Indian–Australian, Dr Pal Dhall, and his wife, Tehseen, lived in Australia but had been travelling back and forth to India for many years. Dr Dhall had been an excellent surgeon in Great Britain but got to a point where he felt he had much more to offer the world. In Australia he ran the Sathya Sai Institute for Human Values in Education. The program is anchored by five core values: love, peace, truth, right conduct and non-violence. From the outset I could see how it could enhance our work back at Cherbourg, particularly as we had started on a positive trajectory with the strong and smart mantra.

Like any new program I knew it needed to be introduced cautiously. I was concerned some people might get caught up and distracted by the program's association with the teachings of Sai Baba. Others might also be spooked by the misplaced notion that this was some kind of religion. For me, there is a sense of spirituality about all of us. Some people choose the frameworks of religion to exercise and practise this; some don't need these frameworks or the institutions. Because of so many conflicting ideas about religions, it was important to get people to understand we were not setting out to *impose* values on the children. The program would simply offer a way to help them articulate their already existing positive values. With this program we would be able to provide sustained opportunities to reflect on what was positive about their lives.

It involved exercises such as mind maps to talk about things like concentration – what it looked like and felt like. The children would make up and sing songs about resilience, communication, tolerance, courage and many other positive values that were sub-values of the core five. The part of the values program I liked best was the silent sitting. It was a simple meditation technique in which the kids would quietly meditate and reflect on the positive aspects of their lives. For many, their lives were so complex and this offered them an opportunity to experience and enjoy the richness, beauty and value of silence. I also felt the silent sitting was in tune with traditional Aboriginal ways of being.

With Dr Dhall's help the program would contribute quite dramatically to the overall transformation of the school. While going to India meant I missed seeing the great Catherine Freeman in that iconic moment of winning her gold medal at the Sydney Olympics, the human values in education program was gold for me. In fact it was gold for all of us. But there was another defining Olympics moment I'm glad I caught on my way back from India. During the fourteen-hour stopover in Singapore I checked into a hotel room, which gave me the opportunity to watch the closing ceremony. Alone in my room I was buzzing and punching the air as Peter Garrett ran onto the stage with Midnight Oil and all of them wearing a black t-shirt saying 'Sorry' on the front. If I had my way I would have given them a gold medal for that performance – or maybe a black one! Some years later, when I knew him, I reflected on this moment with Peter Garrett. Who would have thought in 2000 that he would be sitting on the front bench of the House of Representatives when the Apology was given?

In many ways 2000 was a great year. The school was receiving excellent and positive coverage in the local, state and national newspapers. People were attracted to a positive story, I guess. Then, in November, our daughter Talia Mae arrived. You always feel like you are the only parent who has ever felt this, but when I laid my eyes on her I was instantly in love. Our little family felt almost complete with both Ezra and Talia. Grace and I were truly blessed.

I often think about the exposure our school received. Like others, I watched with some dismay a story on national television about a school going pear-shaped. Similar to us, it was a school on an Aboriginal community and on the move. Most of the story was extremely positive, but there were about fifteen seconds of the fifteen-minute segment in which the principal and an Aboriginal teacher made some comment about the dramatic extent of child sexual abuse in the community. I thought, as I watched, 'Oooh, I hope that doesn't come back to bite them!' It did.

That fifteen seconds would see both of them run out of the community after doing some exceptional work in hard circumstances. I shared their sense of wanting to be brutally honest about the despicable scourge of child sexual abuse in the community, but there is a time and a place and the right forum. In front of a national television audience on a program more interested in airing the sensational rather than considering the wellbeing of those in front of the camera was definitely not it. I could not help but feel sorry for both of them as I could empathise deeply with the challenges they faced, and the unrelenting effort they must have put in to make a difference.

Their unfortunate mistake provided me with an opportunity to reflect on what I might do differently if that circumstance ever came up for us. It was not long after that, in fact, when a national television producer called me.

'Hi, Chris. We've heard great things about your good self and the school and we'd love to do a story for television.'

It was nice to have such interest and recognition but the other experience was fresh in my mind.

'Let me have a think about it and I'll get back to you next week,' I said to him.

I never did call him back and he never followed up with me. What I did do, however, was call my old mate Gary MacLennan. He was still lecturing at Queensland University of Technology but had moved into the media studies area. Gary was still the 'great brain' to me, and I figured he was bound to give me some excellent advice. Gary suggested he bring a film crew from QUT so we could make a short documentary film on our own terms. It turned out to be an exceptional idea.

He drove to Cherbourg and introduced me to his colleague Mark Newman, a world-class and well-credentialled filmmaker from South Africa. Mark and I would become good mates despite his cantankerous, not-happy-unless-he-is-miserable kind of manner. Mark was a perfectionist and this appealed greatly to me. I knew that with his unparalleled experience of working respectfully with black communities in South Africa and his nauseating yet meticulous attention to detail, he would capture our story in a way that was honest and honourable.

The film was called *Strong and Smart: The rise of Cherbourg State School*. It was first played on ABC's *Message Stick* and received a rapturous response from so many people. We received lots of letters saying how much they enjoyed seeing such a positive story. There was one letter that especially meant a great deal to me. It was given to me via an older lady in Cherbourg and was handwritten by her grandson who was in prison in Maryborough. He had a son in our school. He said the story of the school filled him with pride and gave him hope. I still have his letter and keep it close and pull it out and read it when times get tough for me.

There were few positive stories about Aboriginal education but our successes were because we had turned the negative thinking around in such a way that we believed we truly could make a difference. I remember reflecting with our staff about just how important our work at the school really was.

'We're not here to save the community,' I said to them. 'It is not even our place to do that. But we can play a part in helping the community get back on its own feet by doing our best at what we are paid to do: deliver a good education where kids can leave here feeling strong and smart. That's what we're here for.'

I loved those deep moments in our staffroom when our sense of purpose was so clear. We understood also that our work had the potential to influence schooling for Aboriginal children right throughout Australia. It seemed like an extraordinary challenge, but not one that intimidated us. We knew that if we did our best to be excellent in our classrooms and in our school, then we would give others the licence to do the same. Our school was being recognised as a leader in Aboriginal education and this would see us attract many accolades.

It was quite prestigious and an honour to receive many of the awards given to us. Some of the awards were given to the school as a whole, some to the kids individually, some to teachers, and some to me. The NAIDOC Community Person of the Year Award in Cherbourg that I received at my wedding was pretty special. It was an amazing trophy with two painted boomerangs and two carved emu eggs. On my return to the school we had a pizza party for the entire school so we could all share the glory. It was my way of saying this award was not just about me; it was for all of us.

At the end of 2003 I was given the 2004 Regional Local Hero Award for Queensland in the Australian of the Year Awards. My mum came down for the presentation and I think she was most thrilled to meet Stefan, the famous hairdresser. I was excited to meet the great Steve Irwin who was, as usual, bursting with enthusiasm as he took the Australian of the Year Award for Queensland. In 2004 I was ecstatic to receive a Deadly Award for my contribution to Aboriginal education. It was so special because it was voted for by Aboriginal people across Australia. And then as the winter of 2004 kicked in, I was advised that I was a finalist for Queenslander of the Year. To be honest, I was not even aware that such an award existed and so was not sure of just how significant and prestigious it was. I remember feeling stunned when Quentin Bryce, then Queensland's governor, made the announcement. Terry Mackenroth was acting premier at the time, and, as he handed the very big and flash medal to me, all I could think was, 'I knew I should have worn a tie today!'

After making a short speech and singing the Cherbourg School song I was ushered away to the side of the stage and into the firing line of television cameras and radio microphones. It was something of a surreal moment in which I was excited I had won such a grand prize, yet I was feeling guilty that I did not get to say goodbye to the other great finalists, one of whom was Pamela Croft, a well-regarded Aboriginal artist. I spoke to the media from the heart, though, with a sense of conviction because I saw this as a great victory for Aboriginal children and for Aboriginal people, and a great victory for educators.

My mobile phone went crazy with messages and my head was spinning all afternoon. Grace and I took the kids for lunch on the Queen Street mall before heading home. At lunch I got a congratulatory call from Anna Bligh, then the minister of education.

Although I was so tired from all of the commotion and attention and not getting home till one am, I fronted up for school in the morning. I think I might have been running on adrenalin, but I did, after all, have another school pizza party to organise.

With all of the awards I received, I felt awkward with the implication that the success at the school all came down to one man. Me. While it was really great to get the recognition, it was something that always made me tremendously uncomfortable. I wanted people to understand that it really was a team effort, which saw the teachers working in partnership with the teacher aides, the parents and the kids working in partnership with the school, and the community council working in partnership with the school. Of course, we attracted a great deal of attention from a range of media sources. Sometimes this was good, and I would use it to our advantage, sometimes it was not so good.

There are bound to be some people wanting to try and cut us down and to take a swipe at me personally. I still find it hard to comprehend one particular person who became malicious in her personal attacks on me. This lady had done a lot of sound work with the school and the community prior to my arrival.

My first inkling that she was up to no good came when Rob, our Canadian teacher on staff, picked me up for our usual swimming training session at the Wondai pool.

'Mate, what have you done to upset her? She's really got the knives out for you!'

'Oh, that's weird,' I said. 'I've always got on all right with her and she has always been nice to my face.' He said he had basically told her to get lost and didn't want anything to do with any effort to undermine our work. Two other teachers also told me of similar conversations they'd had with her, with similar outcomes. I thought nothing of it until a few weeks later when Hooper came to see me after spending a few days in Brisbane at QUT on professional development activities relating to traditional Aboriginal games.

'You want to get onto her, mate. She's down there running you down, saying you're running the school with an iron fist and abusing the kids.'

I wasn't sure what to make of this, thinking that despite my reservations about her johnny-come-lately sense of Aboriginal identity we got on all right, and the work she did for the school and community was okay.

'Bugger this,' I thought. 'I'll just ring her up and ask her what's going on.'

She was most polite as she took my call.

'It's nice to hear from you. How are you?'

'Yeah, not too bad,' I said, 'but it seems I'm getting some bad press!'

'Oh! Where from?' she asked sincerely.

'Well . . . from you it seems!'

Predictably she got defensive as we talked and I couldn't help wondering why I was bothering.

'Who told you that?'

'Well, actually, I've heard it from a few people now. Some teachers and Hooper when he got back from Brisbane.'

'Oh!' she said as dismissively as any pompous academic. 'Sounds to me like Hooper is doing some muck-raking again.'

Hooper did love a good yarn now and then, but with the school and me his loyalty was absolute. As he said on many occasions, he would literally take a bullet for me and I believed him. So I felt a sense of disappointment and disdain that she had tried to stick the knife into Hooper, but, then, what else could I expect?

'Yeah, well . . . look, why don't you come and see me next time you're up here and we can have a yarn about whatever it is that has got you worried, 'ay?'

She did come to the school for that yarn and it was difficult to make any sense of her concerns. In many ways I found her to be quite incoherent and somewhat manic. Clearly there were some ideological differences about how to manage the behaviour of children when they were playing up. Despite this I did my best to listen to what she had to say and at best we seemed to agree to disagree. I continued to hear from people that she was still spreading the same story but I simply chose to ignore it.

The pattern seemed to be that she would go to someone, they would tell her to get lost, and then she would go to someone of higher authority. This would see her go to the District Office, the Central Office, to the education minister's office and, ultimately, the premier's office. I reckon if God had had a fax machine she would have sent a letter there, too. At every step she was told if she had a concern then she should put it in writing, something she never had the courage to do until she got to Premier Peter Beattie's office.

Peter Beattie had visited a women's group at Cherbourg and given them a very public commitment to support their valiant efforts to attend to the serious challenges of child sexual abuse in the community. Following the visit she drafted a really cunning and malicious three-page letter and deceitfully got two ladies from Cherbourg to sign it. The first page started off politely explaining that the purpose of letter was to update the premier about the activity and progress of the women's group. The final two pages launched into a tirade of accusations that I had physically and verbally abused the kids at the school, encouraged them to be abusive to each other and, to my absolute and most intense disgust, had somehow fabricated the data showing the school's remarkable improvements.

One of the ladies who had signed the letter was a strong supporter of the school. She had grandkids at the school and when she realised what she had done she said it made her feel sick in the guts. It was not her fault, and she didn't need to plead for my forgiveness. Lots of people sign letters put in front of them in this way, trusting the person who is asking you to sign is telling you the truth about what it contains. Peter Beattie saw this for what it was and basically told her to get lost with her crazy stories. He had been to the school and had witnessed firsthand a school full of Aboriginal children beaming with strength, confidence and a voracious desire to learn, something he had never seen before. He also knew of the tendency of some blackfullas to be like crabs in a bucket, where the one at the bottom will readily pull the one at the top down so that nobody goes anywhere.

This chronic saga might have ended there had she not also sent a copy of the premier's letter to Tony Koch, who was writing for

The Australian. It was late in the afternoon and I was in Kingaroy when I had to pull over to the side of the road to take his call.

He asked me whether or not I was being investigated by the department for being a bit rough with kids, and whether or not I'd fabricated the school data. It certainly was true that an investigation was being held, but in futility I tried to explain to him that I thought it was a very good thing that Aboriginal parents had exercised their right to question the role of their local principal. I truly believed this was their right. The story ran in *The Australian* and it started a crazy time in my life.

Central Office's media department was ringing me to make sure I got the message right. They insisted I did not talk about the specific behaviours of the children. Looking back I think they were more interested in covering their own department arse than mine. I was certain that people would get what was going on if I could just tell them that I was being investigated because I had chased some boys who were throwing rocks into a classroom where other children were sitting, had caught them and grabbed them while they were telling me to get fucked, and carried them back into class. I then growled them while I was banging my fist against wall and against the desk, telling them to shut up and get back to work. If only I could have told them all of this, and that after I'd growled them, and after a few sobs, the boys actually did shut up and get back to their schoolwork.

The article started a small frenzy, though, but I found most people were supportive. Talkback radio was going off, apparently. I didn't have time to listen as I was feeling a bit under siege. When I rang Gary MacLennan to tell him what was going on he got on the next train to come up and offer support. On that same day a Channel 9 helicopter was making its way to Cherbourg, landing on the school grounds, making it seem even more like we were under siege. I got the feeling that Alex Smith, the Channel 9 journalist, seemed supportive and I was flanked by steadfast, willing colleagues as he conducted the interview. I knew I just needed to speak from the heart. What hurt me the most about this entire fiasco was knowing that even though this was instigated by a malicious and gutless attack on me personally, other people around me were being also hurt. I will never forget my sense of outrage when my poor old mum, who was in her late seventies at the time, rang me and started to cry over the phone.

I was also furious that this nasty attack was inflicting pain on Grace, too. She was about seven months pregnant at the time with our third child and was up at three in the morning pacing up and down the hallway of our little house, not able to sleep. It was so unfair that others had to suffer in this way because of the nasty and malicious actions of one person with the courage to do so within the confines of anonymity. The questions raised about the validity of our data were hurtful also. The teachers, teacher aides and children had worked so hard and people were raising questions that implied the ability of Aboriginal children to lift and improve wasn't possible.

Throughout the entire ordeal I knew in my heart that I had done my best, and, while the investigation was rightly occurring, I felt I would get through it, albeit with some lessons I was not afraid to reflect upon. At the completion of the investigation it was considered that some of the claims made by some parents should be dismissed, and some upheld. For those claims upheld I was counselled to consider dealing with them in a different way. It was a very fair process in which there were some well-founded lessons for me about how I conducted myself at school.

The questions raised about fabricating the data were completely dismissed.

It did raise some profoundly interesting questions about the difference between abuse and discipline. I believe my actions were borne out of a sense of love and commitment to the kids and a desire to see them understand the difference between what is right and what is wrong. To me this was discipline, not abuse. From my perspective it was a truly dreadful form of abuse to let kids think there were no consequences for throwing rocks into a room full of other kids and teachers, or for telling the principal to get fucked. By the end of the week, though, it had all blown over. As they say, it was fish 'n' chips wrapper. The education department's director general, Ken Smith, wanted to make sure I was okay, and, as I sat in his office, Anna Bligh, the education minister, walked in and gave me a hug. She had known about my work and was very supportive. Like Peter Beattie, she had seen this for what it was.

'What doesn't break you makes you stronger!' she said. I figured if anyone knew about stuff like this then it would be her.

I considered taking legal action but in the end I could not be bothered. It would mean expending energy on something that would take me away from giving my best to the kids and to the Cherbourg community. I just wanted to get back to work and focus on the things that were most important. Some months later I got a call from the ABC. They wanted me to be on their *Australian Story* program. The producer for my story was Caitlin Shea. She and her team spent about three months coming back and forth to the school and my home to put together the program. The kids at the school really enjoyed their time in front of the camera and I was happy the school and the community were being showcased in a positive way. As in any television show, though, there had to be moments of drama.

Particular attention was drawn to the conversation I'd had with teachers when I challenged them about their belief in our children leaving the school feeling proud to be Aboriginal and with academic outcomes as good as any other child. I can see why this would have dramatic appeal, but the tragedy is that it did not really reflect the amount of time I had spent trying to sniff the breeze to determine what was good and could be built upon. The other drama, of course, was around the investigations into the allegations of abuse. I was not so keen to mention it on camera but in some ways I really could not ignore it. As Caitlin put it to me, this was the real drama in the Cherbourg story and they probably would not have been interested in the story in the first place if it hadn't been for this. Fair enough, I thought.

The *Australian Story* episode went to air in October 2004, and, just like with the *Strong and Smart* documentary, I received more than a hundred letters, cards and emails from people saying congratulations, wishing us well, and telling us just how inspired they were by our story. People even sent money to the school. Some even sent money to me, which I sent back with many thanks, explaining that it was not appropriate for me to accept it. What struck me, though, was the generosity of people taking the time to write and offer encouragement.

The school was buzzing the morning after the show had gone to air, especially the kids who had seen themselves on TV the night before. After high-fiving kids here and there before my morning climb up the stairs to my office, I spotted a woman I had butted heads with, so to speak, on many occasions heading straight towards me. She lived across the road from the school and her grandson was a bit of a handful. I had had to be pretty firm with him, determined to get him back on track, and this was the source of our disagreements. On a good day she had a gentle face but on a bad day she could cut you down with just a look. As she got closer, my apprehension diminished as I realised this was a good day.

'Chris, I saw that thing on TV last night . . .'

'Okay,' I said, apprehensively, 'what did you think?'

'No, I thought it was good . . . real deadly, actually. And I just wanted to come up here and let you know that I can see now what you've trying to do with these kids . . . and I think that's real good.'

I wasn't really sure what to say.

She reached out and we hugged. I'm sure in a way it must have been as awkward for her as it was for me, but it just felt like the right thing to do. It was such a special moment for me, one forged with a sense of unified purpose. It was such moments with grass-roots community people that would play a part in inspiring me to keep going. I had a fair idea about what kind of schooling they had endured in the past, and when they were signalling that they were with me on this journey it was really special.

The other interesting thing worth reflecting on was the effect the show had on the claims of those trying to cut me down. The drama they had created actually made me look more like a hero, and a potentially wealthy one at that. People were ringing me wanting to write a screenplay to make a feature film about us, which was a bit strange, I have to confess. I began to joke about who might play me; surely Sidney Poitier would be too old for a role like this and I was not certain they would get Denzel Washington. I put my money on *Different Strokes* star, Gary

Coleman. I could just see it: 'What you talking 'bout Strong and Smart?'

While we laughed about it at the school the offers were deadly serious. At one stage I saw an email from the United States offering one million dollars for the rights to the story. It was one of those situations when you could get starry-eyed and get carried away with it all, but for me there were more important things to do at the school. Maybe one day I might come back to that.

In November 2004, I was due to speak at a conference in Ballarat. I had been booked in some thirteen months before but in the meantime Grace and I were thrilled to find out our third child was on the way. The date of his arrival was after the conference but as it turned out Grace had to be booked in for caesarean. Marcellus Sam Pataleone was born on 8 November. I ended up doing a video link to the conference the next day and we celebrated Talia's birthday on the 10th. It was a very hectic time, but one of great joy as our family was now truly complete.

The school was starting to attract more and more visitors. I thought it was a great thing for the people of Cherbourg. Apart from Peter Beattie, Anna Bligh dropped by. She liked the visit so much she even came back a second time and brought along Andrew Refshauge, the New South Wales education minister and deputy premier. What I most enjoyed about that visit was Andrew Refshauge's profound interest in Aboriginal affairs. He displayed a sense of honesty that made me sit up and think as he wondered whether the efforts of so many well-meaning white people in the 1960s and '70s were actually part of the problem rather than part of the solution. I wasn't too sure about the answer but it got me thinking and about whether I would arrive at some place thirty years from now and think the whole strong and smart attitude would be part of a transformational solution, or part of the problem in some way.

We were also inundated by academics wanting to do research in the school. With academics I was always cautious about ensuring they weren't the type wanting to take, take, take, without any serious prospect of giving anything useful back. It was difficult not to feel some degree of contempt for those who, from my assessment, seemed to have been reasonably hopeless as educators and decided to do research so they could tell prospective undergraduate teachers what works best in schools. Along the way they get some pretty flash letters after their name, but they offer very little to the schools and communities they imposed themselves on.

One inspirational person to visit was the great Olympian Herb Elliott. I was too young to appreciate just how great he was as an athlete, but in the short time I got to know him it was easy to appreciate how great he was as a man. What struck me most about Herb was an encounter he had with a local Aboriginal guy who, despite being blind drunk in the middle of the day, had obviously recognised the great runner.

'Heeeey! Heeerb Elliott,' the guy slurred with tears running down his face, as he hugged Herb and then used him to hold himself up. 'I love you man. I just love you Herb.'

Herb was unperturbed. He just put his arm around the guy and helped him get steady on his feet. He asked him his name and how he was going. They made small talk then Herb explained he had to keep moving and the avid fan gave him one last hug. Herb patted him on the back and said, 'Good on you, mate. Nice to meet you.'

What impressed me about this exchange was knowing that

Herb probably had people coming up to him all the time to say 'g'day' and, even though this guy was drunk, he treated him with dignity. Just as my mum had instilled in us, Herb did not dishonour the humanity of the guy, even though the guy may have dishonoured his own humanity by being so wasted. As we chatted more and more throughout the day and I explained how we were achieving success at the school by working with people Herb took it all in.

'Chris. Nobody is talking like this about Aboriginal education!' he said to me, as he reflected on our efforts. He went on to describe me as a social entrepreneur, a term I hadn't really encountered before. 'Chris. If you ever get to a point where you want to take this to another level and spread this message around, you let me know and I will see how I can help you. We gotta get this message to go further.'

I really appreciated hearing that from such a great man.

If people weren't coming to visit our school then they wanted me to come to them to give a lecture at their university or keynote address at their conference. I really loved going out and telling the story of our school because it was inspiring; I was inspired by the kids. Despite the complexities of their lives they had risen to the challenge. The next step was to get the whole country to understand what we had done. This is why I didn't mind getting on the road to speak about the power of high expectations. It was gruelling, though, with the three-hour drive to Brisbane before flying elsewhere.

In order to minimise the time I was away from home I would sometimes leave at three am to catch a seven o'clock flight to Melbourne, and then fly back that evening and drive three hours home. Hooper and Fred would often help me out by doing the driving to and from the airport; it took the edge off travelling quite a bit and also gave us time to have a really good long yarn. We'd talk about all sorts of profound things. I recall on one occasion we analysed the households in Cherbourg to work out which ones were functional and which ones were chaotic. We established there were probably fewer than twenty homes out of the two hundred and fifty or so that could be considered chaotic or dysfunctional. This gave a good sense of the scale of any problems, which seemed much bigger than they actually were. It was really interesting to reflect on this, particularly when governments were devising blanket policies, such as alcohol bans and quarantining welfare payments, that affected *all* people because of the dysfunctional behaviour of some. As we drove, moments of silence were pierced by these profoundly deep insights. We lamented how lots of Australians were outraged about things like ABSTUDY, arguing it should be based on need not a blanket application to race, but at the same time were silent about the more draconian blanket scheme applied to race.

Some weeks I would be away for two or three nights. The kids at school and my colleagues understood the importance of me sharing our story. By this stage the school was pretty much running itself as I had worked hard to ensure a good depth of leadership so any number of people had the ability to lead in my absence. It was really tough on my family, though. Grace absolutely shared my passion to make a difference and was very understanding, but saying goodnight to the kids over the phone was difficult. Ezra had a way of letting me know how things were for him.

'Dad, when you get home we need to have a talk about all this travelling you're doing.' He was not even seven years old at the time and those words were like a red-hot needle piercing the core of my conscience.

'Okay, son, let's talk about it then. Goodnight. I love you.'

'I love you too, Dad.'

As he trundled off to bed I'd be left feeling so alone in a motel room, sobbing with an aching heart. Getting the balance right between being there for my children and leading a charge to change expectations for all Indigenous children was cruel and seemingly unwinnable. The school's success was a special story that had to be told, but in other ways it seemed like we were just doing what we were paid to do. It was hard work, sometimes, made even harder when others saw us as tall poppies that had to be cut down. This was most disappointing yet not unexpected.

As a group, there were many times when my colleagues and I would regroup and re-energise. We really did work our guts out to make a difference and there was no magic bullet, just really hard work with determination. We also took very seriously the notion that what we were doing was having an impact on schools in other parts of the country. This was not just about the Aboriginal children in our classrooms, but Aboriginal children throughout Australia. There were also times when I had to regroup with the kids, too. It was, after all, their success and the extent to which they had turned things around that was being questioned by the critics. Over the years we had discussed extensively the stereotype of Aboriginal students and the truth about being strong and smart. They knew a negative image of them existed and they also knew that they had a choice about whether to collude with it and made it true or to smash through it by choosing to be strong and smart. For some kids this was really tough.

A few of the students were being punched and harassed on their way to school just for making the strong-and-smart choice. It would have been so much easier for them to fall back into dysfunction and self-pity but they were making the honourable and dignified choice of working hard and embracing higher expectations. Given my research and reflection on notions of identity and stereotyping, this attack on us was to be expected. We were challenging a status quo in which people, black and white, had become comfortable. It would have been much easier to collude with low expectations but we wanted more. There were times when we had to remind ourselves that it was our right to get stronger and smarter. Even kids as young as six understood this when I spoke to them about it at school assembly.

'I need you to understand that it is okay for us to be in this place where we are becoming strong and smart!' I would explain. 'We are getting closer to the truth about who we are as Aboriginal people. Strong and proud to be Aboriginal, and smart enough to mix it with any white people in any other school!'

They knew to be quiet when I was serious like this. I'd scan the room and every small black face in the room would be staring reciprocally straight back into my eyes. So attentive and respectful. So serious. So focussed and into what I was saying.

'People will try to pull us down!' I'd go on. 'They'll try to pull you down because they think this is where blackfullas are supposed to be. So when they see us getting stronger and smarter, they think we're getting too big for our boots. But you know what?' I'd ask, not expecting or getting a response. 'We *are* getting too big for those boots!

'Those boots were never big enough for us in the first place! Those boots were made for us a long time ago by people who thought our place was down on the bottom! Now,' I'd say and could see they were taking in a collective breath, knowing exactly what I was about to shout at them, 'when we leave this school what are we gonna be?'

'STRONG AND SMART!' they would shout with gusto. We did assembly like no other school in the world.

This was a very explicit way of talking with them, and they really did get it. Some people would question my blunt and precise dialogue with them but that never bothered me because I understood the need to face front on the challenge of society's negative expectations. This was about elevating their sense of self as an Aboriginal child. It was never ever about putting white people down. It was, however, about articulating, challenging and realising the impact of their restricted views of us.

Interestingly, when two white girls, Samantha and Zoe, joined our school there were some things about our culture I had to talk through with their parents. They were the daughters of a pastor who had just moved to Cherbourg. I remember well the day he came to check us out. At first he wanted to make sure it was possible to enrol his girls with us and he admitted he was going to check out the other two schools nearby.

'Yeah, go for it. That's cool,' I said genuinely. 'But you won't find them anywhere near as exciting and fun as our school.' He must have agreed with me because a few days later he was back filling in the enrolment forms for his girls. He knew it would be a profound and positive life experience for them.

'Everyone in the school has to be focussed on being strong and smart here,' I explained to him. 'When we talk about strong, though, we all say that means strong and proud to be Aboriginal. Your girls aren't Aboriginal, but they can still be strong, though.

The other thing is in our song we sing about being "young and *black* and deadly" and I'm not sure if you've noticed this . . . but your girls aren't very black.'

'Yes, I noticed.' He smiled.

'There are a few ways around this, I suppose. We could change the words somehow, or your girls could sing "young and *white* and deadly" . . . that could work.'

'No, no,' he said pensively. 'Let's both have a think about it and see what we can come up with.'

The next day he came to see me and said, 'Chris we've been talking with the girls a lot and we really like the strong and smart thing. It made us reflect on our own Irish and English heritage a lot and how we should try to understand that better and take pride in it. And with the school song we don't want you to change it at all. My girls will sing "young and black and deadly", too. For them black will be about a sense of feeling.'

It was an awesome conversation. He was a really impressive guy. His girls were a minority in this school and it would have been wrong for me just to assume they would fit in without having to sit down with their parents and explore cultural or social differences that might have to be accommodated. The need for this was so obvious. Reflecting on this makes me wonder about the extent to which 'mainstream' school principals deal with such a situation when an Aboriginal student is being enrolled into a predominantly white school.

There were a lot of things happening in my life at this time. Looking back I am not exactly sure just how I managed to complete my workload and maintain some sense of sanity. I have often heard people lament on the challenges of writing a PhD thesis, yet here I was, writing my thesis, completing a second Masters, running a complex school, and with small children. Grace was extraordinarily patient and supportive. At the back our small house in Wondai I converted an old wooden toolshed into a modest office. The plan in my head was somehow to finish a Bachelor of Education degree by the time I reached thirty, a Masters by forty, and PhD by fifty. By thirty I had both a BEd and MEd in the bag. In the end I completed my PhD by the time I was thirty-eight and in the process of writing my thesis won a scholarship that would see me completing an Executive Masters in Public Administration with the very first cohort of the ANZSOG, the Australia New Zealand School of Government.

There were many days where I would be up and out of bed by a quarter to five in the morning, when it was still cold and dark outside. There is always something peaceful and calm about that time of the morning. There was also that feeling that I was one of very few up and working at that hour. Eventually the sun would catch up and drag most people out of bed, and by about a quarter past seven I would head back into the house to help get the kids moving, bathed, dressed, fed and ready for school. I'd put in a full day at the 'office' then come home to the family. After the washing up and putting to bed was done, I'd trounce back out to the cold lonely shed and hopefully get a few hours of writing in until about eleven pm.

The act of writing the PhD was quite an experience. Some days I would be in the zone and other days I simply wasn't. On some nights I would feel so into it I would lose track of time. It was an awesome feeling, like I was somehow possessed and the words would just flow from some high and lofty source through me and onto the keyboard. At those times I would emerge from my shed when the sun was rising and think, 'Wow!'

It is hard to explain, but there was something almost spiritual about some of the writing. It truly did feel that some of the words hitting my screen were well beyond my basic level of conscious thought. It was a gift, and one I have always appreciated and never taken for granted. Writing my thesis at the time of running the school made me think more deeply about what I was doing. The thesis in many ways was going to be a case study of my work at the school. It was the only way I could manage doing both tasks, as each was heavy enough on its own. The basic hypothesis was that we would get a positive effect on Aboriginal student performance if we understood and reinforced positive perceptions of being Aboriginal. This meant having to get some sense of mainstream Australian perceptions of being Aboriginal and compare this to Aboriginal perceptions of being Aboriginal.

To get some sense of mainstream Australian perceptions of Aboriginal people, I conducted forums that involved more than two and a half thousand participants. At each I would ask a simple question: 'What are some of the words or adjectives that "mainstream Australia" would use to describe Aboriginal people?' I would always say to them, 'I am not talking about *your* personal perceptions. I want you to tell me what words you think a mainstream Australian, whatever that is, would use to describe Aboriginal people.' From then on I would write the words down on a whiteboard and I would keep a record of such words in order to note how often they came up.

There was a range of words that came up at every forum. These included words and adjectives like 'lazy', 'welfare dependent', 'dirty', 'alcoholics', as well as 'boongs', 'coons' and 'niggers'. It was never a nice thing to have to quantify the existence of such a negative image in such an empirical way, but I felt it was important to do so. While this stereotype existed we would always be held back as a people. For me this was the beast of racism that had to be exposed and killed. As long as this stereotype existed we would always have governments that could simply ignore our plight, or throw money at our challenges without any real concern about tangible outcomes. As long as this stereotype existed, police could 'cause the death' of an Aboriginal man and not have to contemplate any serious consequence. As long as this stereotype existed we could continue to deliver chronic failure in schools and somehow always blame the complexity of the community or an Aboriginal child's household, without ever having to be put under the microscope to question the quality of our schools, teachers or principals.

In my thesis I wanted to expose this as a stereotype that was anchored by misconception and inaccurate pre-judgements. In exposing this misconception I had to make some attempt to articulate what was considered a kind of truth about Aboriginal perceptions of being Aboriginal. I had recorded a series of interviews with a range of Aboriginal people. It was important that I spoke with those whom I knew to identify as Aboriginal all of their life, not simply those who started identifying as Aboriginal because there was money to be got from the government, or good jobs to be had. Time constraints meant that I was only able to conduct a few interviews, but enough to detect an early pattern and identify aspects that were coming up consistently in conversations about what made people identify strongly as being Aboriginal.

The other revelation I unveiled in my thesis, thanks to Professor Roy Bhaskar's groundbreaking Critical Realist theory, was the notion of layered identities. I had the pleasure of meeting

Roy later when I travelled to England and also hosted him in Cherbourg. He is one of those really 'out there' exceptionally bright human beings, a contemporary philosopher who decided to break free of the shackles and limitations of existing philosophical frameworks to create his own.

A lot of things made sense when Roy talked and wrote about identity. At our basic core, whatever our cultural background, is a sense of humanity that unites us all. From there we each have incredible and varied aspects of our identity, or mediations as he called them, that resonate more strongly than others. The extent to which particular aspects of our identity resonated more strongly than others could depend on any number of a complex range of variables such as time, place and context.

Obviously this is a very complex theory, but at a basic level it explained how I could identify very strongly as being Aboriginal, yet also be extremely proud to be of Italian descent. In the context of growing up in Australia around my mum's family, and having been subjected to life experiences such as feeling that connection to country, confronting acts of racism and low expectations – these were experiences that made being Aboriginal resonate more strongly with me. While I was in Italy visiting my family, that sense of being Italian resonated more strongly with me, and I felt really good about that. Despite this, I was still the same person and at my core retained my humanity.

The Critical Realist theory offered an exceptional way of observing the world and having a deeper insight into people around me. It helped me to make sense of those aspects of a person's life that resonated strongly for them. For instance, I could see how someone's religious beliefs, or their sexuality, or a person's lived experience would resonate and inform their sense of identity. It also shed some light on some of the challenges of many Aboriginal people who are pressured by notions of being 'individual' minded or 'community' minded. With this understanding we get that it is, in fact, okay to be both, but at various times in various circumstances, one will resonate more strongly than the other.

The easiest way to explain such a complex theory is to think about how we are as Rugby League fans. When I am watching the National Rugby League competitions I am an ardent north Queensland Cowboys fan. When Queensland plays New South Wales in the State of Origin fixture I am crazy about Queensland, and will even cheer for Queensland players who might play for teams other than the Cowboys. When Australia plays against another country, however, I cheer madly for Australia, and will even cheer for the New South Wales players who are in the Australian team. At every stage I am the same person, yet, depending on the context or who is on the field at the time, sometimes I might identify more strongly as a Cowboys fan, a Queensland fan, or an Australia fan. Importantly, it is always worth remembering that, regardless of who is cheering for what team, we are all still united at our core by our sense of humanity.

Towards the end of 2004 I was starting to feel that, while I had led a very significant cultural shift in the school and there had been a dramatic shift in the data, there was still a need to push harder and the school higher. The majority of my professional career had been in secondary schools and I felt the best way to push the data was for me to make way for a leader who had had good experience leading primary curriculum and assessment reform. I was starting to wonder if it was time for me to hand over the baton. To their credit, when I spoke to the people in the upper echelons of the education department they hatched a plan to bring in someone they thought would be a good successor to work alongside me for twelve months before I left. I appreciated that this would be a hard thing for both of us but I was determined to make the transition work. The new principal was appointed from a small country school and she arrived to start work during the last week of term.

11

Changing the tide

With the national exposure of the school I had been fielding some lucrative job offers from other state education authorities and institutions for more than two years. The salaries were often double or more than my pay at the school. The Cherbourg job for me, though, was far more important than the money and so I hadn't seriously considered the offers. Even though I had now made the decision to move on, I was still determined to see the job through the next twelve months to help the incoming principal take the lead, so any thoughts of what I would do next were put on the backburner.

I met the new principal at the top of the stairs at the school. She had come with good recommendations from former colleagues whose judgement I respected. Clearly, the most important thing at this time was not her and not me, but the kids at the school. We would have to work together and I appreciated it would be a difficult job for anyone taking over a role in a school that had received so much attention.

Late one night Ken Smith, the director general of the education department, called me at home. He had somehow found out I had been offered employment elsewhere.

'Listen, Chris, if you ever get any offers from anywhere in other states make sure you talk to me before you make any decisions, 'ay?'

'Yeah, of course, Ken,' I said, meaning it. I'm a Queenslander, through and through, and it would take a very serious offer to make me think of living in another state.

It was really flattering to get this call and it enabled me to think more boldly about my future options. By then I had completed my PhD and this allowed me to think even more broadly about what the next step should be. The predictable options for me were going into academia, bureaucracy, or another school. An education faculty, surrounded by people who lectured about schooling but often lacked meaningful engagement with the realities faced by teachers, children and parents, made me feel nauseous. I had done bureaucracy and it was equally unappealing. A different type of school was a possibility but another community school would have felt a bit like starting all over again. I was attracted to the idea of leading a larger mainstream school, in some ways just to prove I could cut it. On a personal level I had challenged my expectations about myself. I had led a change at the school, and as a team and community we had transformed Cherbourg School. So now I wondered whether it was the right time to be looking at something much more ambitious: changing the tide of low expectations of Indigenous children in schools right across Australia. But the question was, how?

Whenever I was confronted by a complex challenge I would always go back to that ever-reliable source of wisdom, Dr Gary MacLennan. It was Gary's idea to establish an institute to focus on packaging up what we had learned from the Cherbourg journey to share this knowledge, passion and hope with other school and community leaders throughout Australia and, potentially, the world. I talked about this concept with Ken, and, being the good thinker he is, he could see a great deal of merit in it. The minister for education, Anna Bligh, liked the idea too, and they agreed to keep a dialogue open about it. They also began discussing the idea with Peter Coaldrake, the vice-chancellor of the Queensland University of Technology. As if paving the way to leave the school and moving on to establish an institute was not overwhelming enough for me, an incident occurred that would make everything pale into insignificance.

Late on a Saturday night in April 2005 I got the call from Hooper. The children, Grace and I were watching *Whale Rider*, the great New Zealand film that resonates so strongly with its message about the importance of cultural identity to young Indigenous children. At first I ignored the phone, like I had done on so many other occasions. I was used to the guys giving me a call late on a Friday or Saturday night after being on the charge a bit. This night was different, though. Usually they got the hint not to bother about ringing more than once or twice, but Hooper kept ringing.

'Hooper, what's up?' I asked.

'It's Michael, man. He's not good. We're taking him to the hospital now,' he told me with a serious tone that made me realise this was bad.

'Oh shit! What happened?'

'He got whacked on the head and knocked out cold. We're just taking him up there now but they shoulda took him up straightaway,' he said.

Michael Blackman was my cousin. I had asked him to come

to Cherbourg to teach with me. There was not much I could do right now but I told Hooper to ring me back to let me know what was going on. He rang back later to say Michael was being flown to Brisbane by helicopter. I hated that helicopter. Every time it was heard at Cherbourg it usually meant bad news for someone and their family. I woke up the next morning not knowing what news to expect but naively assuming it would just be okay.

Hooper called from Brisbane. The news was not good.

'Brother, he's not good. They got him in a coma. He's got bleeding on his brain and they were gonna try to drill into his head and take the pressure off his brain . . . but they think it might be too late!'

'This can't be happening,' was all I could think. 'Not Michael. Not Mr Blackman!'

Grace and I grabbed the kids, got in the car and drove to Brisbane. At the Princess Alexandra Hospital we met Michael's family, who are also my family. It felt strange embracing members of the family whom I hadn't seen for such a long time amid such tragic, confusing, and surreal times. We were all so bewildered and so confused. It was so hard as we began to realise that while he lay there on the bed attached to a machine, he may not be coming back.

I suspect his spirit had already gone and it was just the machine that was furnishing false hope, but allowing us time to steady ourselves enough to stand and let him go. His immediate family then made the harrowing decision to turn the machine off. As distressing as it was, it was the right thing to do.

I was hit by a wave of emotions, from the depths of sadness to a quagmire of confusion, and on to a furnace of rage. Michael had just been drinking with his so-called mates and they got on the charge quite fiercely. There was nothing unusual about this. They had done it heaps of times before. Afterwards they had a bit of a dust-up and one of the guys punched Michael and knocked him out. Sadly, there was also nothing unusual in having a dust-up either; it had happened many times before. But this time, Michael had been knocked unconscious and then left unattended, lying on the pavement, for several hours. What person with the slightest grain of humanity would do that? You wouldn't leave a dog unattended if it didn't move. There is no polite way to describe it but to me it signalled just how fucked up some people were. The doctors said that had he been taken to hospital immediately they might have been able to release the pressure from his brain and he could well have survived. We will always be tormented by such speculation. Our brother was gone! The one we used to tease all the time yet admire for his gentle and skilful way with the kids and with other adults was gone. Michael was gone.

I was conscious of how this might affect the staff and the children. A crisis or traumatic event is one of the hard things about leading in a school, or any situation for that matter. It is almost as if you have to put your own emotional fragility on the shelf in order to see everyone else is guided through. There is also the risk of stories blowing out of proportion as people try to make sense of the various truths and half-truths circulating.

I let everyone know there would be a whole staff meeting before school started on the Monday morning. I remember going into the meeting in a very matter-of-fact way, without any emotion, and simply laying out the facts, as I understood them. By now most knew what had happened, but some were finding out for the first time. People broke down and started to cry while others consoled them. As they consoled each other I mapped out a plan for how we would proceed with the day, how we would discuss this matter with the children, how we would organise support for those who needed it, and how we had arranged for additional support from District Office. As a team we steeled ourselves for the day. I said to them that, as difficult as this day was going to be, we should not let ourselves be overwhelmed or somehow feel discouraged. If anything, this truly was the time to be strong and smart for our children. They needed us; we needed them. We all needed each other. Sombrely they shuffled out of the staffroom to start what was always going to be a precarious day.

Somehow I felt the need to appear strong and stable in such a way so that I could lead us through this difficult and traumatic circumstance. I felt like I was acting in some type of crazy movie and somebody would yell, 'Cut,' and we could just go back to how it was last Friday. But the truth was I was hurting just as much as anyone in that room. In some ways it was because of me Michael was in Cherbourg.

In spite of such thoughts going through my mind I breathed deeply and tried to look like I was standing strong until everyone had left the room. I walked down the long dark hallway to my office where Cecily Anderson, the district director, was already sitting. I closed the door, sat down to bury my head in my hands, and I cried and I cried and I cried. I could feel Cecily embrace me like a small child in a way that was comforting yet futile. I had lost a wonderful and gentle friend and cousin. I just could not comprehend why they would leave him lying like that. I cried because he was an Aboriginal man dying on an Aboriginal community, and I didn't believe the matter would be taken seriously by the judicial authorities.

Even in 2005 I had little faith in the system to deliver any sense of justice to Aboriginal people. What hurt me most about Michael's untimely death was that those dynamics of dysfunction that we sought to break would be those very dynamics that would conspire to contribute to his demise. Michael was one of the gentlest men I had known. He was passionate about teaching Aboriginal studies to the children and they loved him. The parents really loved what he was doing, too. I remembered one day watching him from my office window, sitting out on the grass with a bunch of Year 2 children. As he sat cross-legged on the grass and yarned with them, occasionally pointing to various things here and there, it was obvious they were engrossed in whatever he was saying, hanging off every word. I thought that if we travelled back three hundred years all of the buildings and modern landscapes would not be there but somehow he and the children would remain unchanged. Michael would be sitting cross-legged on the grass, telling the stories, pointing here and there occasionally to embellish his points, with the children sitting in that same way, hanging off his every word.

I had always planned to see out 2005 as the principal but my last day at the school would come much sooner than I expected. Events conspired to usurp my plan. Anna Bligh was promoted to deputy premier and a more senior ministerial portfolio, and it was understood that she would eventually take her director general, Ken Smith, with her. With both of them I shared a sense of appreciation about how they understood and were receptive to the strong and smart culture we were building in our school. Together they had used it as a platform upon which to challenge other schools and senior education bureaucrats around the state and country. I recall harbouring a degree of apprehension at the time, wondering if this progressive time was more of a window of opportunity rather than a new horizon in Aboriginal education.

In February 2005 I got a call from Gary Barnes, the director of human resources in the Queensland education department. Gary was one of those guys who appeared laid back but was actually quite intense and focussed. He told me Ken Smith didn't want to wait until the end of the year, he wanted the Indigenous Education Leadership Institute to be set up and running by Easter.

I was never sure how the kids would react when I told them that I would be leaving the school. I wasn't even sure how I would react. In some ways I believed I wouldn't be leaving entirely because we had designed the Institute in such a way that it would be based in Cherbourg and still have a connection to the school. The school would become the living, working laboratory for the Institute. The idea was for people from all around Australia to come to the school and hear about the key factors that underpinned our success, and then walk around and talk to the staff, students and parents about the concepts. Anticipating that sense of ongoing connection made it a little easier to talk with the kids about my leaving, although it was still difficult in some ways.

'Good morning, everybody!' I screamed out to them in my usual way.

'GOOD MORNING, MR SARRA!' they hollered back.

'I need to tell you something. Now listen up. Today is my last day here as principal of the school.'

Even today I still recall that look of shock, confusion and disbelief that made its way upon their gorgeous faces. In some ways I felt guilty and like somehow I was betraying them. As I cast my eyes around the sea of faces, I made direct eye contact with each of them as I had done more than a hundred times before. On their faces I sensed their burning question, 'Who's gonna give us strong and smart now?'

'Strong and smart is not something I gave to you,' I explained. 'It's not something anybody gives you!'

I let them dwell on the silence for a moment, while inside I was feeling immensely proud of just how they truly got what I was talking about in that deep moment.

'I want you to understand this! It's not something anybody gives you. It was inside you before we even got here. It's inside all of us. It's inside every black child in Australia and you proved this. What I have to do is take what you have done . . . what you have proved . . . and get everyone in Australia to understand this. You have made it okay for young black kids all over Australia to stand up and be strong and smart. Remember what I said to you now, and don't ever forget it.'

I paused again so that my next words had extra weight.

'Strong and smart really has been inside you all along. Nobody gave it to you . . . and nobody can ever take it away!'

With that I walked away from my final school assembly with them, feeling like I had done what I came here for. With a heavy heart I went back to my office and sat alone with the door closed. It was time to move on.

With the confusion and trauma surrounding Michael's death, my sense of being a bit worn down and tired after six and a half years at the school, coupled with a feeling that I had taken the school as far as I could as a leader, I had decided to take six weeks off. In that time I would create some necessary distance between me and my successor, have a break, and come back as the director of a newly established Institute that was going to change low expectations of Indigenous children in all Australian schools.

Soon after Easter 2005 we launched the Institute. It would be the first institute to be based on an Aboriginal community so that we could have an ongoing relationship with the school as the living laboratory of the stronger smarter philosophy. QUT and the Queensland education department would each put in one hundred and twenty thousand dollars to get us started. It was enough to employ myself as the director, Michal Purcell as the admin assistant and Dr Merv Wilkinson as a project manager. We remained within the department of education under the HR and Strategic Planning Division. This meant we would be working under the supervision of Gary Barnes. We were also well supported by Claudia Whitton from HR, who was instrumental in the early stages of sorting the logistics of getting established. Claudia was extremely efficient and business-like, having worked for Anna Bligh as her chief of staff, but, most importantly, she had a good heart.

Michal and I had made a pretty deadly team at the school and forged one of those working partnerships where she just seemed to know what I was thinking, even when I wasn't sure myself. I'd walk into the storeroom behind her office and forget what I was looking for and say to her, 'Miss, what did I come in here for?'

She'd stop what she was doing for a moment to think and then say something like, 'Um . . . stapler!' And it really was what I was looking for.

'You know what, Miss,' I'd say on my way out, 'one day when I'm finished here as the principal I'm gonna have a big flash job somewhere and you're coming with me!'

'Yeah right, Mr Sarra,' she'd say, not entirely sure whether to be disbelieving.

Merv came to know us through his relationship with one of the teachers at Cherbourg. He was a tall gentlemanly type, whose father was English and mother was Papua New Guinean. He had a genuine interest in helping us to make a difference. We would tease him heaps about looking so much like Walter Matthau. Eventually, we were also joined by Zona Hussey-Smith and my old mate Fred Cobbo, both of whom I had worked with at the school. We were a small but determined team. Together we shared a relentless interest and passion in changing expectations across Australia and all we had to do now was work out how we were going to do it.

Due to the profile of the school and the Institute I was invited to a range of leadership programs and activities. It enabled me to consider opportunities beyond education, such as the invite to sit on the Australia Council for the Arts as the chair of Aboriginal and Torres Strait Islander Arts Board. The federal minister for the arts, Senator Rod Kemp, called for a chat. He seemed a pretty decent guy and was unperturbed when I confessed my limited aptitude in the arts arena.

'You know, the only dancing I've done was in my night-clubbing days, and I've not done much painting since Year 1 at primary.'

'That's fine, Chris, I'm not concerned about that,' he said. 'I've read a lot about you, and I've seen what you can do in driving a strategic vision. That's really what I am after, someone who can bring a real sense of strategic direction to the council, particularly to the Aboriginal and Torres Strait Islander Arts Board.'

I was pretty confident in my ability to plan and implement. In all of the work I had done so far I'd been involved in working out the direction and leading the development and of good strategy.

We chatted for several minutes about the role and what it would entail in terms of demands on my time. Some years later he would confess that, as with many other recruits to the Australia Council, he had underplayed the discussion about time demands, but that was okay as it was a role I greatly enjoyed.

I was highly influenced by my involvement as an inaugural student of the Australia New Zealand School of Government in their Executive Masters of Public Administration program. I was doing this program while I was running the school and finishing off my PhD. Looking back I am not sure how I did it. The Executive Masters programs offered the opportunity to live in at the facility while we participated in lectures and other activities with lots of intellectual rigour. As a small team at the Institute we thought we could develop something similar to this. We discussed meeting with ministers of education around the country to convince them to mandate principals to participate in our leadership program but I was not fussed on this notion. I had lost patience trying to work with people who needed to be convinced it was important to put in some extra effort to deliver a better education for Indigenous children. I saw them as a waste of time and energy, and, while I knew I would not touch them directly, they would ultimately be touched indirectly by our work. Our logic was to engage those who were ready to be engaged with us, and expose those with low expectations.

We knew we could not get to every Aboriginal student or parent, or even every school or community, so we set out to engage school and community leaders who were ready to engage with us. It made sense to us that if we could inspire them to transform their school, arming them with the belief, capacity and skill to go back and make a difference, then we could highlight their success as a way of shooting down all of the excuses that try to justify failure with Aboriginal children. We wanted to work with leaders of large metropolitan high schools right through to the tiny and remote primary schools. If we could play a part in nurturing success with Aboriginal kids in every type of school, then we could effectively expose every teacher and principal with low expectations, leaving them no place to hide in any model of school, in any part of Australia. It was a lofty ambition but we truly felt we could do it.

We started off slowly with our first leadership program, which attracted participants from Western Australia, north Queensland and New South Wales. Those from north Queensland came to the program as a result of very strong support from my respected friends and colleagues Ian Mackie, Leigh Schelks and Don Andersen. Each of them was a strong and significant education leader in the region. The West Australian participants were encouraged to come by a senior Aboriginal school leader and WA education director, Kevin O'Keefe. Kevin was a man I respected and admired greatly. He had visited us at Cherbourg School to see what everyone else was talking about. He then invited me to several forums to offer lectures and keynote addresses to challenge his West Australian colleagues. Strangely enough, he had to fight with other Indigenous bureaucrats in his own department in order to send some of their principals along to that first program, a phenomenon that would play out in other states as well. The New South Wales participants were encouraged to come along by my close colleague and associate Maree Roberts, a former senior Queensland education department employee who visited our school and became a great supporter of my work. Another advocate from New South Wales was Karen Jones, a strong and well-credentialled Koori woman working as a school education director.

If it had not been for the good relationships with these particular people and their support, we might have really struggled to get our leadership programs going. Thankfully we did and were able to develop a powerful and experiential learning experience that would see participants reflecting deeply on their roles and questioning whether or not their actions, beliefs and behaviours were about colluding with the negative stereotype of Aboriginal students, rather than about smashing through this in the pursuit of stronger smarter students.

The question everyone asked me at our leadership programs and on my travels around the country was, 'What happened to the school after you left?' It was a valid question but one that would always cause me grief to reflect upon. I had had to give up quite early the initial concept of having the school as a partner in our venture as it seemed to me that members of the school staff were threatened by my presence. There was some confusion, I'm sure, about whether I had any say in what was going on there or whether I had no say at all. It was a shame in many ways, as the people who came in for our leadership programs were desperate to see the school in action. I was keen to show them, but as time unfolded I was losing confidence in the school as a model of the strong and smart philosophy, where high expectations were at play and where locals were embraced as fundamental to the school's success.

It was impossible to just switch off and move on for many reasons. The emotional investment I'd made into the school over six and a half years was obviously substantial and so this alone made it hard. To make matters even more complex, Grace was still teaching at the school and our two eldest children, Ezra and Talia, were enrolled as students. As a parent at the P&C meetings I would challenge the principal about her expectations. At one meeting I recall an exchange with her as she tried to justify what was occurring with the parents.

'Most of these grade seven kids are not going to have the same literacy levels as other kids. You just have to accept that!' she tried to assert with some authority.

I was fuming inside and working extremely hard not to swear or raise my voice in front of some of the elders in the room.

'Well, no actually. We DON'T have to accept that! But you have to explain to us what you intend to do about it!'

It was so infuriating and such a soul-destroying experience. The hardest part was hearing from the Aboriginal teacher aides about their experiences. They were coming to me and begging me to do something about the slipping standards and expectations about student behaviour. Some of them were also quite animated as they articulated a concern about the dramatic increase in the number of children being identified as 'special needs' when there was no apparent need for such an assessment. There were claims that some parents were being told, 'You have to sign this form so that we can get more support for your child.' Of course, any parent would sign a form if it was explained to them like that. To me it seemed to be done so that the school could get more resources, but parents really didn't seem to have much of an idea about what they were signing.

The question of special needs identification was interesting at Cherbourg as indeed it is in many Aboriginal schools. When I arrived, no children had been identified, and statistically I knew that this could not be the case. People at the school would say the tests were culturally irrelevant, but, while there was some truth in that, it is useful to consider these tests as just one of the pieces of information you can use to make assessments. As an ex-guidance officer I felt it was important that we test some of the kids who just seemed a bit out of kilter compared with others. When we got to the point of having parents sign forms, I would invite them into my office for a lengthy conversation about it. I wanted them to completely understand what they were signing. As it turned out we had a few kids identified as special needs students, but after I left there was a dramatic spike in the number of kids identified. The issue of identifying Aboriginal kids as special needs, not only in Cherbourg but throughout Australia, was something I intensely disliked. It may not have been a new wave of child abuse, but there certainly was a filthy undercurrent to it.

Parents had started to pull their children out of the school to send them into Murgon, just as they had done previously. I did my best to raise concerns with the most senior people in the education department and the government champion for Cherbourg. None of them really wanted to know about it. The minister for education said to me, 'Chris, you can't really expect someone to come and take over and keep it up at the level that you had it!' If there was one thing that we proved so profoundly at the school, you usually always get what you expect. They expected it to slide backwards and, in many ways, it did slide backwards. They got what they expected.

The Queensland education department seemed to me to have a head-in-the-sand approach, and anyone who dared question or challenge them was likely to get cut off. In my time at the school I was the pin-up boy in some ways for the education department. They would invite me to lots of forums to speak to other principals and bring me to various functions to meet important people. Now that I was outside of the school, and in a role where I had to challenge others about how well we were going in Aboriginal education, I felt like I was being treated more like a leper. I was being invited to speak at conferences all around the world, but I was being actively shunned from my former school just four hundred metres from my office.

Most of the Institute's early work involved me having to travel interstate so I would do the arduous three-hour drive to Brisbane airport, fly out and back, and then make the long drive home. It was like I was a prophet in another man's land. Looking back it might have been a blessing in disguise. At the Institute we gave up on the original idea of Cherbourg as the laboratory for the stronger smarter philosophy, but we now had a range of schools throughout Australia that took on that mantle. The best I could do for Cherbourg was reflect on what I'd learned there, think about what I could have done differently, and share those reflections with other school leaders so they didn't make the same mistakes that I did.

There were several mistakes I'd made, and, looking back, the most fundamental was not working hard enough with community people to embed their voice and authority into the governance processes of the school. I'd feel good when I took the school's strategic and operational documents down to the mayor for his signature and try to explain what was contained within it and he would just say, 'You're right, brother. We trust you. Give it here and I'll just sign it now!' It was good to have such trust but what I should have done instead was insist that I sit down with the entire council and the school's P&C and explain all of the strategies and targets, and got them to challenge me, so they would know what to look out for when the next principal came along.

The other mistake I made was tiptoeing around a few of the local Aboriginal people on staff. There were two in particular that were underperforming and were never likely to perform adequately, but both were, in their own way, somewhat prominent in the community. I had backed off challenging them because I was concerned about what effect it might have on the school's relationship with the community. I lacked courage here and it was the kids in the school who paid a price for this. As things transpired it was these two staff members who got into a cosy relationship with the new principal, protecting her from my challenges, and leading the charge back to mediocrity. It was a place at which they would be unchallenged and comfortable.

Another reflection on that time was that there were a few teachers who had worked so hard for me, yet as soon as I was out the door they took their foot off the pedal. I'm not sure how I was supposed to see this at the time, but it was something that I just did not predict. It has taken a long while for me to think about all this and in some ways forgive myself for the mistakes I made. Some people try to suggest the downturn of the school means the stronger smarter approach is unsustainable. I never accept that view. The truth from my perspective is that we had put in six and a half years hard slog at the school with the strong and smart approach, and in that time we delivered dramatic changes with authentic data. As a result, other schools and communities around Australia were inspired by our story and applied the stronger smarter approach with great success. So while it may not have been sustained at Cherbourg, it was an approach sustained by its influence in other places.

Even within Cherbourg, the community did not let up on its demand to retrieve that sense of being strong and smart. While the fire might have diminished somewhat, the embers remained, awaiting that fresh new breeze of high expectations. Today the school is back on track, and strangely enough is being led by an old school buddy of mine, Peter Sansby from Kepnock High. He is working hard at the school and doing a really good job.

Other people question the sustainability and value of the stronger smarter approach by looking at the progress of former Cherbourg students when they got to high school. Many did well, but many not so well, following the trajectory expected of them from some teachers at the high school. Stepping back, I realise the success or failure of students at Cherbourg after my departure, or their success or failure at high school, does raise questions about the validity of the stronger smarter approach. It raises profoundly more questions, though, about the quality and integrity of the people who followed me or who were at the high school. There is no doubt that if our children had been met in high school by a team that got what strong and smart was all about, then who knows what exciting trajectory those students might have been on after another six years of stronger smarter schooling?

When I took the question to one of the high school leaders, arguing they should run a strong and smart stream for our students in his school, he said such streaming would be apartheid. Like many other schools, though, they had no problem whatsoever streaming these kids away from mainstream classes into an annexe program, which by amazing coincidence was filled almost entirely with black students. Somehow it was acceptable to stream black kids downwards and into lower standard maths and English and life skills programs, but streaming black kids for excellence was somehow morally incomprehensible.

In my quieter and more reflective moments I look back on

those exasperating times, and, rather than get angry at those individuals in question, I realise they simply lacked the capacity to understand the sophisticated and complex insights to the entire stronger smarter approach. In some ways I look back on them as decent people as I suspect they were probably trying their hardest. While the stronger smarter approach is a simple message, to raise expectations, it requires a great deal of energy and thought to work out how to implement it. Some people have the ability to do this, some people don't.

Grace and I decided there was no point staying in Cherbourg. I didn't really want to leave as I would have been more content if the original plan had come off – that we could have had that strong and smart laboratory at the school, with the Institute based on Cherbourg, and with us continuing to live in our little three-bedroom country house in Wondai. In the end it seemed there was little choice. The hardest part was leaving the people and the kids of Cherbourg. I felt in some ways that I was betraying them, and in other ways that I was giving up. The best I could do was walk away but retain a connection with the community by bringing people back there for our leadership programs. My relationship with the school leaders had broken down and I never really did have the chance to say thank you and goodbye properly to the kids. Even today I look back on this with a sense of despair and sadness.

Given that I was travelling a lot, the Institute decided to try to retain something of a base in Cherbourg where we could run our leadership programs, but I would have to be set up closer to the Brisbane airport. Peter Coaldrake, the vice-chancellor of QUT, offered an office at their Kelvin Grove or Gardens Point campus, both of which were in the Brisbane CBD. Grace and I were not so keen on moving our kids in to the city and I was aware that QUT had started a partnership with Caboolture TAFE on the northern outskirts of Brisbane. I elected to set up at the Caboolture campus.

Grace and I then bought a big house just outside of Caboolture with a nice pool, a bit of acreage and a lovely creek down the back. We sat back with a sense of disbelief on the first night in our huge new house, looking up at the high timber ceilings where the kids were asleep upstairs in their bedrooms.

'Wow. Can you believe this flash big house is actually ours?' I said to her. Coming from where we had come from we never really imagined growing up and owning a house like this. It wasn't as though we felt like we didn't deserve it because we both knew very well just how hard we had worked for it. The tobacco fields, college doing two diplomas, a Bachelor's degree, two Masters degrees and a PhD, running the school and all the travel while trying to be a dad to the three littlies was hard work. Grace had also just finished her doctorate, and after many hours juggling parenting, teaching, studying and writing, it was nice for us to stop and appreciate what we had accomplished.

For me it was also great to look back on the times when my family lived at Whittred Street. I wanted our kids to have that same feeling of attachment with lots of fond memories of one particular house that they'd remember as the one they grew up in. The kids settled into the new surrounds well. Despite our nervousness about Talia starting grade one in a school with more than a thousand kids, she strode into it with confidence with just one hiccup, when her special needs teacher rang us to enquire about her 'condition'.

'We didn't know Talia had hearing problems and was blind in the right eye,' they said.

'What are you talking about?' we asked.

It seemed that when they got the student transfer forms from Cherbourg School she was listed as being visually impaired and deaf in her right ear. Grace and I were both furious. She rang the school and their response was, 'Oh, it's just a typo!' I couldn't help wondering how many other typos had occurred for other students whose parents had no idea what was going on.

At the beginning, Ezra was unsettled in such a big school but once he had cleaned up on sports day and was named Age Champion for athletics, he was away. Marcellus was ever exuberant as usual and feeling very pleased about going to a kindergarten that was right next to a train station. My big sisters Tracie and Mandy had moved close by with their families and Tracie offered to help us out by picking up the kids after school. With a new house, a new school, a new town and family around, life was great.

From modest beginnings and a frugal budget, the Institute was starting to travel well. Herb Elliott made good on his promise to support me in any way that he could to get our message out. At the time he was chairing the Telstra Foundation and he asked the foundation manager, Georgia Simmons, to come and speak with us. Georgia was another person who just knew in her heart that we could somehow find a way to deliver excellence to Aboriginal children and communities. She had been to Cherbourg many times, and, having seen and experienced the euphoria of strong and smart kids, she was keen to support us.

This was not the only corporate interest in the work of the Institute. Elaine Mogilevski and Maree Shelmerdine from the Sidney Myer Fund and Myer Foundation, two more very decent Australians with high expectations for Aboriginal children, approached me to ask what I would do if I had a million dollars to invest in Indigenous education. They explained that their foundation was more interested in investing significantly into a large project they felt would make a difference, rather than offering lots of small amounts in piecemeal ways and achieving nice outcomes, but nothing substantial.

I explained to both Telstra and Myer, our intention was to change the tide of low expectations of Indigenous children right across Australia. Both foundations were respectful and receptive when I explained how we intended to set about doing this and that we would not be changing course for the purposes of attracting dollars. I was never very good at asking people for money. I would have been more content if someone had come along and set up a substantial fund that would sustain the Institute so that we would never have to ask for money again. It would mean we could speak freely and with greater truth and conviction, rather than having to choose our words carefully so that we didn't upset whoever was in government at the time – not that I have ever been too good at telling governments what they wanted to hear when there were things they needed to hear. In this job, however, I guess it was expected that I would be out there pressing the flesh and asking people for thousands and millions of dollars. It would make me think back to those days in Bundaberg when we might have done it tough at times with no money, but we would work and earn what we needed rather than ask others. I realise there were different dynamics at play here but I still felt uncomfortable about asking for rather than earning money. Such times also caused me to reflect differently on the qualities of wealthy people and I began to realise that many, not necessarily all, harboured a genuine sense of decency and desire to make a difference to the lives of others less fortunate.

I knew that with such big dollars being discussed I needed an expert to walk with me. Rebecca Hazell was working with QUT's corporate and philanthropic area and she was an expert at handling such matters. I'd watch with envy as Rebecca would do much of the talking to the corporate people and bring me in whenever I was required. She was fantastic and she knew exactly what she was doing. Rebecca and I flew to Melbourne to meet with each board individually to explain what the Institute could do with some serious money on the table. I talked about how our approach had worked at Cherbourg and how we intended to enhance the activity of the leadership program by recruiting other people into the team to enable us to get a broader reach. We would also use the money to subsidise the cost of participating in our leadership program as we were not really in a position to run it on a straight fee-for-service model. Both the Telstra and Myer foundations agreed to invest $1.2 million. Rebecca and I were both stunned.

We found a restaurant in some trendy side street and even had a glass of champagne to celebrate. It was hard not to feel very emotional at the time. Here were some serious corporate people who were prepared to invest heavily into my work and my ideas. It was a similar feeling to when Mike Primmer and Lyn Healy signalled they absolutely trusted me to take on the role as principal at the school. I took the interest and investment of both boards seriously, and I was determined not to let them down. The only catch was we'd have to move the Institute out of the education department and into QUT as both Telstra and Myer were not so keen on sending their money into a government department.

From the outset it was clear that the people of QUT were very keen on having us in their stable. But in my discussions with

QUT leadership I was being told that I needed to be protected. In some ways I understood this, given my increased profile around the country, but in other ways I would have liked to be trusted in the same way I was trusted by others; the Aboriginal protection act had been gone for some time, after all. From my angle there was no doubt we would always deliver on what we promised. I was an Aboriginal man in charge of a significant amount of dollars, and on these matters I have always been hypersensitive about accountability and transparency.

Despite not having the most ideal governance arrangements in which we had a true sense of autonomy in our decision-making and ability to be more financially independent and transparent, we got on with the job that Telstra and Sidney Myer Foundation people had trusted us to do. With them we assembled an exceptional team of people. I poached Sharon Grose from the New South Wales education department and she would become the programs manager. She brought great skills to the Institute and with her leadership we went from delivering just four leadership programs per year in Cherbourg to fourteen. Some of these were in Cherbourg but some were held in other regional parts of Australia.

The leadership team, led by Sharon, consisted of David Spillman, Scott Gorringe and John Davis, who focussed on the delivery of the program, while Michal and Fred focussed on community engagement. I had met David and Scott in earlier days, when our paths would cross and cross serendipitously. There was always something inevitable about us finding a way of working together. David had taught for a long time in the territory but he was not one of those who think that because they had spent time there they somehow become an expert in all things Aboriginal.

But while he was in the territory for a decent period of time he developed some authentic relationships and actually did get some results that were worth hearing about. Scott was from out west. I first worked with him when he was at Roma. He and Dave had been mates for a long time and so they came to the Institute as a very good package. John had also been on my radar as a young Aboriginal educator and leader worth keeping an eye out for. He had rung me out of the blue several years earlier to find out what I was up to and if there was any opportunity for us to work together. At the time he was working in Central Office and feeling frustrated. In my mind anyone who gets frustrated working in Central Office is always worth keeping on your radar.

The injection of serious dollars and new people into the team created some growing pains as an institute. Suddenly we went from just three of us to five, and then to about fifteen on staff. There were challenges. There was less time to just sit down and chat as freely as we had done in the past, and we now had to make appointments to meet. It took some time for us to get used to that but we still got on with our work, which was building the Stronger Smarter Institute into a respected and effective organisation.

The programs we set up challenged people to take a long hard look at themselves and their practice before they pointed the finger at the complexities of Aboriginal children and their communities. The courses comprise a range of sophisticated and experiential processes and those who undergo the challenge have become quite unanimous in their determination to go back to their schools and do things differently and with high expectations. It is always interesting work as we find people at different levels of an important journey, and all of them realise after a while that quality schooling for Aboriginal children is in many ways the same as that for any child. Some people come to us searching for magic bullets with no idea about where to start and then leave realising they have to look deep inside themselves and understand some very basic, yet sophisticated, insights.

The first insight is really about understanding the existence of a negative stereotype of Aboriginal students, and the toxic influence that has on both teachers and students. It can be confronting getting participants, both black and white, to realise that each of us as individuals, through our own beliefs and behaviours, are either colluding with or being complicit with that negative stereotype. A teacher who allows an Aboriginal child to run with a snotty nose is actually colluding with the notion of Aboriginal children being unhealthy. A principal who doesn't ever engage or challenge parents about why their kids are frequently missing from school, simply accepting this as the norm for 'that' family, is actually colluding with the notion that Aboriginal children are chronic truants. Regional directors, director generals, ministers of education who are content with failure or, at best, mediocrity allow the status quo to go unchallenged and are guilty of colluding with low expectations. We learn by reflecting on our own actions or inactions around Aboriginal education.

'Why should we go out of our way to make an effort for them if they're not making an effort?' some would ask.

'Because we are the ones being paid to be in the relationship,' I usually respond.

'Why should we slog our guts out if the parents and the kids don't value education?' others would ask.

'What have you got in your school and your classrooms that is worth valuing?' I would usually respond.

The second important insight for participants is getting them to understand the importance of acknowledging and embracing positive community leadership. This was one of the resounding success factors of the Cherbourg story and it is always great when we run the program in Cherbourg and bring in some of the Aboriginal people who were central to the school's story. People would hang off every word as they spoke with such wisdom and enthusiasm. Pop John knew the significance of such forums and he always gave more than his best. There was a time, after all, like when he and I visited that regional director in Maryborough all those years ago, that many would speak and nobody would listen.

The legendary and great Hooper would be in his element, too, on these programs. He entertained people from all around Australia with his rogue streak, but within moments he would captivate them with his wisdom. Sadly, he passed away in 2007 from throat cancer. I sat with Hooper and his family in the Cherbourg Hospital in his last moments, knowing he had passed on reasonably content with the change that he wanted to see to conquer the cancer of low expectations.

As part of this insight, it is also important to understand some complexities about Indigenous leadership. Some Indigenous leaders lead in a way that can be about nurturing and perpetuating victim status. For me this is a status that lacks integrity and surrenders power. Other Indigenous leaders get caught in a seductive relationship with those in power and get handsomely rewarded when they boot the victim. Again I see this type of Indigenous leadership as lacking integrity. In the interests of a more honourable and stronger smarter future we assert the importance of embracing Indigenous leadership that is about transcending victim status.

We promoted high expectations, and I always explained the need to understand that the most important place in the entire education system was the space where a teacher stared the child in the face. This made the classrooms sacred places. Our belief is that everything that goes on in an entire education department had to be designed to enhance that most profound relationship. I knew that the principal's office is not the place where student data changes. As principal I was important in that I had to support teachers, develop their capacity and confidence, monitor their performance, challenge them, and intervene when I had to. But it is the relationship between the teacher and the student that is paramount. We'd talk a lot about this in our programs. Most people were good at doing the supporting and developing and even the monitoring, and I'd raise questions to challenge how they did their monitoring.

If a teacher had been teaching for ten years to classes of twenty-five kids, with about five Indigenous kids every year, did they ever wonder about the performance of those fifty Indigenous kids with that teacher? Perhaps they might have discovered that forty-five of those kids had failed dramatically, a ninety per cent failure rate. Was this a statistic they would be comfortable with if it was with non-Indigenous kids? These were all questions worth considering when talking about monitoring. There is always room to nudge people about how good they are at challenging their colleagues, or how courageous they were at intervening when they needed to. The challenging part meant making room for the hard conversations and to wonder about whether or not we, as individuals, our teachers, our classroom, or our schools were designed or operated with a culture of high expectations or whether we simply colluded with a negative stereotype.

The challenging questions we'd kick around were the same as I'd kicked around when I ran the school.

'What are you doing as a teacher that might be contributing to poor student outcomes?'

'What are you doing as a teacher that might be contributing to student absenteeism?'

This line of questioning simply offered a differing and more honourable angle from which to reflect on how we might contemplate making a difference. Asking such hard questions at first was often confronting for some teachers, but when I reflected back on our time at the school, we had developed a high-expectations culture in which that type of questioning did not shock anyone. They were seen as an opportunity to reflect and develop professionally rather than a time to be defensive and blame others.

On notions of intervening we'd simply ask whether or not we had the courage to exercise the hard processes to performance manage or get rid of poor performing teachers, or whether we would take the usual, and easy path of simply tolerating such teachers, thus compromising any sense of integrity and high-expectations culture. We'd also discuss the need for courage to suspend kids if it was appropriate and the difference between being culturally sensitive and colluding with low expectations. On the whole, though, we got them to understand that a high-expectations relationship was not just about carrots, and not just about sticks. It was about having the courage to be firm as well as fair, and understanding the need for courage as well as compassion.

The final insight was just about the need for innovative approaches to school modelling and school staffing. Here we'd say if we always did what we always got, then we'd always get what we always got. It's a simple message that encourages educators to have the courage to try new things if the established ways of doing things in classrooms and schools is returning data that we would never accept for our own children, but somehow we've accepted for Indigenous children.

The Institute quickly developed a national profile as Australia's leading agency in Indigenous education. With an excellent team to work with I could afford to be involved more in challenging, influencing and reviewing education and Indigenous policy agenda on a national scale. There were many occasions when I would get a call from someone saying they had the next best literacy or numeracy product that was going to fix everything in Aboriginal communities. All they needed from me was an endorsement or to open up some doors to key politicians to let them know how great they were. They'd also offer a percentage or some kind of generous monetary reward for being a strong advocate of whatever program they had to offer. It got to a point where we had to develop our standard line for such people and their products: the Institute does not endorse products! It might have been a very lucrative source of revenue but it was just not right to think that one particular product could offer the solutions to literacy in communities that we were not extensively involved with. It was also not right to get in the way of school principals, whose role it was to examine in consultation with their staff and communities which literacy or numeracy program was best for their children.

In 2007 the Victorian department of education invited me to review their four Koori schools, which were located at Morwell, Glenroy, Swan Hill and Mildura. As I had signalled from the outset I thought the VCOKE (Victorian College of Koorie Education) concept was an excellent one with exceptional potential, but it was established with mindsets and personnel that were anything but exceptional. My instincts at the time told me that they knew the schools were a train wreck and, knowing I would have the courage to call it as it was, they could take dramatic measures based on my considered opinion.

What I saw was chronic collusion with low expectations. The schools were attached as annexes to mainstream schools from the outset, and this led to them usually being staffed with teachers that could not cut it in the mainstream part of the school. Some were okay and trying really hard. Not only were they a dumping ground for teachers that would not be tolerated in mainstream schools, they also became a dumping ground for students, black and white, who became a little bit hard to manage. Of all of the conversations I had as part of that review the line that stuck most prominently in my mind came from a parent reporting what a teacher from a mainstream school had said to his child: 'If you keep playing up like this you're gonna have to go down to the coon school down the road!' It adequately summed up what many people thought and how they felt about this concept.

Clearly dramatic measures were required as there was a heavy financial investment in the schools. All of the VCOKE schools were exceedingly well resourced but the quality of the education was mired in the culture of low expectations. As a result, many parents had pulled their children out of the school, just like they had done at Cherbourg, and went looking to other schools for a better education for their children. In some schools there were more staff than students.

We spoke to parents whose kids went to the school as well as parents who had put their kids in other schools. The parents with kids in the school were fierce in their support of it. They wanted it kept open, right or wrong. The problem as I saw it was they were being told their kids were getting a great education, but from where I was sitting it looked like very expensive, yet poor-quality, babysitting, apart from the cultural programs that were being run. Cultural programs are really great in schools and this is what can make kids strong, but on its own this is not enough. Schools have to ensure that kids are smart as well.

I felt sorry for these parents. In the community consultations they really went for me in some places. With my ego left outside I didn't mind this so much as underneath all of the shouting and placards was a deep sense of concern about their kids' education. You can hardly knock them for this. There was no reason to doubt, too, that the education experience they were getting prob-ably was better than anything they'd had in a mainstream school. In spite of this I maintained that they deserved even better and there was the potential for them to thrive in an environment with an authentic high-expectations agenda and culture.

There is no evidence to suggest that an all-Indigenous school would produce better outcomes for Indigenous kids. The evi-dence is clear, however, that Indigenous kids do very well in a school where there are quality teachers, quality leadership and quality relationships with parents and the community. The school culture had to be intent on nurturing a positive sense of student and cultural identity as well as high expectations about student learning.

What I liked most about doing this review was seeing the tenacity of the Koori parents and community to retain something of an education facility in their community. Even those parents who had abandoned the school still signalled the importance of having something. Against this background I had recommended the VCOKE schools be refocussed on early education and getting kids well prepared for schooling, with a substantial amount of the funds in question being redirected to better support the mainstream schools that many of the Koori students had already turned to. To me it made good sense to focus on the kids in that zero to five years bracket to get them engaged in early literacy and numeracy so they can sight-read, know the alphabet, love books, write their name and count to a hundred, before they even got to grade one. Despite what I considered reasonably bold yet sound recommendations, it seems the government of the day was more content with a mediocre status quo that was less politically charged.

The other major review I helped lead was in the Northern Territory. Marion Scrymgour, a really sharp and charismatic Aboriginal leader from the Tiwi Islands, was the deputy chief minister and education minister at the time and she asked for me specifically to be involved in a major review of the structure of her education department and comment on its effectiveness. Not long into the review, and to no surprise at all, it was clear that remote Aboriginal schools in the territory had been left to starve at the end of the vine. Some places had lots of great kids, but not even a full-time teacher available to them.

At one of the schools in a large remote community we were picked up at the airstrip by the principal and almost immediately we were informed about all of the dramas and dysfunction in the community. Sadly, I was accustomed to this kind of diatribe, as I had heard it so many times before. It is always refreshing to be greeted by someone bursting with enthusiasm to tell you about the good things and the strengths that exist in such places.

At the commencement of the school tour I asked the principal how many kids were enrolled in the secondary school.

'Well . . . we made sixty lunches today,' she replied.

'Okay,' I said, but I was thinking, 'I didn't ask you about lunches. I asked about kids. When I was fifteen I could eat three lunches so why the smoke and mirrors?'

We stopped by to see some kids jamming on drums and electric guitars with a few young Aboriginal men who had come in to volunteer and show the kids some cool beats.

'Good stuff,' I thought. 'That's as good as anything you'd see in other schools.'

We meandered on through the arts room. With anticipation loaded by knowing that artists from this community were world famous and hung their work in the best galleries in Europe, I asked her about how they integrated local artists into their arts program.

'We don't really have much involvement from local artists and their work doesn't really fit into the curriculum.' In her next breath she was telling me just how frustrating it was to get local involvement in the school. If I was a world-renowned artist being ignored and dishonoured in this way I'm not sure that I would be too keen to be involved with the school either. The day was not going so well, it's fair to say.

At morning tea, like in a few remote Aboriginal community schools I have seen, the white teachers all sat inside enjoying their space on a comfy lounge in air-conditioned comfort, having a conversation about what crazy thing some kid had done, or how many fish they caught, or what their plans were for the next holidays. The Aboriginal staff sat on the ground outside under a tree. Sure, they were having a good laugh and they were allowed to come into the staffroom, but there was something despicable and something telling about why they were not all sitting together. Observing this did not put me in a good frame of mind for the conversation I was due to have with the principal and her two deputies.

'The teachers and the programs are really good here. It's just that the kids don't want anything to do with them,' she led with authority. It's probably a line that had worked consistently for her with others in the past, and it's one I'd heard before.

'So how good can these programs be if kids don't want anything to do with them?' I asked, with a slightly belligerent tone fuelled by the images of all those black staff sitting outside under a tree. Their reaction was one of slight shock and defensiveness as I'm not sure they'd been asked such a question.

'Oh, well . . . you don't really understand what it is like here. You're not from here!'

'Here we go,' I thought. I had heard all of this before, too.

'There's a lot of alcoholism and gambling in the community. There's lots of sexual abuse and violence that goes on here. It makes it hard to get kids engaged when you've got all that going on!'

'Okay . . . so let me get this straight,' I responded, taking a deep breath and trying to calm myself down at the same time. 'You're telling me that the kids in this community choose to locate themselves among alcoholism, gambling, sexual abuse and gambling, rather than turn up to your air-conditioned school and access these programs that you say are so great!' I was livid. 'If that's where they choose to be instead of at your "great" school, then what the hell does that say about your school, do you reckon?'

The three of them were stunned. They offered no response and I didn't allow them time to.

'Anyway, look. I gotta go to the toilet,' I said, as I got up and walked to the door. 'I'll meet you guys outside,' I said to my colleagues in the room with us. I didn't really need to go to the toilet. I was just so furious I felt it was better to walk out before I started swearing or saying anything unprofessional. Of course, it was true that there were dramatic complexities in the community but these were the same things that existed in Cherbourg, as they do in lots of communities struggling to throw off legacies of an ugly past. Surely, we owe it to vulnerable children swamped by such complexity to give them at least one place in their life where the environment is positive, productive and predictable – an environment where they are praised for their efforts, rewarded for good behaviour and delivered consequences for inappropriate behaviour. Surely, in such places we can offer them an environment that offers intellectual stimulation and integrity so they might dream big dreams and actually have a real opportunity to transcend such complexity.

It does not seem a lot to ask, and the needs in the territory are just the same, in many ways, as they are for Koori kids in Victoria: quality schools with quality leaders and teachers, and quality relationships with the community. But a political football, in the shape of the Northern Territory Intervention, was heading the way of these communities and that still has a lasting negative effect on their ability to rise above the low expectations society has of them.

12

A world beyond expectations

In 2007 I was working in Perth with educators from the Catholic Education sector when the Northern Territory Intervention was announced. With no Tampa boat on the horizon, no way to conjure a children overboard story, and no September 11-type attacks to scare the voters, they seemed desperate for an electoral rabbit to pull out of the hat. After eleven years in office the prime minister decided he cared deeply for Aboriginal children – it seemed there might be votes in appearing concerned, and there are always votes in sinking the boot into blackfullas. The Northern Territory Intervention was born out of political desperation and engineered by people who had no idea.

My phone was running hot with media asking my thoughts about it.

'Yes, we want things to change in remote communities. Yes, we want to see an increased injection of funds to make a difference. But change will only happen if we do things with people not to them!' I would say with futility to journo after journo.

The Intervention rolled on like a juggernaut, inflicted on Aboriginal people of the Territory. To me it had seemed a despicable approach that lacked any sense of humanity. Of course there was a need for some type of intervention, but not in a way that just assumed everyone was hopeless and not worthy of being treated like people. Even to this day, I have seared in my mind the memory of a young Aboriginal guy in Alice Springs. I was there as chair of the Aboriginal and Torres Strait Islander Arts Board reviewing how we were doing Arts funding across Australia.

'Chris, you don't know just how hard it is to be an Aboriginal man in this town! You walk down the street here and these people just look at you like you're some kind of paedophile or like you're just comin' from bashing your woman at home.'

He spoke with a deep sense of hurt. My heart broke for him.

I recalled a similar sense of hurt and bewilderment from three old Alice Springs ladies who came to see me after I delivered a keynote address at a Newcastle University conference. It is difficult to know what to say to such dignified and honourable women who had worked tirelessly in their local school for more than twenty-five years, when they explained how they wanted to buy some gifts for their grandchildren while in Newcastle but couldn't. They had money in their bank accounts but the government decided which shops they could spend it in, and those shops were back in the Northern Territory.

I became more incensed as I thought about the architects of this dreadful policy. They would never be interested in hearing the testimony of people who actually lived in a remote community unless they told them what they wanted to hear. Disappointingly, there were some blackfullas who were losing faith in the ancient strength and wisdom of their people and they had jumped ship, dancing to the tunes of the corporate and political masters, telling them what they wanted to hear with their booting-the-victim leadership. The government was only interested in picking up a few anecdotes here and there to justify this expensive and ineffective approach. Even today they spruik on about how they are listening, telling us about how some old ladies whisper to them, 'We want this,' while thousands upon thousands of others are yelling in the street, 'STOP THE INTERVENTION!'

To make it worse there was a great deal of hot air blowing around about evidence-based policy, while all the evidence was actually screaming out that such approaches were dramatically expensive and ineffective. This was Passion Pop policy for Dom Perignon prices. Somebody must have been doing well from it, but it certainly wasn't the blackfullas who bore the brunt of it.

With much fanfare Kevin '07 rolled John Howard and this brought a great deal of hope for Aboriginal Australians. It also brought promise for the Institute and our high-expectations agenda. So far we had established ourselves with a good reputation across Australia, primarily with funding from Telstra and Myer. Finally, we had a federal government that knew we existed, and were interested in hearing from us. It also seemed like they were interested in Indigenous education, too. Within one week of them winning the election I had a call on my mobile from a senior staffer from the office of the deputy prime minister and minister for education.

'We're just wanting to open a dialogue with a broader range of people, and people we think have something to offer,' he said. This was fantastic, particularly given there was absolutely no interest from the previous government. Through this dialogue I was keen to support the 'education revolution' agenda because it was refreshing to hear the government, especially someone as high as the deputy prime minister, actually talking about and having a serious interest in education.

I'd always had an interest in greater measures for transparency and accountability for schools, more so in relation to remote Aboriginal schools. I had seen too many school leaders telling their communities that everything was going great, when the reality was things were dramatically substandard. Aboriginal parents with kids who were at the top of the class and getting As on their report cards would sadly often discover that A was worth little more than a D in a mainstream school. This had to change, and so I welcomed new measures that would let parents in Kowanyama, Yuendemu, Wingelina, Kalumburu or any other remote location truly know how their children were going compared with places like Sydney, Melbourne, Bundaberg, Orange or Geraldton.

Of course, there are limitations with national and statewide diagnostic testing regimes, particularly with kids of different ethnic backgrounds. There has been for the past fifty years and there will be for the next half-century. But I would rather have something than nothing, in this case, so that parents can at least have access to a comparable yardstick and benchmarks. It's fair to say there was a lot of kickback from our profession about such national measures, although I found that it was often those who were threatened by a greater sense of transparency and accountability. It became pretty much impossible for a teacher with low expectations to hide in a school anywhere in the country now without some inevitability about being challenged about the data they were responsible for. The hardworking teachers were generally not the least bit threatened by these measures.

In a conversation with the legendary Queensland Rugby League State of Origin coach Mal Meninga, I found a useful analogy about NAPLAN and the MYSchool website that I often shared with other principals and teachers. He had just finished saying to me, 'No thanks, Chris, but keep your phone handy just in case,' after I let him know I still had my old footy boots and mouthguard and was still available for Origin selection.

'Mal, you know how your boys have been winning so consistently over the last few years? How do you get them focussed so that you get the best out of them, without them getting complacent?'

Mal is an exceptional and profound thinker and he said to me, 'It's not about the scoreboard, Chris. When I send my boys onto the field all I ask of them individually is to give their best and a bit more if they can. We never worry about the scoreboard because if they focus on giving their best and a bit more, then the scoreboard will take care of itself!'

It struck me as an excellent message for teachers and principals worried about NAPLAN and the MYSchool website. To me this was the scoreboard, and our classrooms and schools were the field. As educators, if we each focussed on giving our best to our children, then the scoreboard would take care of itself. It is a gem of an analogy and I refer to it often. I also keep my phone handy during the lead-up to State of Origin just in case Mal needs me!

The other profoundly significant moment I was so lucky to be a part of was Kevin Rudd's Apology to members of the stolen generations. I sat in the public gallery of the House of Representatives chamber, just behind New South Wales Premier Morris Iemma. We made small talk about our shared Italian heritage, but there was nothing small about the moment in that house. For a long time I had publicly supported the notion of a public apology, even during the time when it was not popular. Others had been well lauded for huffing and puffing, suggesting that saying sorry or walking across a bridge would not help people in communities get a job. I can see why such posturing appealed to the previous government as they created a binary in which we were all supposed to appreciate the need for 'practical reconciliation' rather than 'symbolic reconciliation'. To me this is a classic manoeuvre that is often deployed to cloud important or complex issues by those where courage and leadership is required. I could never see why there should be a choice. Surely we were a sophisticated and mature enough nation to deliver on both practical and symbolic reconciliation simultaneously.

It was a wonderful and euphoric day. In a strange way I think Howard's nagging and persistent yearning for the past in relation to this, and his barren sense of ability to take Australia to a newer and more honourable future, somehow contributed to the excitement of the day. He had nurtured a period in which the genuine pain and hurt of fellow Australians was ignored, with no idea that when you do this those raw emotions are exacerbated. It was like a balloon getting bigger and bigger with more tension built each time the pleas for acknowledgement were ignored. Kevin Rudd's apology and acknowledgement of that pain, hurt and anger was like the pin that would finally burst that ever-tense bubble of raw emotion. With that many, not all, were able to move on in life not getting so frustrated about this lie we were all living.

After this phenomenal occasion I made my way to the morning tea just outside the chamber. On my way I dropped in to see Maxine McKew in her office. At the time she was parliamentary secretary in the education department and she was keen to hear about our high-expectations approach. I went out of my way to also meet Jenny Macklin, and thanked her for the invitation. Kevin Rudd was like a rock star that day, and as I sat and listened to him making another speech I noticed another politician who awed me: Gough Whitlam and his tall and graceful wife, Margaret. Normally I am too shy and introverted to go out of my way to say hello to people on such occasions but for Gough I just had to make an effort. He was sitting in a wheelchair to my left and so I reached over to shake hands with the great man.

'Hello, Mr Whitlam. My name is Chris Sarra and I am very honoured to meet you,' I said, feeling out of my comfort zone but buzzing with excitement.

'It's very nice to meet you,' he said in a way so manifestly statesmanlike.

'He's doing a great job today, 'ay, Mr Whitlam?' I said of Kevin Rudd, without trying to annoy him.

'I think he's going to be one of Australia's great prime ministers,' he replied, with that voice and tone I had tried to emulate with friends so many times before.

'Yeah,' I said.

'But you will always be Australia's greatest prime minister, 'ay, Mr Whitlam?' I added.

It brought a wonderful smile to his face as his eyes looked up to engage mine.

'Well, that's very nice of you to say so, son!' he said, with his voice tapering off in a way that would render his remaining comments inaudible. I think he was agreeing with me.

While the change in government brought fresh and innovative approaches to education, the dreadful stench of the Intervention remained, despite a great sense of hope for more honourable approaches to reform. There was also a lot of hot air and huffing and puffing about 'mutual' responsibilities, but the restrictions being inflicted, draconically, on Aboriginal people in remote communities only, with absolutely no questions being raised about the quality of non-Aboriginal service providers in those same places. There was nothing mutual about this.

With the thought of those old ladies I'd met at Newcastle and the hurt in the voice of the guy from Alice Springs, I could not sit by and say nothing. By now I had something of a profile with the media and with the Australian public. In my heart I felt that if I had at least some scope to speak up and be heard on behalf of others, then I must speak up.

On many occasions I had visited communities and had the opportunity to have a good look at what was really going on. It wasn't hard to get a sense of the quality of some of the teachers, principals, shopkeepers, council managers and gatekeepers, who had landed a job in a remote Aboriginal community, probably because they were unemployable in mainstream locations – the saying rang true: missionaries, mercenaries, misfits and madmen. Of course, it was not true of all white people in remote communities. There were some very decent, very authentic white people who were deeply committed, deeply passionate, highly effective and extremely hard working, but you could not say this about all of them.

I wrote an article to run in the *Weekend Australian* that raised a simple challenge: if we are going to have a conversation about 'mutual responsibilities' then let's be completely honest. Rather than be one-sided and only run strategies and processes that inflict restrictions on Aboriginal people, let's start questioning the quality of non-Aboriginal service providers in those communities. Like a lot of blackfullas, and those hard-working white people in communities, I was absolutely fed up with this situation where a warm body that was upright and with a heartbeat was considered good enough to be a teacher in a remote school. It was time these people and the people who put them there were challenged, especially when it seemed that only blackfullas were being blamed for disastrous education outcomes and other types of social dysfunction.

I was resolute about this challenge for a number of reasons. I had seen the pitiable quality of some of these people; I had read and thought deeply, intellectually and philosophically about these challenges; but the most significant reason of all, is that I had watched with my own eyes, a school and a community transformed by flushing out the deadwood and replacing them with exceptional people. Furthermore, the drama and dysfunction that people would describe in relation to some of those schools and communities was the same as that used to describe Cherbourg before I got there. I knew from my heart and from what I had seen with my own eyes, that a different, more honourable, and more effective, approach was possible.

Justine Ferrari from *The Australian* rang me to run a story alongside my article for the weekend paper as I was saying something different from the usual propaganda being peddled. We had built up a good relationship over time and I trusted her, despite numerous people telling me to never trust journalists. In her usual insightful way, she was quickly onto the challenge I was raising.

'So, you're saying that if the quality of teachers and principals in remote schools was better, then results would be more likely to improve?' she clarified.

'That's precisely what I'm saying,' I replied.

Drilling down further she asked, 'So how come remote schools end up with the poor-quality teachers and principals?'

'In a really crude way, Justine,' I said, cringing, as I knew what I was about to say, 'it's a bit like remote Aboriginal communities are the place where you tuck away your white trash, and it's not only teachers. There are all sorts of second-rate-performing white people tucked away in remote communities because they are not considered good enough in other places. It's not a nice thing to say, but if we can't have an honest conversation about mutual responsibilities, if we are not prepared to question the quality of these people and the people who put them there, what's the point?'

I had to go to Weipa for a few days to visit the school and talk with the teachers and students, and to catch up on my good mate and colleague Ian Mackie. He had just been appointed executive principal at Western Cape College after putting in some hard yards at Aurukun. We had done a bit of work with him and a lot of his teachers through our leadership program. Aurukun was renowned as one of the hardest schools in Queensland and under his leadership things had turned around dramatically; for instance, attendance jumped from below forty per cent to above seventy. Ian's wife Liz took over from him as principal and was building on his momentum, attracting quality teachers and forging a positive relationship with the community. Ian and I drove up from Weipa to Aurukun, mainly to visit the teachers and offer them some words of encouragement. It was a school heading in the right direction, where both Ian and Liz had built a good team of committed young teachers. There was still a lot of room for improvement, but after many years of extraordinarily hard work, things were finally heading in the right direction.

I flew out of Aurukun at lunchtime on Friday and had a stopover in Cairns. Reluctantly, I turned the mobile phone on, anticipating a text saying I had lots and lots of messages. Before I'd actually dialled to hear them Justine Ferrari was calling me.

'Hi Chris, how's it going?' she asked.

I was feeling great and I explained to her just how good it was to see that Aurukun school finally seemed to be on the move and heading in the right direction after so many principals and teachers had tried and failed there.

'Hey, Chris, the reason I'm calling is because you know how in our conversation the other day you talked about remote communities being the place where we tuck away our white trash?'

'Yeah,' I said, not too certain about where this was going.

'Well, they want to run a headline using that term and it will probably be controversial, so I just wanted to check if you would be okay about this. We can change it if you want to but I just wanted to check and see how you felt about it.'

Strangely enough I'd had some kind of premonition about being embroiled in a scandal about using the term 'white trash' in the public media arena.

'Hmm . . . okay . . . let me think!'

A swift and sophisticated conversation started in my head. I really hated the term and any other such derogatory pejoratives, having known what it feels like to be called a black cunt or coon or boong. I really hated that feeling of being stereotyped and being unfairly judged according to the stupid actions of others. I then thought about those people in the Northern Territory. Infinitely more than any of the name calling and stereotyping, I hated what was happening to them. For a moment I was concerned that I had just been in Aurukun talking and rallying up the morale of teachers, and if this came out in the next day's paper they might think I was talking about them. But I was really sticking up for them and all of those other hard-working white teachers who slogged their guts out in a community school, while the other teachers got the same pay for letting kids watch videos or play games all day. I reflected on the relationship and the level of emotional credit I had with the Australian public. By my reckoning I had enough emotional credit to say something like that and attract enough attention to this issue, without damaging my reputation and going into the red. Overwhelmingly it felt like something I had to do. As an educator I knew the most profound learning occurs when we can invoke an emotional response in an individual, and then capitalise on this as an opportunity to reflect on those feelings and learn from them. There was no question this would invoke an emotional response and I saw it as an opportunity to help other people understand what it felt like to be stereotyped or called names.

After what seemed like just short of an hour but was in reality was more like seconds I got back to Justine.

'Okay, let's do this!' I said, with confidence shadowed by apprehension.

'You're sure about this?' she asked again.

'Yep, let's do it!'

It wasn't so much wanting people to have a taste of their own medicine, because not all white people engage in such despicable ways of talking. It was more that I wanted people to have a moment to feel what it was like to be stereotyped. I knew that if I made people angry in this way, then I could ask them to take those feelings of anger and frustration, and imagine that multiplied by the number of times a black person might be stereotyped in life. I thought if they could do this then they might be able to understand and appreciate just how frustrating and infuriating it is. Even so, and in spite of their moment of anger, those people would still have the luxury of simply turning the page and moving on, with little happening. I knew that when a black person is stereotyped things really do affect their lives, and they can't take off their black skin and move on in the same way.

The conversation and the potential ramifications of this occupied my mind on the entire flight home, and still persisted as I lay down in bed that night.

'People will be going crazy over this!' I thought, as I did a lousy job of going to sleep. I just kept thinking of those old ladies and that guy in Alice Springs, and all of the other blackfullas being treated unfairly and inhumanely in remote parts of the territory. I was also mindful of those Aboriginal women and children in complex circumstances and I knew we could do better. Somebody had to stick up for them.

I had switched my phone off, anticipating lots of messages, and when I turned it on the first message I got was a text from my good mate and colleague Catherine O'Sullivan. Catherine was a charismatic high flyer in the Commonwealth department of education, but we had been buddies from way back in our school principal days. She had transformed schooling at Goondiwindi State High School when I was at Cherbourg.

'Stay strong. I'm here to support you if you need it.'

By this stage I hadn't even read the paper. There were also voicemail messages from Leigh Schelks, Don Andersen and Ian Mackie, all offering strident support. These were people who knew exactly what I was talking about.

I went up to the shop to buy the paper. Despite knowing the crassness of the headline I still could not help cringing again when I actually saw it on the front page of *The Australian* in print: 'White Trash Let Aborigines Down.'

'Actually,' I thought, 'that kind of says it all succinctly.'

The tragedy in all of this was that the story I wrote was pretty good, I thought. It was thoughtful and challenging, yet polite, and not the least bit controversial. When I got home the next call on the home number was my mother-in-law.

'Good on you, boy! Somebody had to say it like it is. And don't you dare apologise to anyone.'

I always loved getting calls from her about things I'd said or written in papers. My mum called me also. She is as feisty as anyone on matters like this but on this occasion she was decidedly more apprehensive. She was worried about my safety.

'Chris, you can't just talk like that. You gotta watch these white people. You don't know what they'll do!' There was a genuine fear and concern in her voice. I wasn't going to argue my case with Mum. She knew very well what this was all about given her journey in life.

Among the many other calls of support, and those from journalists, was Jeff McMullen. Jeff had become like a big, wise and worldly brother to me. He described my comments and my article as like a red-hot poker into the conscience of white Australia. It was a vivid and truthful analogy, although I still really hated having to do this. The journalists were asking me if I resented my comments and whether I wanted to apologise. Without apologising, I did give some ground to them by conceding that instead of using the term 'white trash' I probably should have said 'lazy and incompetent'. I'm not sure this would have sparked the same level of debate, though.

Lots of people on the blogs went absolutely nuts, just as I expected them to do. My nemesis that led the attacks back in Cherbourg, from behind the signatures of others, joined in with much delight, albeit under a pseudonym, just as I expected her to do. I tried to engage people online to provide a deeper context to my comments. Some people were swayed, which was good, but some were just downright crazy.

In response to assertions that I was being racist I felt like saying, 'I'm not a racist. Some of my best friends are white people!' I wanted to get at that dynamic of when some white person having an Aboriginal friend is a passport to running other blackfullas down or somehow makes it okay to harbour racist views and ignorance or tell offensive and pathetic racist jokes.

Most of all, though, I just wanted to say, 'Yes, calling people nasty names is wrong. Yes, stereotyping is wrong. And you know what, it really hurts, doesn't it? So now that you have a little insight into what it feels like, stop doing it to others!'

It was a bit pious, and a bit nasty in some ways, but I didn't want to miss this opportunity to help people learn. Of course it created discomfort for lots of people, but I just kept thinking the discomfort those people felt on that Saturday morning was nothing like the discomfort of those brave people from the Northern Territory, or the discomfort of a fourteen-year-old Aboriginal young person who cannot read or write because they have never seen a quality teacher in their life. It was nothing like the discomfort of those young Aboriginal boys or girls I had known who decided suicide was a more favourable option to continuing life.

On the Monday morning there was damage control to be done. While it was an uncomfortable message, the Australian Education Union and the Queensland Teachers' Union understood exactly what I was trying to do and the need to challenge such teachers who undermined our professional reputation. They rallied in behind me as the Queensland education department continued to stick its head in the sand and pretend that such criticism was unfounded. What I didn't anticipate, and I truly regretted, was anecdotal reports of some Aboriginal students using the term 'white trash' with some of their teachers. While the context of this issue was extremely complex, I didn't want to be a kind of leader that validated the use of such terms. As someone pointed out to me, though, an Aboriginal child would not ever use such a term if the relationship with their teachers was respectable.

On balance there was much more support for me than against me, and, while it was a difficult and dramatic period, it was something I felt I had to do. At the time the catchcry to attract teachers to the Northern Territory was something like, 'Come to the Northern Territory and have an adventure!' with some veiled reference in there about teaching kids somewhere. Today the catchcry for the Territory education department is, 'Are you good enough?' This represents a profound and essential shift in thinking and I like to think my efforts to expose the quality of teachers and a principal has influenced this. Today, teachers are told they are not good enough to teach in a remote school, and it is understood that for remote schools a teacher must be a top gun, which is what the data demands, which is what Aboriginal parents and children demand, and which is how it should have been all along.

Now that we were on the radar of the federal government and we actually had a positive relationship with them, there was room to contemplate how we could take the work of the Institute to the next level. It was a relationship in which our good work and actual results were acknowledged and respected, as opposed to one in which we'd swear at, bully or intimidate politicians or bureaucrats. If we wanted to see stronger smarter, then we had to be stronger smarter.

I take being an Aboriginal leader seriously. For me it is about demonstrating I have good intellect, integrity and humility to offer rather than just my blackness. It is also about climbing the ladder of success so that we can put out more ladders for others to climb, rather than feeling threatened and turning to kick those below us.

We had been very effective with our leadership programs so far, but there would always be some inevitable challenges to respond to. The content of the leadership program was based on the work at Cherbourg School when I was there as principal, and inevitably with time, the story would get old and lose its currency, and I would become ever distant from actually being a practising school principal. It was also obvious that we would still be unable to get a broad reach across Australia unless we modelled some new ways of engaging other educators and community people.

Annette Rutherford, my cousin and colleague, had done one of the early leadership programs and she floated the brilliant idea of taking things to the next level by developing a series of stronger smarter learning communities across Australia. It was a bit like an Institute's associates model in which we could identify at least sixty schools throughout Australia that were living and breathing stronger smarter. They had to have a school culture that nurtured a positive sense of identity, embraced positive Indigenous leadership, high-expectations relationships, and flexible and innovative approaches to school modelling and staffing. The Institute could then be in a high-expectations relationship with them in a way in which we would support and develop their capacity to support, develop and challenge three or four schools around them.

As part of the stronger smarter philosophy we talk a lot about strengths-based approaches to reform. This applied not only to individuals and communities but also to bureaucracies. As cumbersome as they can be, it would have been hypocritical for us to assume that everything about education department bureaucracies was useless, and so it was worth identifying the good. With the learning communities project we could work with aspects of the bureaucracy that were working soundly and then build upon that capacity to make a difference. This was a more sustainable approach to making a difference as well as a notion I had learned from watching others trying to making a difference by creating massive and expensive new quasi-bureaucracies to do what the initial bureaucracy was supposed to do in the first place. That was an approach that just didn't make sense to me. The trick here was to get the existing structures to work more effectively, and this way the positive changes could be extrapolated in a way more sustainable, affordable and logical.

It was a model that was very well understood by people in Julia Gillard's office. They saw great merit in it as a project that would create vibrant learning and sharing hubs across the country with opportunities for stronger smarter teachers to lead and influence other teachers, for stronger smarter principals to lead and influence other principals. It's one of those things you come to learn as an insider to the education profession – teachers and principals are most influenced by other teachers and principals who are in schools now, and who can show both what they are doing, and the results they are getting.

In October 2009 our Stronger Smarter Learning Communities proposal was approved and Julia Gillard, who came to our inaugural Stronger Smarter Summit to announce the sixteen-million-dollar project. She would also announce a name change from the Indigenous Education Leadership Institute to the Stronger

Smarter Institute. This significant funding announcement would mark an important moment in my career and the history of the Institute. It represented an opportunity to really shift the dialogue about what education standards we as a nation consider good enough for Aboriginal and Torres Strait Islander children. Although it meant I had to reflect seriously on the responsibility of being in control of this substantial amount of money, and it was public money. After the announcement I was open with the media and made it very clear that I took this matter very seriously, particularly as I had watched other Indigenous leaders crucified by allegations of misspent funds.

It was also a moment in which the leadership at QUT, with tremendous enthusiasm about our ability to attract such a significant amount of funds, continued signalling grave concerns about our ability to execute this large project successfully. I had been defiant about our ability to deliver on this project, given that we had been overwhelmingly successful in the delivery of the leadership program, and I made this clear as I stood confidently by the deputy prime minister taking questions from a barrage of radio, print and television journalists. It felt as though we were giving them something they had never heard before. We were telling them that Indigenous children did have a right to a good-quality education. We told them we did believe that children, no matter where they came from, or how complex their lives were, had the ability to fly high, given the right conditions of a quality school with quality people around them.

Margaret Wenham, a *Courier-Mail* journalist whom I had known from previous interviews and lengthy conversations, jumped in when she could.

'Dr Sarra, what is the significance of the name change from

Indigenous Education Leadership Institute to the Stronger Smarter Institute?'

'Well it's much easier answering the phones now! That's significant!' I replied candidly. I then went into a more profound response describing how the stronger smarter approach is not only effective for Indigenous kids, it is effective for all kids, particularly poor white kids from tough suburbs. Somebody had to stick up for them, too, and the new title would enable us to encompass them with a broader reach. And then she nailed me.

'So what do you think about the federal government supporting initiatives to link welfare payments to school attendance?'

'Not today,' I thought. It was a question I wanted to avoid so we could remain positive and focus on the stronger smarter approach. I forced a wry smile at her and she returned one. She knew that she'd nailed me, but not in any malicious way. In response I offered unremarkable weasel words like, 'There are different people with different points of view on this, and I guess we have to try a range of ideas see what works.' That even made me cringe a bit when I said them. The truth is I absolutely despise the notion of linking welfare payments to school attendance.

From my perspective it has always been an approach that assumes the true cause of disengagement from school resides entirely with the child or their family when, based on my experience, this just isn't true. There are often complex reasons for kids' truancy and it has always been my belief that as teachers and principals, because we're paid to do a job, we must reflect on our own practice first before we point the finger elsewhere. As policy rhetoric it might appear to work because it is politically sexy to be seen to be going tough on welfare recipients, but in reality it is an approach with dramatically exorbitant financial costs but dramatically insignificant results. Through various media forums I have tried to argue the ineffectiveness of this approach, which is based purely on the shabby economics. It is an approach that undermines what is so fundamental to the successful engagement of kids in schools: a positive relationship with the school. We would get far better results spending a few thousand here and there creating jobs for people in communities to liaise between the principal and their family groups to develop more positive relationships. It would be far better to nurture positive relationships between schools and parents, rather than dramatically undermining it by turning school personnel into watchdogs who have to report people to the welfare department. It often prevents teachers and principals from reflecting on what they need to change in their schools; instead they say, 'If we can get away with blaming the kids or the parents, then why not?'

I've watched millions of dollars wasted on the salaries of bureaucrats to execute these policies when far better results would occur spending just a few hundred dollars here and there to reward and promote attendance as a positive behaviour. As a taxpayer I despise that it costs so much yet is relatively ineffective and inefficient compared with more positive and honourable approaches.

At times, though, it seems to me that some would rather see millions of dollars wasted on ineffective policies that demonise Aboriginal people and poor white people, rather than hundreds of dollars spent on ways that honour and invest in what is good about them.

The positive stronger smarter approach is more efficient, more honourable and far more effective. We have seen unexplained absenteeism fall, with attendance jumping from sixty-two per cent to ninety-four. I have watched children from some of the toughest, most chaotic home environments one could imagine be at school at half past seven every morning without fail. A girl who missed almost half of the first six years of school because her absence went unquestioned missed only six days of Year 7 when we challenged her to realise she was smart, and to be stronger and smarter, she needed to go to school. She went on to finish among the top students at her high school. We saw a situation where parents had no idea their kids were missing from school to submitting medical certificates to explain why their child was away because they didn't want their kids to miss out on a good education or the rewards being offered for students who attended regularly. I know it works because our team and the community worked together on even the most intractable challenges. I have watched it happen with my own eyes.

The other policy in Indigenous education that has to be challenged is the notion of private school scholarships. Some schools have had a long association with remote Aboriginal communities and families, and this is commendable. But from what I have observed there is plenty of room for questions. I usually respond to media questions about this with more questions. Why do private schools turn up only when the government puts lots of money into a scheme? If the money wasn't available, would they still be interested in helping Aboriginal children? In some ways these questions can be a little harsh, but they have to be asked. Schools that come riding out of the sunset to save Aboriginal children by offering them scholarships might think they offer a bridge to a brighter future, but it is often a tightrope fraught with difficulty. Consider the ramifications of a child leaving their community and failing, then feeling too ashamed to go back. On many occasions there is no going forwards and no going back for these kids.

I became even more cynical about these scholarships when I watched two of our strongest and smartest girls at Cherbourg take up such a scholarship, only to find it was not such a rosy experience. One of the girls went to an exclusive girls' school in Brisbane and was booted out the moment it got hard. She was backed into a corner by some of the other girls, who taunted her with racist remarks that went continually unchecked. When she lashed back in the only way she knew how, she was the one excluded. I got the feeling the school was glad to see her go, and they had already received the funding for her placement for the year. The other girl went to an exclusive school in Toowoomba and her experience was even more infuriating. When she came back to Cherbourg after being shown the door when it got a little bit hard, she said to me, 'They didn't really care about us. The only time they were interested in us was when the TV cameras and the newspaper and magazine people came to the school. Then they would bring us right up the front to be in the pictures.'

These were just two stories among many more about kids being sent hundreds of kilometres away from home and family, to a school that has no idea about how to accommodate their social and cultural needs. Despite this, I will admit it is an option that has worked for a few children. There are some decent Aboriginal supporters of this approach. Waverley Stanley, whose father is Pop John, and Joe Ross from the Kimberley are two Aboriginal men who have been strong advocates. I have always had a good and respectful relationship with them, and we have our differences of opinion on this matter, yet maintain a healthy respect for each other and our opinions. I confess, too, my thinking has evolved. I'm still not convinced that elite private school scholarships are the answer, far from it, but I have come to think there is merit in opportunities being offered to children to be housed in boarding accommodation that is close enough to home so they can get home on the weekend if they choose to, or family can visit them, too. I respect Waverley and Joe, but the same cannot be said for one dishonourable advocate who reacted aggressively to my comments to a journalist.

The journalist rang me to ask my opinion about the boarding school scholarships. I gave him my usual response, as I had done with many other journalists who had approached me: 'Sure, it might work for some Aboriginal children, but it doesn't work for all of them! There are almost forty thousand Indigenous children in secondary schools and if we offer two thousand scholarships it is still only less than five per cent. So what about the other ninety-five per cent? Don't they deserve quality education if they haven't been cherry picked for this "magical" opportunity?'

It lets corporate people feel a warm glow about investing in Aboriginal education but it is an investment with a minute and questionable focus. It reminds me of the starfish story where the guy feels good about throwing one of thousands of starfish into the water saying, 'I saved that one'. The only thing here is these are not starfish we are talking about. They are Aboriginal children, and I want to get them all back in the water. Reflecting on the experience of my two girls from Cherbourg, I wanted to add, 'The culture of some of these places is "fit in or fuck off".'

It is one of those comments loaded with the potential to be controversial. In this particular case there was no need for me to be so controversial as I had genuine concerns for the Aboriginal kids who had taken up such opportunities and flourished. The last thing I wanted was for them to be caught in the crossfire of an ideological argument. The other reason I didn't want to be controversial was because of my great respect for Waverley, and for his father, who in many ways was like my own father. So I toned down the language and said, 'The culture of some of these places is "fit in or farewell".'

Despite this, this advocate launched into an email campaign that challenged me on my views to try to undermine my reputation as a successful educator. In his initial tirade he copied in all of the key people from the Myer Foundation and Sidney Myer Fund and the Telstra Foundation and suggested it was important to do so in the interests of making them aware of this issue in case it appeared in the paper.

I responded by calling him on his motives, suggesting that it was not to make them aware of the issue, as they had been aware of it already, but rather to undermine my relationship with the people who were key partners and investors with us.

He replied with an obsessive email that ran for three and a half thousand or more words, which must have taken him ages to write, and he copied in many people from around the country. I didn't actually read it all as I skipped to the end of the diatribe straightaway, finding some words that resonated strongly for me: 'If you do not want to be included in this dialogue, please ignore this email.' I did.

It was a really sneaky and dishonourable way of doing business, and it also emerged at Kevin Rudd's 2020 Summit. On that occasion I was part of the productivity working strand but obviously I knew many of the blackfullas in the Indigenous working strand. After a weekend of lengthy and robust discussion we sat at the conclusion watching the key ideas from each strand put up for consideration. For the Indigenous strand, one of the key ideas presented was 'Scholarships for Indigenous children'. Most of the blackfullas I knew reacted with disbelief.

'Where the hell did that come from?' they said in unison. 'I don't remember anyone saying anything about that!'

To me this is a questionable way of doing business and it turns me off just as much as the concept. I never really like having to play the politics and games to convince people we have some solutions. It was disappointing to find others ready to attack or to try to denigrate our approaches in order to elevate their own. It is also disappointing to find moments of realisation that I am 'in the game' and getting into personal attacks, when I should really be focussed on engaging others intellectually rather than personally. There are times when I have to stop and remind myself it is more important to focus on the work that we do, and be confident about our stronger smarter philosophies and processes.

My involvement with the Aboriginal and Torres Strait Islander Arts Board offered many great opportunities for me to travel around Australia and on some occasions to other parts of the world. It was an excellent time to talk with others and take on board many insights. I attended the Festival of the Pacific Arts, which was hosted by American Samoa. I had a memorable trip to Paris for the opening of Jacques Chirac's Musée du Quai Branly. It was his presidential swansong, a museum designed to honour and celebrate Indigenous cultures from around the world. With an entourage of accomplished Aboriginal and Torres Strait Islander artists, who represented our people well, we stayed in Paris for several nights. Alexander Downer was the senior government representative on the tour and he was accompanied by his wife, Nicky, who was at that time an Australia Council colleague of mine. Alexander made sure I got to meet the French president and also Kofi Annan, who was Secretary-General of the United Nations at the time. It was such a thrill, of course, but what I enjoyed most of all was seeing Aboriginal and Torres Strait Islander artists, some young, some quite old, being recognised and embraced so enthusiastically. They truly deserved to be honoured in this way.

I made note of this in a speech I made to a large crowd at the Australian High Commission, taking time to emphasise the irony of seeing our people embraced and honoured like rock stars abroad, while at home some of the same people were being subjected to the dishonourable and disempowering processes of the Northern Territory Intervention. The somewhat defiant speech got a rousing reception for the content, but I think also because I had made the time and effort to be coached in order to speak some sentences in French.

In some ways I felt a bit like a fish out of water in the Aboriginal arts arena. My years as chair of the board made me realise that the same dynamics of low expectations was just as toxic here as it was in any other policy arena. There were many meetings, but one that sticks in my mind was in Sydney in June 2007. We were engaged, as we often were, in heavy discussion about the priorities on the table at the time. Richard Frankland, an accomplished and well-credentialled Koorie filmmaker and artist from Victoria, was partly focussed on our discussion and partly on the internet via his laptop. As the chair it used to niggle me a bit how he would be on his laptop during the meetings, but he had the kind of character that enabled him to get away with it, and he always added a tremendous sense of richness to our conversations. On this particular day he stopped, almost stunned, and with a gloomy gaze looked towards the rest of us.

'Not Guilty!' he said, with a dark tone. 'They just found Chris Hurley not guilty!'

We were stunned. I found it really hard to proceed with the meeting even though it was one of those issues that had very little to do with any of us at the table, yet it affected all of us so deeply in some ways. It was the first time ever a police officer had been charged with anything relating to the mistreatment of Aboriginal people or any Aboriginal death in custody. To me it seemed the Police Union was demanding some kind of unquestionable right to cause the death of Aboriginal civilians, without having to endure any kind of scrutiny. It was an emotionally charged time that sent shockwaves that would affect so many Aboriginal people. I couldn't even begin to imagine what it must have been like for the people of Palm Island and the families that were at the epicentre of this tragedy.

Some years later, in a McDonald's in Townsville, I got to meet the greatly admired Lex Wotton, the Palm Island man thrown in jail amid allegations he caused the riots that saw the police station burned to the ground. To me the question was really about what caused the anger that led to the riots in the first place. What struck me about Lex Wotton was how he was so *not* the man portrayed on the television and in the papers. He was a gentle, hardworking family man who loved his kids and wanted them to have a good education. In fact, the reason he came up to me in McDonald's was that he had heard about my work at Cherbourg and he just wanted to say 'hi' and to also share his passion about education for our children. Some described him as akin to a terrorist, but this always reminds me that the great Nelson Mandela was also described this way.

As a blackfulla, when you meet such good people and when

you watch such tragedies unfold in communities, even from where I sat, it is so hard to endure such a sense of exasperation and hopelessness about the prospect of this 'fair go' that is so often referred to in Australia. At the board meeting, I rounded up our discussions and closed the meeting. It was impossible to have any constructive dialogue given the overwhelming sense of anger, frustration and exasperation we were feeling. It happened some three thousand kilometres away and we had no direct connection to what was going on, but we were gobsmacked by the news. I was silent all the way to Sydney airport and I waited until the plane got to the right altitude so that I could pull out my laptop and just write. Not to anyone in particular, but just to write.

Waiting for the Hurley verdict to emerge was like waiting for a relative with a terminal illness to pass away. You kind of know that things just won't be right, but when it happens you experience shock, hurt, frustration and dismay. In this case throw in an intense sense of outrage.

For Aboriginal Australians all we can say I guess is, 'Well what else did we expect?' This case simply articulates one of the despicable realities in which we are located. The reality that seemingly asserts that with White Might, She'll be Right! I challenge any white Australian leadership uncomfortable with this assertion to disprove it!

We can only salvage respite from knowing that while Hurley may be found not guilty in a court, he will never ever be free. His conscience will remind him of the real truth surrounding that time when he went into a room with another human being, knowing exactly what it was that caused the death of another. He will be reminded of this every time he sees another Aboriginal person; every time he sees some Aboriginal icon or motif; every time he hears the sound of an Aboriginal instrument. Every time he hears the wind blow his conscience will remind him of the real truth of that time!

The day will come when enough white leadership in this country is evolved enough to know, understand, and be receptive to this frustrating dynamic, to the extent that we can celebrate their true freedom. Sadly we just have to wait longer. White Australian leadership thinks that when things are 'fixed' in Aboriginal communities, then they set Aborigines free. The truth is that white Australia will set itself free . . . and, like always, we will be here, ready to share a sense of dignity that is worth much more than a 'technical' truth.

My deepest condolences to the family of Mr Doomadgee and the proud people of Palm Island.

Dr Chris Sarra

I took many flights to many places in my time and they were not all serious. Most were routine but some were fun. One evening I was on a plane trip to Canberra with two colleagues and there were a lot of other Aboriginal people on board, so something must have been going down the next day. The three of us were seated in seats D, E and F, behind some older Aboriginal ladies. Like schoolboys going away on camp, we laughed and giggled all the way. As we filed into the aisle to get out of the plane I held my ground politely to let the older Aboriginal ladies before me.

'Gorn, missus!' I said pointing down the aisle. 'You go 'long there!'

'No, love,' she replied. 'You go.'

With that I took off down the aisle ready to be stiffened by the

Canberra chill on arrival. Later I heard about the most wonderful exchange that occurred in my wake.

'Who is that happy young chappy laughing all the way to Canberra?' the old Aboriginal lady asked my colleague. He puffed up his chest with a great sense of pride that his boss had been recognised.

'That's Dr Chris Sarra, madam!' he replied with enthusiasm and more pride.

'Oooh!' she said, with intrigue and enthusiasm to match. After several moments taking in the information she had just been offered she looked up at my colleague and asked, 'And who is Dr Chris Sarra?' with an apparent look of bewilderment on her sweet elderly face.

With that my colleagues bust out laughing and raced to catch up and tell me. Even today I laugh out loud when I think about that story. It is a great reminder that regardless of how important I might think I am, there are always good people out there who never know who I am. Besides, there are plenty of other really great educators in Australia who are also important and worth knowing.

It is fair to say I got to a point where I was knocking back invitations to present keynote addresses at various conferences around the country, not because of any sense of arrogance but rather because I felt it was time to make room for other people to step up. There were several other good-quality Indigenous educators that deserved the limelight and prominence as much as I did. This included Aboriginal school leaders like Dyonne Anderson, who led significant positive change as principal of an Aboriginal school at Cabbage Tree Island Public School in Northern New South Wales. Donna Bridge was a participant in our very first leadership program, and she then returned to East Kalgoorlie Primary School and dramatically transform it. Her husband, Paul, was also a prominent and experienced senior Aboriginal principal throughout remote parts of Western Australia – Donna and Paul were known as the 'Posh and Becks of Indigenous Education' in that state and I said to them that Grace and I were 'Barack and Michelle'. All jokes aside, Dyonne, Donna and Paul, along with several other highly successful Aboriginal or Torres Strait Islander educators, certainly deserved to be recognised as prominent voices worth hearing.

There were several other non-Indigenous school leaders that also deserved to be heard. This included people such as Jane Cameron, who led with great success Glenroi Heights Public School in New South Wales, a school with a reputation for being 'hard', supposedly from the wrong side of the railway track in Orange. Jane led and developed an exceptional teaching and community team that delivered a quality education in a place where most people thought it wasn't possible. From the more remote parts of Australia, Jenni Greenham at Mount Margaret Remote Community School in Western Australia and Neil Gibson from Minyerri in the Northern Territory both led schools where student attendance bounced to well above ninety per cent, when most imagined this was impossible. There was also Ian Mackie and his wife, Liz, who did most of the heavy lifting to get Aurukun school in Cape York on track. In the larger and more provincial areas of North Queensland guys like Michael Hansen, who led Cairns West, and Tony Whybird at Atherton State High School were really giving their all. Further south in some of the metropolitan and larger centres you could find exceptional school leaders like Belinda Leavers of Loganlea and Peter Hoehn of Tullawong in Caboolture, who were in for the long haul in metro schools noted for their toughness. Mark McConville and Paul Tracey both led great schools in some of the tougher parts of the Hunter Region of New South Wales, and in Victoria Graham Blackley re-engaged Koori kids and parents in East Gippsland, as did Greg Phair at Rokeby Primary School in Tasmania. There are also so many others who are working towards change.

Whenever ministers or other senior bureaucrats rang me looking for advice or representation at various education forums, it was always good to re-direct them to such great people. In part I enjoyed this because it took a lot of pressure off me personally. I could not be everywhere and be a good husband and father. I also liked the fact that there was a broad range of people from an equally broad range of schools. Their respective stories enabled us to move well beyond any suggestion that the only reason we saw such dramatic change at Cherbourg School was because somehow I was a man, or an Aboriginal man, or it was only an Aboriginal community school with a mono-cultural environment, or whatever other excuse could be conjured. What was important was they were educators with a story to tell about what they did and what they were planning for their schools. Clearly I had been gone from a school for a long time now.

Their stories firmly put other educators throughout Australia on notice. It didn't matter what type of person you were or what type of school or community you were in, we had within our national stronger smarter network someone who had cracked it in similar circumstances. There truly was no place to hide in any school in Australia for any educator with low expectations of Aboriginal children.

★

I have always subscribed to that saying, 'The harder you work, the luckier you become.' For a long time I have been content to work really hard and content to embrace opportunities as they inevitably emerge, rather than feeling the need to chase them. In July 2011 a fantastic opportunity emerged and I grabbed it with both hands. Just like the job at Cherbourg I was not expecting the call from Deputy Premier Terry Mackenroth. He was on the board of Queensland Rugby League and we first met in 2004 when he was with Governor-General Quentin Bryce to present me with the medal for being Queenslander of the Year.

'Chris would you be interested in being a commissioner on the Australian Rugby League Commission?' he asked, with his usual gruff voice.

Without trying to sound too exuberant and jumping down the phone to yell, 'YES!' I did my best to sound calm and said, 'Hmm . . . Yeah! What would be required of me in terms of time commitments, et cetera?'

He told me the commission was to be established with seven other prominent Australians who had already been selected via a rigorous headhunting and screening process. We would meet every month to determine the strategic directions of the game at the highest level.

Truly, I didn't really care about the time I'd have to commit, there was no way I would knock back this opportunity to lead in the game I loved so much. I clearly had some questions that needed answers, though.

'So, Terry, if I take this role on do I have to be diplomatic at State of Origin matches?'

'No, mate . . . you're a Queenslander!'

Correct response!

'So, what about Rugby Union? Do I have to be diplomatic about Rugby Union?'

'No, mate, they've got nothing on our game!'

Correct response, again! With that I said, 'Terry, I reckon I can do this. In fact, I'm going to love doing this job!'

We agreed that I should say nothing about the appointment until it was all made official, but, despite this, it was leaked and in all of the papers the next day. As my family and friends found out about my appointment there were two standard questions: 'Is it really true?' and 'Can you get me some tickets?'

It was a great honour to be asked to be an inaugural commissioner in this very important role. I hadn't truly realised the significance of my appointment until I read Stephen Hagan's article about it in his *National Indigenous Times*. Stephen made the point that I had broken the glass ceiling in sports administration. As I reflected on this, it further reinforced my view about just how great the game of Rugby League is.

In 1973, Arthur Beetson ran on to the field as the first Aboriginal Australian to captain his country in any sport in Australia. In the Rugby League world the playing field is truly level and Aboriginal excellence is recognised, embraced and celebrated. Beetson showed great guts, determination and hard work to reach such a lofty pinnacle. When you reflect on how Aboriginal people were being treated in other parts of our society at that time, you begin to appreciate the magnitude of such extraordinary achievements of not only Beetson but the entire Rugby League society. This is what makes the game great for Aboriginal Australians, and for all Australians. It truly does represent an aspiration of what our society should look like. In the Rugby League society, if an Aboriginal person is prepared to work hard and show a level of guts and determination to succeed, they usually can. It is a place where hopelessness and despair does not exist as it does in other places for Aboriginal people.

I was in grade one when Beetson became Australia's first Indigenous captain of our national Rugby League team. While I've never been anywhere near as flash as Beetson on the field, I hoped that in some ways I could emulate his legacy off the field by inspiring other Indigenous people to work hard and earn their place at other significant corporate tables. I am confident that we certainly will see Indigenous excellence acknowledged and embraced at other corporate tables, and we should all be grateful to the game of Rugby League for continuing to lead the way.

Having a great team is so important, which is why it has always been important to me to acknowledge the profoundly important efforts of those who have worked with me at Cherbourg School and at the Institute. While I might get to enjoy recognition and access to lofty heights, I never forget them, carrying them always in my heart. At the Institute Toby Adams had become my new right-hand man when Michal spread her wings and deservedly became our Senior Community Relations person, setting up national leadership programs across Australia for the Institute. I first met Toby back in 2003 and was immediately impressed by his commitment and professionalism. He was also a very proud young black man and together we made a great team.

In October 2011, Toby rang me and said, 'Hey, you won't believe this! I got an invitation here for you to have lunch with her Majesty!'

I knew she was coming to town after the massive floods had wreaked havoc in Queensland in the summer of 2010/11. I wasn't sure, though, whether he was winding me up or not.

'True God!' he replied, and with that I knew, like most black-fullas do, that he was telling the truth. 'You want me to RSVP to say yes?'

'Yeah, go on, then!' I said, wondering whether or not it was the right thing to do as a blackfulla. I figured I could have some kind of little protest in my own lunchtime by saying no, but absolutely nobody would have noticed.

On the morning of the luncheon I was driving to work when I got a call from the office of the Governor of Queensland.

'Good morning, Dr Sarra. I am just ringing to advise you that you will be sitting at the table today with her Majesty.'

'Okay,' I said, but I was thinking, 'Oh, my God!' I immediately pulled the car to the side of the road to continue the conversation because there were some things I had to get clear about. 'Um . . . would you mind explaining to me some of the protocols and etiquette things because I'm not really up there with all that five-star stuff?'

She was very nice and proceeded to explain the 'outside in' rule with the cutlery, that I should wait until her Majesty started eating before I started, and that I should not eat too quickly so that I finish at around the same time as everyone else does.

'Hey, thanks,' I said, sincerely. 'Just as well you told me as I'm youngest of ten and when we sit at the table to eat we don't wait for anybody!'

At the luncheon at South Bank there were about a hundred and fifty important people, including Anna Bligh, the premier, and many other prominent Queenslanders. Normally at such functions I am always too shy to talk to people, but I went out of my way to say 'hi' to Archbishop Phillip Aspinall, a very decent man whom I have come to admire greatly. The Queen arrived amid much pomp and ceremony, and we, her guests, watched each other nervously, making sure we were getting our gestures and greetings right. There were about eight people at my table. The waiters brought in an impressive looking crystal glass containing a reddish-pink drink for the Queen.

To my immediate right was Sally Pearson, the great hurdler. On my immediate left was the governor for Queensland, Penelope Wensley. We remembered each other fondly from the time we had met many years before on that great trip to Paris for the opening of the Musée du Quai Branly. At the time she was Australia's Ambassador to France. To her immediate left, just two seats away from me, was the guest of honour, Her Majesty.

We didn't get to talk much, but she was quite a lady and I was really glad I took the opportunity to be in her company. I couldn't help thinking that she was so close I could just reach across and touch her, but of course I never would. In the deep confines of my own head I was wondering just how people might react if I had said something like, 'Your Majesty . . . any chance you could give the country back to us before you take off?'

It's fair to say I am no monarchist, but after having lunch with her and seeing her in action I really respected what she was doing at her age. Her visit to Queensland was in response to the chaos and havoc wreaked upon us by a vicious summer of natural disasters. She didn't have to come but she did. In doing so she prompted a huge lift in the morale of Queenslanders at a time when we really needed it.

At the end of the lunch she got up with the governor and made her way off to the next regal function. On the table she left that impressive crystal glass still two-thirds full. I just couldn't help myself. Reaching out I sort of grabbed the glass and sniffed it. My fellow dining guests asked me what it was. I couldn't be sure, so I had to take a sip! I still couldn't work out what it was and I passed it on to Sally Pearson. She had a smell and I urged to try it, too. She was way too apprehensive and so I pushed her.

'Do it!' I urged. 'You will never get the chance to drink from the same cup as the Queen ever again!'

With that she took a small sip and we passed it around the table for the others to do the same. I still don't know what was in the glass, but for me I think it is pretty cool just to say I have lunched with Queen, and drunk from the same cup she used.

The following month I was in a taxi in Sydney when Toby rang me.

'Brother, you're not gonna believe this but I got a dinner invitation here that will top lunch with the Queen! Have a guess who!'

'Missy Higgins,' I said. I have always loved Missy Higgins from the night I saw her on a music awards show jumping all over David Hasselhoff.

'Nope.'

'Oh, come on, what could be better than dinner with Missy Higgins? The Pope?'

'Nope. You have been cordially invited to have dinner with Barack Obama!'

'Holy shit!' I squealed in disbelief, feeling a bit like Julia Roberts in that spa scene from *Pretty Woman*.

'True God,' Toby said.

The occasion was in the Great Hall of Parliament House with six hundred others. It was nowhere near as intimate as the lunch with the Queen, but still it was good to sit at a table and chat with Peter Garrett and his wife, Doris, Penny Wong and her partner, Sophie, and another older Aboriginal lady, Ms Anderson from

South Australia. As the evening progressed and the speeches were done, people started lining up to meet the president. By this stage Ms Anderson and I were standing around yarning, and the line was getting longer and longer.

'I'd like to meet that president, you know, Chris,' she said.

'Well come on then, missus,' I said, 'let's go.'

As we got closer we realised the line was so long that there was every chance we might never get to shake hands with him.

The prime minister was doing her duty by waiting with the president and introducing people to him as they filed past. I thought to myself there might be an underhanded way to get in to say hello.

'Here, come with me, missus. Let's just stand at the side here and if I can catch the prime minister's eye, she might just call us in!'

Angelo Gavrielatos, the head of the Australian Education Union, joined us, saying, 'I'm coming through on your coat tails brother!' That was fine with me but things did not go to plan.

Prime Minister Gillard was focussed on her duties and it was difficult to catch her eye. We also had to contend with a rather large bodyguard who was putting his big frame to good use by blocking us from coming in at the side.

'Stay here, missus. But you stand in front 'cause if she sees me and calls me in I will drag you in there with me, okay?'

We must have waited patiently for about twenty minutes. I was chatting to Angelo and Ms Anderson started making small talk with the bodyguard.

'So did you fly out from the States with the president, love?' I was not paying too much attention until I heard his response.

'No, actually, I'm an Indigenous . . .'

On hearing that my head snapped back around almost instantaneously. Not wanting to hear where he was Indigenous to, I said, 'Brother! Why didn't you say something before? We're blackfullas, too! Can't you cut a break for another blackfulla?'

On fielding my desperate and well-founded plea he whispered something into his hidden microphone, stepped aside, and ushered us through to meet Barack Obama. Angelo, good to his word, cruised in with us. As I looked up and shook hands with the president, I was struck by just how engaging he was. Like many commentators have noted, he really does make you feel like you're the only person in the room.

Epilogue

These days I am content to listen more than speak. When my calendar permits I still present at conferences, although I tend to enjoy smaller occasions, when you can get close to others and have more meaningful conversations. I particularly enjoy being able to accept invitations to speak and present at various forums back home in Bundaberg, as it lets me feel like I am giving something back to my community. At every conference, though, whether large or small, flash or not so flash, I never take these opportunities for granted or let myself feel complacent. There have been many times when I have stared myself in the face, reminding myself to be at my best and choose the words I share. You can never know just how or when you might have some influence on the way some people think and act and then go on to make a difference in the life of some child in a school somewhere.

I still get a buzz when other educators come up to me to say how they saw the *Strong and Smart* film years ago and it prompted them to rethink what they were doing. Some tell me they showed it to their kids, and I really love it that schools and classrooms right across Australia have the words 'strong and smart' somewhere to remind them of what they should be focussing on. What I love most about this is that it was the kids of Cherbourg, and the elders, parents and community, who worked so hard with us all those years ago to start the ripple that would eventually change the tide of low expectations right across Australia.

I really do think it is time for Aboriginal people to assert our place in the nation. For a long time we have been the 'other' in Australian society. Many of us have always known, however, that we are more than this. A different truth about us has always existed and it is our time to assert that truth in a way that should not threaten white Australia, but instead set us all free.

Some Australians think the answer lies in abandoning this sense of being 'other' so that we can all be the same. This is not a future to which we should aspire. We must be content to being 'other' with no desire to be the 'same' as mainstream Australia. We need to stand on grounds where *we* as blackfullas decide who we are. We will triumph as Aboriginal Australians when we assert ourselves in Australia as the Strong, Smart, Young Black and Deadly Australians that we are. In doing this it is crucial that other Australians do not feel threatened or divided by our actions. While it may be a different circumstance from the historical status quo in which we were often powerless, embracing our blackness and celebrating the notion that we are the only Australians who are connected to the oldest human existence on the planet, and the true descendants of the very first Australians, has never ever been about putting white Australians down.

As a people we have known what it is like to be put down. This is not something that is good to inflict upon other people.

Of course, we must never forget the sacrifices of our elders, who walked in the long grass to lay a solid platform upon which many of us Aboriginal people can stand proudly. We must keep in our minds the times when some of us had to fight – the Redfern Riots, the courage of Lex Wotton and the Palm Island riots. We should never want to re-visit such times, but they serve as reminders to all Aboriginal people that our children still have a journey to make into a stronger smarter Australian future. It is a journey they must be armed for. Not with rocks and sticks and petrol bombs, but with intellectual, psychological and spiritual integrity.

To appreciate where we can go we must never forget where we have come from. That is why I will never ever forget the tenacity, courage and hard work of the team I worked with at Cherbourg – in particular, the parents and, most importantly, the children of Cherbourg School. What a journey they started! Their efforts created a ripple that has changed the tide of low expectations of Aboriginal children in schools throughout Australia. I will always remember that.

I was first encouraged to write my story by my very good friend Jeff McMullen. We had been brought together by our passion for making a difference to the lives of Aboriginal people, in particular, our children. Jeff and I sat together and chatted for hours one night under a big Weipa sky. With dismay we both lamented the effect inhumane policy approaches, such as the Northern Territory Intervention with its Basics Card and cutting welfare payments to parents in communities where the schools are failing them, were having on us.

'We have to show there is another way of doing this!' we agreed. While neither of us pretended that great complexities and challenges didn't exist in Aboriginal communities, both of us had seen with our own eyes many positive things that were worth acknowledging, learning from, and building upon. I am still in my mid forties and even to me it seems too early to have written a memoir. My intention here, though, has been to offer an insight into a different and more honourable way to contemplate policy reform for Aboriginal Australians, and indeed for all Australians.

The Stronger Smarter Institute has grown significantly, as has the demand for our leadership programs and activities. From just running two leadership programs a year we've had to respond to demands from educators throughout Australia to run up to fourteen. One of the things I like best about where the Institute is at now, in terms of the leadership programs we run, is that people are turning up not because they have heard about Chris Sarra but because they have heard about the stronger smarter philosophy.

The Institute's challenge is to consolidate better and more transparent arrangements in which governance and financial processes are more open than they are currently. It must also get better at telling the story of its impact on schools and communities. This remains a tough challenge, but it has been so all along. The rhetoric of evidence-based policy rightly swirls and for us it creates reasonable demands. As an institute that has received significant levels of public funding and had much success, we have a very good story to tell. Many schools throughout Australia have seen dramatic improvements, although I have always been reticent about over-claiming the effect of the stronger smarter approach. It is not as clear-cut as suggesting that if a school leader completes our leadership program then they are guaranteed a twenty per cent improvement in literacy and a forty per cent improvement in Indigenous student attendance. There are many variables at play in the complex challenge of making a difference in schools and communities.

The one thing I am certain about is that, when it comes to making a difference in Aboriginal education, we now know what we need to know. We know that in schools embracing a stronger smarter approach, the seemingly intractable challenge of engaging and transforming the lives of Indigenous children, and poor white children, can be relegated to an undignified history where they belong. More recently we have been able to articulate what we mean when we refer to the stronger smarter philosophy.

The stronger smarter philosophy honours a positive sense of cultural identity, acknowledges and embraces positive community leadership, and enables innovative and dynamic approaches and processes anchored by high-expectations relationships. High-expectations relationships honour the humanity of others, and in doing so acknowledge a person's strengths, capacity and human right to emancipatory opportunity.

For us it is about doing things 'with' people not 'to' them. At one philosophical level it is quite easy. At the level of reality, as I have said all along without pretending otherwise, it remains extraordinarily hard work to overcome the challenges we contemplate. It is a way of engaging in authentic dialogue with patience and listening. It also requires us to leave our egos at the door.

There is room for people working in other policy areas to learn from and apply this philosophy in their respective areas. In fact, one of the things I like about the stronger smarter philosophical approach is that it doesn't mean that as an Aboriginal leader I have to encroach upon other people's areas of expertise. There are plenty of other experts in Aboriginal health and other complex human policy areas doing great work already. I have watched so-called leaders make this mistake with disastrous effect and from this there are many lessons to learn.

For me, personally, I am interested in a future that takes on the challenges of Indigenous housing, armed with the stronger smarter approach. There are several reasons this appeals. During my time on Kevin Rudd's Social Inclusion Board, I watched with frustration how remote communities were being promised housing, yet being delivered very little. While millions may have been spent, the reality was very few houses were provided. As I watched on I just know a more honourable approach would see much better outcomes delivered.

The other thing that appeals to me in the area of Indigenous housing is that the outcomes are more tangible than they are in education, where we focus on delivering and entrenching a sense of hope. Hope is an amazing entity that manifests its glory in unmeasurable ways. It brings joy when you sense it enters the psyche of those you set out to inspire, yet hope is so glorious and unfettered by a need for tangibleness.

I guess it is my humanness, and not my humanity, that sees me yearning to experience the sense of satisfaction in seeing something like a bare block of dirt, and then three months later a house, for which you are handing over the keys to a young Aboriginal father or mother with a family. Despite such yearnings I suspect I will always continue to play a role as an educator. For me it remains, after all, the noblest profession.

As I reflect on my life I can't help feeling content with what I have achieved so far. Sometimes I think it is funny to know that one of my first jobs as a young, barefooted blackfulla from East Bundaberg was delivering papers. Today I have the good fortune to be invited to places all around the world, and at various conferences, I am still delivering 'papers'. I hope others can be inspired by my story. As a student I was not necessarily expected to go on to great heights. Despite this I was able to achieve beyond expectations with a diploma of Teaching, a Bachelor's Degree, two Masters degrees, a PhD, and a Company Directors Diploma. I suspect more will come. I never did get to represent Queensland or Australia in Rugby League, but I did manage to land among those at the highest echelons in charge of the entire game.

As Cherbourg State School's first Aboriginal principal, I was able to lead in such a way that would see its students, parents and community achieve well beyond expectations. This in turn would see other schools and communities licensed to have high expectations and believe in themselves and their right to a quality education. Ultimately this would change schooling right across the entire country, and, without getting too carried away, in my quietest thoughts I think it is humbling, yet pretty cool to be described as the man who changed the tide of low expectations of Indigenous children in schools.

I continue to value the lessons I learned as the youngest of ten, of a proud Aboriginal mother and a hard-working Italian father. Work hard. Don't stop until the job is done. Stick up for yourself and for others who have difficulty sticking up for themselves. Be proud of being Aboriginal. Be strong. Be smart. These are worthy lessons worth cherishing, lessons that have put me in good stead so far, and I am certain will continue to do so into the future. In life I have learned some lessons of my own.

In 1985, my long-time friend, and the greatest teacher I've known, Gary MacLennan, exposed me to the toxicity of low expectations. As I said before, he threw the petrol on the fire my parents kindled in my belly. It fuelled my sense of rage that would drive me to play my part in changing expectations for all Indigenous children in schools. I learned, though, that this could not be achieved with rage alone. There are times for anger and times for brutal honesty, but there are also times for quiet and compassion. Over time I learned, sometimes the hard way, that not every white person was there to cut me down, and not every Aboriginal person was necessarily there to help me fly. I've learned that family can be your greatest source of support and also your greatest source of hurt. I've also had to learn to guide with good leadership and not with ego. Hubris is an ugly beast that can attract dynamics that bring your world crashing down around you. These are the lessons I reflect upon each morning and each night.

I do my best to ensure my actions and behaviours are driven by motives that are more pure rather than malicious. I recall my mum's words here about 'being more of a man if you can walk away from a fight'. Sometimes this is excruciatingly difficult, especially in a role that others set out to cut you down from, saying you are a tall poppy. Today, I look back on those times when I have been attacked in various ways that were quite malicious and I just have to be content that I was able to rise above such behaviour and not get caught in such a game that lacks integrity. This is not to say I am perfect as there have been times when I may have not been as strong as I should have been. It is not to say also that such attacks are not hurtful, especially when you are being attacked by those closest to you. There have been times when I have failed and there have been times when I have been hurt; here I bring my humanity to the world as much as the next person.

I have also learned to live with criticism to the extent that I now see it as an opportunity to grow. In the leadership programs we run with others, we ask this question: 'When offered feedback or criticism, do you respond with defensiveness or opportunity?' I try my best to respond with opportunity. With a somewhat public profile and as someone who has been trusted with public money, I have come to accept the need for scrutiny and criticism. On such occasions I try to reflect on such criticisms in order to pick out the gems, which are the lessons that might help me get better. Of course, I will question the motives of those who criticise as this will give me clues as to the validity of their criticism.

I've also realised through time, though, that there is no integrity in putting others down to elevate yourself. In an ideal world we should all feel elevated. This is the aspiration of leadership. As one described as an Aboriginal leader, I have watched and learned that it is not about bullying and smashing other people around so they subscribe to my point of view; it is about capturing the hearts and minds of others in a way that inspires them. The truth is I can only control what I do. I can only be the captain of my own soul. As a father, as a teacher, as a leader, I owe it to those around me to be the best I can be. When I am at my best, I give licence to others to be at their best. If we can all be at our best then all of us truly can have a world beyond expectations.

Acknowledgements

At forty-five years of age it seemed too early to be writing a memoir but with so much going on in Indigenous policy and politics it also seemed the right thing to do. I want to thank those people who have encouraged me to write this piece in order to signal that there is a different and more honourable way to approach the challenges we face together.

I want to thank Jeff McMullen for encouraging me to have a voice in this space. Thanks to my old mate Jean Bourke for helping me to get started on this massive task and to Madonna Duffy, my publisher, and the team at UQP, and Joanne Holliman, my editor, who all helped me get finished.

I am forever grateful for the ongoing love and support of my parents and family and Dr Gary MacLennan, the greatest teacher I ever had.

Thanks must also go to those who have worked with me over the years as part of my story, our story: at Cherbourg School, at the Stronger Smarter Institute and all of those educators and community workers across Australia who have become an important part of the stronger smarter journey. Let me make special mention of the people of Cherbourg and their precious children who rose with such courage, strength and tenacity to create the ripple that really did change the tide of low expectations of Indigenous children throughout Australia.

To my wife Grace, and my amazing children, thank you for your ongoing love, support and inspiration. Thank you also for your patience and forgiveness as I continue to wrestle with the challenges of getting the balance right between being a good husband and father, and playing my part in building a stronger smarter future for all Australian children.

To all of those friends and colleagues who believed in me, prompting me to believe in myself, thanks.